The New Four Winds Guide to Indian Weaponry, Trade Goods, and Replicas

Preston E. Miller
and Carolyn Corey

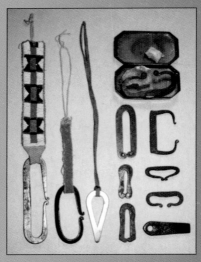

Schiffer Publishing Ltd

4880 Lower Valley Road   Atglen, Pennsylvania   19310

The authors and their dogs are ready for a parade in Preston's old 1932 Chevrolet truck in front of Four Winds Indian Trading Post. The truck is decorated with many fine pieces from their collection. *Photograph by Craig Tice.*

Other Schiffer Books by Preston E. Miller and Carolyn Corey
The New Four Winds Guide to American Indian Artifacts

Other Schiffer Books on Related Subjects
Rugs and Posts: The Story of Navaho Weaving and the Role of the Indian Trader (Revised & Updated 3rd Edition), by H. L. James
Indian Dolls, by Nancy N. Schiffer
Indian Baskets (Revised 3rd Edition), by Sarah Peabody and William A. Turnbaugh
Native American Fetishes (Revised & Expanded 2nd Edition), by Kay Whittle

Copyright © 2007 by Preston E. Miller and Carolyn Corey
Library of Congress Control Number: 2006939319

Designed by Mark David Bowyer
Type set in Benguiat Bk BT / Zurich BT

ISBN: 978-0-7643-2634-9
Printed in China

Published by Schiffer Publishing Ltd.
4880 Lower Valley Road
Atglen, PA 19310
Phone: (610) 593-1777; Fax: (610) 593-2002
E-mail: Info@schifferbooks.com

For the largest selection of fine reference books on this and related subjects, please visit our web site at
www.schifferbooks.com
We are always looking for people to write books on new and related subjects. If you have an idea for a book please contact us at the above address.

This book may be purchased from the publisher.
Include $3.95 for shipping.
Please try your bookstore first.
You may write for a free catalog.

In Europe, Schiffer books are distributed by
Bushwood Books
6 Marksbury Ave.
Kew Gardens
Surrey TW9 4JF England
Phone: 44 (0) 20 8392-8585; Fax: 44 (0) 20 8392-9876
E-mail: info@bushwoodbooks.co.uk
Website: www.bushwoodbooks.co.uk
Free postage in the U.K., Europe; air mail at cost.

Contents

Introduction

How to Use This Book

The American Indian collectibles in this book were sold by Four Winds Indian Auction in St. Ignatius, Montana between 1990 and 2006. Included in this volume are Indian-made weaponry and cases, horse gear, ethnographic pieces, and pipes. The trade goods section includes trade beads, trade cloth, Hudson's Bay collectibles, blankets, weapons and tools. There is a separate section on replicas made by contemporary craftspeople. Genuine Indian-made items of both new and old vintage are featured in the companion volume to this work, *New Four Winds Guide to American Indian Artifacts.* The full range of items in each category with **descriptions, dates, price estimates, and prices realized** will provide useful information to both sellers and collectors.

The **title** of each item is named using terminology that is most accepted by experienced collectors. This is followed by a **date** approximating the year in which the item was made. Without certified provenance, it is difficult to be completely accurate when assigning dates to Indian material based solely on appearance, so that a date of "c. 1870" assumes that an item could have been made ten years earlier or later.

Information on provenance, when available, is *italicized,* following the date.

The **descriptions** contain pertinent construction details, such as a detailed list of bead colors and materials used, as well as the size and condition of the item. All are very important factors in determining the value of an item. For instance, certain bead colors can help verify the age (see Bead Glossary p. 7); usually the older a piece is the more it is worth. Also, the use of thread or sinew, brain tan or commercial hide (see p. 8), and whether or not the item is in good sound condition can be very important when assigning values. Many price guides fail to take these things into account when establishing an item's value. It is important to realize that a pair of moccasins with half the beads missing is worth considerably less that an intact pair with little or no damage. The same applies to torn rugs, damaged baskets, broken pottery or stone artifacts; often the damaged item can be worth less than half the value of a similar but intact one. Sometimes an item will be so undesirable that you might have difficulty finding a buyer. The exception could be when an item has a provenance or rarity that makes it one-of-a-kind. For instance, a stiff torn moccasin that has positive provenance proving that it was picked up at the Battle of Wounded Knee or a damaged but a very rare early incised buffalo hide parfleche would continue to fetch a high price.

Finally, we list the price for which each item was sold at our auction preceded by the estimate range. Example: "Est. 400-800 **SOLD $250(98).**" The dollar amount following the word **SOLD** is the amount for which the item was sold and the numbers in parenthesis indicate the year that it sold. This is an accurate method for assigning values to artifacts. At auction, the highest price realized is determined by the bidders. It means that at least two people had similar ideas as to the value of an item. Also, it can be assumed that because participants in any one auction are limited, there must be other buyers outside the auction realm who will pay as much or more. The **estimate range** reflects **the current (2007) market value** as determined by our personal opinion guided by many years of experience. (Preston has been selling, buying and collecting Indian artifacts for over fifty years). Sometimes the range can seem quite broad; for instance, "Est. 400-800" might leave you a little doubtful as to the real value. As the seller, you can always ask $800 and come down but you can never ask $400 and go up when a customer is ready to buy. This principle works vice versa for the buyer. If you can buy or sell an item within our suggested estimate range, you can feel secure that your transaction was financially acceptable. **There are so many variables to every situation that it would be impossible to assign one price value to each artifact.**

Prices realized for the most desirable items in the current auction market seem to be getting higher and higher. The reasons are a bit obscure, but seem to be based on the fact that some bidders have unlimited funds with which to make their purchases. The only way to keep abreast of this trend is to watch the prices realized at larger auction houses.

It is important to note that if an item sold for a certain amount in 1998 it should have appreciated with time. Since there is no scale that can be assigned to evaluate the appreciation that accrued with time you will have to use your own personal judgment. Because some items appreciate slowly, some not at all, and some even depreciate, this can only be determined by knowledge of the current trends in the marketplace.

Any omissions are due to information that was not available or could not be verified.

Reasons for Collecting

Beginning in the 1970s, the collecting of Indian artifacts reached new levels of popularity, perhaps encouraged by the fact that several major antique and art auction houses began selling collections of old Indian-made items to high paying buyers. Prior to these auctions, Indian-made relics seemed to be viewed as merely craftwork, having little or no art value. Because of this new demand, many old and heretofore unknown treasures were gradually unearthed from old family trunks, attics, and museum storage areas to be placed into the collectors' market. Today, there are more people collecting Indian artifacts, and the number continues to grow. The reasons for collecting include investment potential, historical value, art and craft appreciation, home and business decoration, and personal adornment. See the companion volume, *New Four Winds Guide to American Indian Artifacts*, pp. 4-5, for an in-depth discussion of these categories.

The authors cavort in a Sioux-style courting blanket while their dog Brownie looks on. Carolyn made the blanket and her Cheyenne-style dress out of "saved list" wool trade cloth that she dyed. *Photograph by Craig Tice*.

The authors pose in Canadian attire: Carolyn wears an original early 19th century capote (*see description and photos in Four Winds Guide to Trade Goods, p. 47)* and Preston sports RCMP hat and buffalo coat. Their dog Brownie wears a faux Metis dog saddle. They are standing in front of a Metis cart replica. *Photograph by Craig Tice*.

Bead Glossary

Terms and abbreviations used in descriptions of GLASS BEADS in this book:

Bead Sizes
(refer to color bead chart)

"Seed" beads are the smallest beads, varying from Czech 10° (largest) to 22°. Czech 12°-13° and Italian 4° (see bead chart) were the most commonly found sizes on pre-20th century pieces.

"Pony" bead, more correctly called a "pound" bead, is a large seed bead (Czech size 5° or "I"—see largest beads on the bead chart—to Czech 9°) that usually pre-dates the use of smaller seed beads on Plains and Plateau items.

"Crow" bead is larger still and has large hole for stringing on necklaces or thong decorations on objects and clothing, etc. "Old-style" size approximately 7mm. to 9mm.

Bead Styles

"Basket" beads are cylinders cut from longer tubes manufactured since the mid-1800s (not currently being made to our knowledge). Very versatile use in sewing and stringing. Usually transparent or "lined" (with interior color), or satin, a gleaming satin-like finish.

"Bugle" beads are thin tubular beads.

"Cuts" or cut beads are single-faceted beads resulting in a sparkling effect. The best are still being made in Czechoslovakia in transparent, opaque, pearl (lustre), and iris (multi-color metallic). 19th century pieces frequently have "Czech" cuts in t. (transparent), gr. (greasy) and in even smaller sizes (even 20° and smaller!)

"Tile" bead is an opaque molded cylinder bead with straight sides. Primarily used strung in loop necklaces and thong decorations as early as the mid-19th century.

"Tri-cuts" are 3-cut faceted beads, larger than a cut (see above) and often used on Indian items made after the turn of the 20th century to the present. Usually pearl (lustre), iris (multi-color metallic), or lined (see below); also transparent and opaque.

Bead Colors

No adjective with the bead color refers to an opaque or a solid color bead; i.e., red bead.

"C. pink" or Chey. pink is the abbreviation for Crow or Cheyenne pink. Both refer to the same old-time bead color—a dusty muted pink, popularly used by those tribes in the 19th century and earlier.

"gr." or "greasy" refers to translucent (transl.) or cloudy (semi-transparent). Many old beads were made this way, and many have been re-made in Europe recently. Gives an old piece (or modern reproduction) a richly varying beadwork texture.

Opalescent (opal.) is a varying iridescent color, like an opal.

"Pony trader blue" or Trader blue is a rich "greasy" medium blue, in many color variations (darker than greasy blue and lighter than cobalt). This color was popular on the Plains in the early 19th century in a "pony" bead size along with white, black, and rose w. heart. Also Bodmer blue," an intense greasy blue named for Karl Bodmer, 1830s painter of Plains Indian subjects.

t. or trans. is the abbreviation for transparent or clear.

w. (white) lined (w. heart or w. center) all mean the same thing and refer to the color (in this case white) of the interior of a bead. Outer color is usually red, sometimes brick, pink, orange, green, yellow, or bright blue in modern reproductions. Can be any size of bead. A very old style of seed bead was a highly desirable rose or rose-red.

Beadwork Styles

Flat or appliqué. Used to cover large areas with solid beading; sewn straight or in curved rows. Overall appears flat and used by many tribes, i.e., Blackfeet, Plateau, and Cree.

Lane-stitch (previously called "lazy-stitch"). Multiple beads (5-12) strung and sewn down to create humped or raised rows; often used to cover large areas. Principally used by the Sioux, Cheyenne, Arapaho, and Ute; a modification used by the Crow.

Embossed or raised. Beads sewn in a crowded arched stitch for a 3-D effect, as found on Iroquois and other Eastern tribes beadwork.

Peyote or gourd. A netting technique usually used to cover solid objects, i.e., fan handles, key chains, ballpoint pens, etc. Common on contemporary Indian beadwork items. The term "peyote" is derived from its use on numerous peyote religious articles that are used by the Native American Church.

For further information on tribal styles and how-to techniques see:

Miller, Preston. *Four Winds Indian Beadwork Book.* St. Ignatius, Montana, 1971.

Dean, David. *Beading in the Native American Tradition.* Loveland, Colorado: Interweave Press, 2002.

Whiteford, Andrew H. *North American Indian Arts.* New York: Golden Press, 1970. Concise visual and factual guide to quick identification of material culture objects.

SIZES

Size
14/0
5/0
13/0
4/0
12/0
3/0
11/0
2/0
10/0
0
9/0
c
8/0
7/0
d
e
f
g
h
i
l

COLOURS

Colour
Cristalux
Cristalux extra
2
41

3	732
Snow white (4)	616
28	18 1/2
823	507
824	18
828	102
828 1/2	63
11	64
13	735
801	103
806	27 1/2
807	27
807 1/2	20
808	20 N
812 1/2	31
813	30 1/2
810	30
811	464
803	448
805	49
38	695
6	Black (40)
7	
678	
523	
22	

STRIPED BEADS

CSS 1 R
6599
6697
6721
CSS 2
6631
205
6687
6657
06671
06679
06686

SLIGHT DEVIATIONS FROM COLOURS AND SIZES TO BE TOLERATED

MADE IN ITALY

Card #1, Edition 1962 from Societa Veneziana Conterie, Italy in 1970. This card displays both Italian sizes (0° to 5°) and Czech. sizes (7° to 14°). Notice that bead colors are identified by numbers. 19th century bead cards also use numbers for identification of colors. Notice the many shades of blue, green and red. #28 is greasy yellow; #810 and #811 are white lined reds.

Abbreviations and Definitions

Definitions of materials used for artifacts:

HIDES: "Brain-tanned" or **"Indian-tanned"** buckskin refers to the original hand-worked and organic process of rendering a hide white, soft, supple, porous, and easy to pierce with a needle for beadwork. *The saying goes that each deer has enough brains to tan his own hide!* Considerable time and effort are expended in scraping and stretching by hand. Smoking darkens and water-proofs it.

"Commercial (comm.) hide tanning" is a modern mechanical and chemical process that doesn't break down the grain (in comparison to brain-tanning), so that the hide is not porous, as supple, or easily pierced with a needle; also, it has a chemical odor. Usually has a smooth and rough side. The color is usually not a tan or light brown like a smoked hide, but more of a gold tone. Costs much less than a brain-tan hide.

TRADE WOOL: "White Selvedge" Trade Wool or **"Undyed Selvedge"** or **"SAVED* LIST."** Wool of this terminology is usually navy (indigo) or red; it is distinguished by the white (undyed) selvedge (edge or LIST) that made it the most popular and widely distributed trade cloth to North American Indians as early as 1700.

*Saving is the hand-done process of leaving the selvedge white. The term "saved list" was used in early fur trade ledgers, and is the most accurate description.

"Rainbow" Selvedge Trade Wool has a woven multi-colored edge also called "fancy" list in the early fur trade journals.** It was especially popular on the Southern Plains and later, after "saved list" was no longer available, it was widely distributed in the North in the 20th century. *Shown here is a close-up of a c.1900 three band rainbow list breechclout from the Preston Miller collection, obtained from Pat Read, Oklahoma trader.*

*Corey, Carolyn. *The Tradecloth Handbook.* St. Ignatius, MT, 2001. Details the saving process and history of trade cloth; "rainbow," "stroud," and "saved list."

**Corey, Carolyn. "Coveted Stripes," in *The People of the Buffalo,* Vol. 2. Wyk, Germany: Tatanka Press, 2005: 131-146.

Special tribal designations and terms used in this book:

Intermontane refers to a geometric decorative beadwork style shared by Plateau, Crow, and some Basin tribes (spanning a large geographic area).
See Conn, Richard. *A Persistent Vision.* Seattle: University of Washington, 1986: 128-131.
Blackfoot or Blackfeet. In modern times, Indians of the Blackfoot Confederacy refer to themselves as **Blackfoot** from Canada; and **Blackfeet** from the United States. We use this designation in the book.
See Hungry Wolf, Adolf & Beverly. *Indian Tribes of the Northern Rockies.* Summertown: Good Medicine Books, 1989: 2-4.

Abbreviations used in this book, listed alphabetically *(see also bead definitions for bead color abbreviations)*:

alt. = alternating
apx. = approximately
avg. = average
betw. = between
bkgrd. = background
blk. = black
c. = circa
char. = characteristic
comm. = commercial
cond. = condition
Czech. = Czechoslovakia
D. = deep (depth)
diam. = diameter
diff. = different
dk. = dark
ea. = each
ex. = example
exc. = excellent
excl. = excluding
Fdn. = Foundation
H. = high (height)
incl. = including
Is. = Island (place name)
L. = long (length)
lt. = light
mocs = moccasins
nat. = natural
No. or N. = North

nr. = near
opal. = opalescent
pred. = predominantly
pr. = pair
prob. = probably
prov. = provenance
pt. = point
R. = River (place name)
Res. = Indian Reservation or Reserve (Canada)
So. or S. = South
transl. = translucent
turq. = turquoise
VG = very good
w. = white
W. = wide (width)
yrs. = years

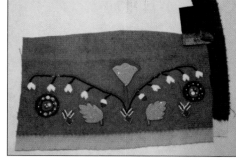

Bright green **saved list** was referred to as "grass green" in the 1828 American Fur Co. orders. Today, it is still sought after on the Crow Reservation to make a prestigious elk tooth dress. In contrast to the indigo dyed wool, green is very fugitive and fades dramatically with exposure to light. As a result, most 19th century cloth is now a drab olive green, not the intense original Kelly green. The c.1875 example (upper right in this photo) has been kept from light; it is shown next to a 19th century Nez Perce breechclout fragment that has faded. (Far right is old hand-woven cloth dyed by the author.)

The following photo essay on TRADE WOOL is excerpted from a presentation by Carolyn Corey at the 8th Annual Plains Indian Seminar, "Artifacts-Artifakes," Buffalo Bill Historical Center in Cody, Wyoming, September 1984.

Indigo (navy blue) **saved list** was the most common color and was used for women's dresses, men's breechclouts, leggings, and blankets. This photo shows three 19th century indigo dyed swatches surrounding a modern reproduction—which was dyed (by the author) using the same dyeing technique with new wool and synthetic dyes. NOTE: new wool selvedge is **white**. The old cloth has turned yellow with age and exposure to light. Also, the texture, dye color, and weave show significant differences: modern mills make wool with diagonal weave, NOT the usual old-time (known as "plain") square weave. The new woolen goods are not coarse, but soft, as dictated by the fashion industry. The natural indigo actually darkens with exposure to light, so that early cloth is rarely faded. (Not until at least 1897 was a synthetic indigo used.) Modern navy is not so intense and deep nor as color fast as the old indigo. *Swatches of old cloth in the author's collection are from the Milton Chandler Coll., courtesy of the late Richard Pohrt.*

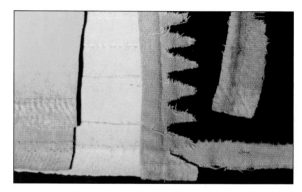

Yellow also fades readily, although many shades were used—from deep mustard to lemon yellow to the pale yellow of the old Sioux legging (faded) binding. (NOTE: the white edge is barely discernible.) It was also used as trim on blankets, bonnet trailers, etc., and rarely seen made into whole garments.

Red **saved list** cloth. There were many variations in shades of scarlet* and red, especially after the invention of synthetic dyes in 1862. The only new example in this photo is the striped selvedge trade cloth on the bottom row; this cloth was known as "Hudson's Bay stroud." The piece shown was purchased from Canada in 1976, the last year for its production (dyed by the author). Note the differences in the old selvedges and backs of selvedge (some have red bleed-through); also note differences in texture, sizes of scalloped edge, and degrees of yellowing. The yellowing from age also affects the red cloth, resulting in a dull red-orange from age.

*Bright scarlet was a very early color (popular for military uniforms) named "Stroudwater Red" for the vicinity in England where a superior wool and shade of red was achieved.

Cheyenne Breechclout. c.1890. *Author's collection.* Rare use of yellow as a garment. Although the ribbon trim is now cotton, the previous hand-stitched lines have fragments of old silk ribbon. Magenta and purple **saved list** were also found on the Plateau, although with less frequency.

Photo Essay –
Is it Real or is it an Artifake?

By Preston E. Miller

Collecting
and Identifying Replicas

In today's marketplace, the replica Indian artifact deserves your attention. Understanding this area of collecting is important, regardless if you wish to own any replicas or not. Without knowledge of this phenomena you will, at some point in your collecting, undoubtedly become the owner of an artifake thinking that it is an authentic historic Indian made relic. It may even cost you a lot of money and will most surely be a disappointment to your collecting pleasures. This can all be eliminated if you take the time to learn about the types of replicas being made and the artists making them. Who knows—once you increase your knowledge, you may even find reasons to add a few replicas to your collection.

An Indian replica is the re-creation of an item to duplicate or resemble something Indians would have made and used in the past. When a replica receives additional efforts to make it appear as though it were actually made in the past it becomes an "Artifake." The value of such an item is not the same as the old original. For instance, the value of a fully beaded vest, in excellent condition and made in 1870, is higher than an exact replica or artifake made in 1990. The value of the replica is determined by the expertise of the maker, the rarity of construction materials, and the amount of construction time (hours, days, or weeks).

Some collectors would prefer that this process not be used to change an item's appearance. The fact is that some items are more attractive and sellable if they look old. Many collectors seem to equate dirt with wear and age. This, they feel, makes an item look like it was made by Indians long ago. On the other hand, let us suppose that a pair of moccasins, made in 1870, was purchased by the local Indian agent and immediately stored in a trunk. This trunk has remained in the agent's family for three generations. If all conditions, such as no light, no bugs, no dampness, no dust, etc., have remained stable, the moccasins should look the same one hundred years later. Some collectors will value these moccasins for their excellent condition while others would prefer a little dirt and wear (patina). The choice is up to the individual collector. The trick is to know which items have an original patina and which are replicas with an artificially applied patina. Experience and observation will help you learn to see the difference. The answer is, don't make a purchase unless an item satisfies you completely.

The importance of whether or not the replica was made by persons identifying themselves as American Indian must be determined by the purchaser. Generally, this does not make a difference in the value of the finished item. Buyers seem to be more interested in the quality of the work and value finished items accordingly. Currently, most replicators are of non-Indian heritage. Most Indian artists are busy making contemporary items for the Indian and non-Indian markets. However, both Indian and non-Indian replicators are gaining a reputation for their skills, and their ability and fame usually determines the monetary value of their replicas.

The lack of authentic old relics and the high prices they command are the reasons for the large number of replicators at work today. Suppose you would like to purchase a fine old Sioux beaded and quilled pipe bag; not only would you find few for sale, but the price would probably be over $2,000. A comparable, expertly made replica would be available for under $1,200. A more dramatic example would be a rare original shield, too costly to purchase or in a museum. Why not a beautiful copy

These photos show close-ups of pony beads that have been sinew-sewn to buckskin and aged to look old. The beads were painted with a water color solution. If you look carefully you can see dark water color lines on the buckskin next to some of the white beads. (Hide also has red ochre stains.) The maker's brush slipped off the beads and left this stain. After the water color dries, the excess is wiped off with a damp cloth. Look carefully and you will notice dark and light colored areas, which result from how heavily the color was applied and how completely it was wiped off. Individual beads will often have a clean top surface with a ring of darkened stain that proceeds to the underside of the bead *(see second photo on white beads).*

instead made from authentic new materials? Hand-made rawhide, brain-tan leather, and saved list trade wool looks wonderful over your fireplace but costs less than $300. Originals can be expensive, whereas replicas are more affordable. Also, original relics are sometimes rather fragile because the materials are old and demand special care. The high cost alone can be a reason for special handling. However, replicas are fresh and durable. You can handle, wear, and play with them. In fact, limited use usually makes them look even more authentic. Suppose you would like to have a beautiful war shirt you have seen displayed at the Smithsonian Institute. You can't buy it, but you can have a replica made. Suppose an old black and white photo you own shows a Crow warrior holding a beautiful beaded knife sheath. Not only does no one seem to know what happened to the original but you probably couldn't own it if they did. For a minimal fee, you can have a replica made. The reasons for having replicas made include many such examples.

Most replicators are good, honest, trustworthy folks who want your business and have no interest in selling you a replica as being old and authentic. They want you to be pleased so that you will buy more. But, be careful because there are replicators, dealers, collectors, and sometimes questionable friends who will try to sell you an artifake as being genuine and authentic. Granted, it is possible they sometimes don't know, or aren't sure if it is genuine or not. Your best protection is education. Look, listen, study, and learn to know the origin of what you are buying.

A **restoration** is an old item or some part thereof that has been restored to its original appearance. If there is not enough of the original piece present to indicate what it looked like, you cannot do an honest restoration. You can still use the part to make something else but it will have to be labeled as a replica made with some old parts. Sometimes, parts from several old pieces are combined to make a new piece. This would be a replica and not a restoration. It is interesting to note that Indians did this long ago. Look carefully in museums and collections and you will find many items made from one or more original pieces re-combined to make something new. Examples would include a strike-a-light pouch made from a little girl's fully beaded legging or a knife case made from the beaded side of a saddle bag. Many things were re-combined into something useful. If it was done long ago by Indians, we would call it an authentic relic.

Sometimes the question is how much of an item must be present before a restoration becomes a replica. For instance, if all you have is one rawhide moccasin sole and you use it to make a pair of beaded moccasins, it is not a restoration. This would be a replica because you had no insight into how the original moccasin looked just by viewing the rawhide sole. This moccasin would be a whole now creation. An example of a restoration would be a Sioux pipe bag with most of the porcupine quills eaten off the rawhide slats by carpet beetles, and the replicator replaces the missing quills using good old colors and an authentic pattern. This would be a restoration. The *integrity* of the original pipe bag is till intact.

Ideally, restorations should be done so that the process can be reversed and the item returned to its original condition. This is the only kind of restoration that would be allowed in most large recognized museums.

Cleaning

The cleaning of artifacts is a restoration process that should only be undertaken by persons who have complete knowledge of the final outcome. For instance, the washing of white brain tanned buckskin in soap and water is irreversible. I once owned a beautifully quilled child's vest that had been washed with soap and water. What a shame to see the buckskin turned into a board-like stiffness that could never be returned to its beautiful soft condition.

Be careful, because items can be ruined and their value greatly or sometimes completely lost if you cause any irreversible change in the material structure or stability of the object. Every item has its special patina or appearance, which has been acquired through years of use or just natural aging. This can be a certain coloring, texture, smell, feeling to the touch or look. If the patina is good, do not change it as you will most surely reduce the value.

DON'T, DON'T, DON'T do any of the following:

- Wash Navajo rugs in soap and water. The colors will bleed together.
- Wash white buckskin in soap and water. It will turn board stiff.
- Use glue to repair damaged beadwork, quillwork, or baskets.
- Restore painted colors with magic markers.

The best practice is to seek the advice of a reputable authority before doing anything that might change an artifact's visual appearance.

Authenticating Relics By Bead Colors

One of the first things to consider when authenticating the age of a beaded relic is the color of the beads. It is good to think about the color choices as if you were the Indian craftworker. One hundred and fifty years ago your life would be centered around natural things. The colors you preferred would reflect those surroundings. They would probably be similar to the forests, mountains, or deserts near where you lived. A good test is to think of the beadwork you are trying to authenticate as if it were hanging on a tree in the forest. Does it blend into the natural surroundings or would it blend in better with the colorful cereal boxes in your local grocery store? If it looks better in the forest, chances are good that it pre-dates 1900, and if it looks better in the grocery store it could be more recent.

It is interesting to theorize why color choice might be an important guide in helping collectors determine the age of a beaded object. There can only be two reasons: the Indians' preference or the availability of the beads. Certainly, traders could not stock every bead color. We must assume they stocked the beads that were most in demand. But on the other hand, if bright oranges, pinks, yellows, reds, and blues had been available in 1870, how do we know the Indian people would not have used them? They certainly are popular in modern times. It is interesting to note that, presently, bright orange is a very popular color among Indians and very unpopular among non-Indians. However, orange seldom shows up on pre-1900 artifacts. Was this because it was an unpopular color or because it was not available?

This is a section from an 1870s Ojibwa garter displaying the use of subtle old time colors. Three different reds are visible. Transparent rose is used on the teardrop portion of the larger flower. The center of the large flower and two of the teardrop designs contain ruby red white center beads. The middle teardrop design uses rose-red white center beads. The center of each teardrop contains a row of gold metal faceted beads. Cheyenne pink is a popular old-time color. The white flower stems use an interesting style of barbs that identify this piece as Ojibwa.

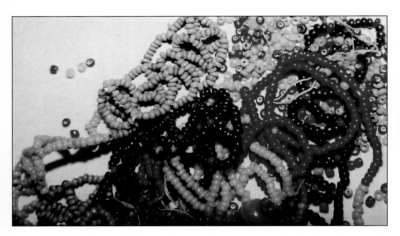

An assortment of **old** seed beads showing colors of white lined ruby red, greasy yellow, black, and light blue.

Greasy yellow and greasy blue are good old colors that are often found on older pieces. Even though they have usually been available, Indians seem to have not used them much after 1915. Perhaps the brighter opaque yellows and blues became more popular. Presently, there is a trend back to these colors but they are still a good indication of a relic's age and authenticity.

Red bead types can be loosely dated as follows:

• a ruby red bead with white center dates before 1870
• a rose-red w/white center dates between 1870 and 1900
• a bright red w/white center dates from 1890 to 1920
• a greasy opaque red dates from 1915 to 1940
• transparent rose-red (various shades) dates from before 1870 to the present
• various shades of opaque reds date from 1920 to the present.

If these dates don't coincide with your beliefs, don't be too disappointed, as my data is based on my own personal observations. Because there is no accurate data to substantiate what years certain bead colors were produced, we can only make observations and estimates. There is no time limit between the year a bead is made and when it is used; Indians sometimes collect beads for many years before using them. Also they often tear an older used item apart and use the beads to make a new item. Some old beads are still being used today by Indians and replicators. So, these dates are only intended to give you an idea of when certain colors of red appear to be most popular.

In this photo, a string of old wire-wound white center red necklace* beads is shown next to four *new* white center red beads*. The old wire-wound beads were made one at a time by melting glass around a copper wire and slipping the finished bead off after the glass cooled. This type bead was already being traded to Indians prior to 1870; their use on a relic is a good indication that it is old and authentic. The four new beads, from France, were made from a long glass tube that was cut into small tubes and tumbled in sand to make the edges smooth. Because of this they retain a rather tube-like square shape. Notice that these have white centers and that the colors are two different shades of red. This style bead is not as common on early relics and seems to have been most popular after 1900.

(*popularly known as "Crow" beads)

Beads are like dye lots of yarn, in that each time a color is made the shade will vary. Even though the factory assigns a number to a certain color, the shade will usually vary slightly each time they are made. White and black are the only colors that stay the same. Blues show the most variation. Bead workers who haven't accumulated enough beads to finish a project will often find it difficult to match additional colors exactly. Many times you will find old fully-beaded items with the background color changing shades and sometimes sizes before it is finished. This is because the bead worker ran out of beads and the trading post couldn't supply the exact same color.

Look and learn, take photos, compare objects, ask questions, and in time you should develop a sense of how to authenticate and date a relic by looking at the colors of the beads.

Trade Ornaments and Materials Used on Indian Artifacts

Comparisons of Old vs. New

Brass hawk bells were attached to many old Indian items as decorative ornaments. They show up on horse gear, dresses, pipe bags, war bonnets, dance bustles, medicine items, etc. As old and new bells are somewhat different, they can often be a tell-tale indication of a relic's authenticity. Old hawk bells are made from two sheets of brass that have been domed and crimped together. The top is perforated to produce a tinkling sound and the underside has a hole into which a brass wire attachment loop is loosely inserted. Hawk bells come in many sizes, with most being under 3/4" diam.

(Left to right) Here are four recently manufactured, and still shiny, hawk bells. Notice the smoothness of the crimped edge. On old bells, the crimping will be less smooth. These bells have wire loops. On the first two, both ends of the loop are inserted into one hole. On the third and fourth bells, the wire loop is triangular shaped with each end stuck into its own individual hole. I have never seen an old bell with two holes for the wire loop or this triangular shaped wire. Remember that an artifaker will antique these bells to look old and the patina will no longer shine. If you want to be able to recognize the difference, try tarnishing one yourself. Just soak it in vinegar for a day or two and see what happens. Keep looking and in time you will learn to recognize the difference between a natural old patina and an artificial modern patina.

Indians obtained brass tacks from traders as early as 1773. (See Hanson, Charles, *Museum of the Fur Trade Quarterly*, Vol. 18, #1 & #2, 1982: 20). Tacks were also salvaged from worn out leather trunks that were made in abundance by Eastern trunk makers beginning in the 1700s. Indians used tacks to decorate gun stocks, quirts, knives and sheaths, war clubs, leather belts, mirror boards, etc.

(Left to right) The largest bell (apx. 1.75" diam.) was dug up by G. B. Fenstermaker at the Daisy Site on the Fry property in Washington Boro, Pa. It dates before 1700 and is of Spanish manufacture according to Mr. Fenstermaker. It has an unusual attachment loop that is solidly attached and made from a strip of brass. The second bell has a nice aged patina with brass wire loop. Notice the interesting raised ridge that circles the loop hole. The remaining bells show a nice patina and still have buckskin thongs attached. Notice that one of the smaller bells still has some of its original red gilt finish near the crimped edge.

(Left to right) The first tack is new. It has a steel shank and a finished edge on the dome. Even though records indicate steel shank tacks were being made by 1870, they do not show up on many Indian made items until about 1900. Many collectors believe, falsely, that items decorated with steel shank tacks are artifakes. The second tack is a very old example of a cast brass tack with a square brass shank. It was pulled from an old leather trunk. The square shank and the rough edge on the dome are proof to most collectors that a relic containing this type tack is old. These tacks are not being made today, but old ones are being found and sometimes used to decorate replicas and artifakes. So, be careful!

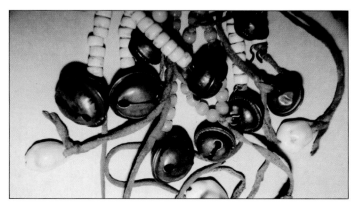

This photo shows an assortment of various sized hawk bells attached to the bottom of an old Flathead necklace. Notice the red and green gilding that is still visible near the crimped edge on some of these bells. Originally, they were completely colored but most of the gilt plating has worn off. We do not know of any recently manufactured examples with color gilding. To identify old bells, look for the crimping to be more rough looking, the loose wire loop, possible gilt coloring, and a nice even patina. Don't forget to look inside to see if the patina is evenly distributed. Also notice the old cowry shells with hand filed holes on this necklace.

This is an old beaded musket cap holder with square shank tacks decorating the edge.

Brass beads have been a popular Indian trade item for nearly two hundred years. The old beads were manufactured by pressing the ends of a brass tube until it bulged into a round hollow bead. Solid brass beads were not made until after the invention of the metal lathe and probably didn't show up in the Indian trade until after the 1950s.

Old bone hair pipe necklace strung with old hollow round brass beads.

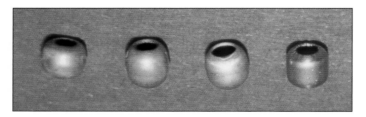

The four beads in this photo are hollow and were made since 1985. These new beads often have straighter sides and appear more square than the old beads.

Tin cones, ranging from apx. 1/2" to 2", were made by Indians to ornament pouches, knife cases, dresses, moccasins, etc. Most often they were cut with shears or chisels from old tobacco tins, kettle tops, tin cans, etc. Because they were individually hand made, the tin cones found on old Indian items are usually crudely cut and bent.

(Left to right) The first old tin cone is 1-1/8" long with protruding black horse hair. The second is 1-3/8" long with protruding horse hair that has been dyed red. Notice that the fourth and fifth cones are attached to buckskin thongs and have red feather fluffs protruding. The two small cones on the left are 3/4" long. These and the larger cone next to them were found at the site of old Fort Bennet along the Missouri River in South Dakota.

These tin cones are attached to the bottom of an old Sioux beaded awl case with buckskin thongs and have dyed red horse hair protrusions. Notice the bottom edges do not come together perfectly. This is a good sign that they were hand-made; the evenly distributed patina is also a good indication of their authenticity.

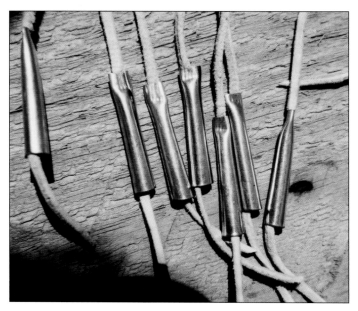

These commercially made tin cones demonstrate the most obvious way to detect old from new. The tops have been crimped with a pliers to keep them from sliding off the buckskin thong; I have never seen this method of attachment used on a genuine artifact. This along with their uniform construction and size are certain proof that the tin cones were recently attached.

(Left to right) **Cowrie shells** were often used as ornamental attachments on dresses, vests, necklaces, pouches, etc. They were usually imported from the Pacific Islands and traded without holes to Indian people. By rubbing the sharp edge of a file or stone against the shell, a hole could be worn into the upper portion so a buckskin thong, sinew string, or thread could be passed through. The old shells with holes, probably dating before 1920, were filed by Indians. After the invention of speed drills and small sharp bits, commercial companies began drilling round holes into the shells. Remember, a round hole is an indication that the shells could be of recent manufacture. Notice that the fourth shell has a round drilled hole and is modern. The first two shells are of the bulbous/lumpy type called Yellow Money Cowries, which were the most popular style in the early American Indian trade. The smooth oval type, called Ring Top Cowries, could be an indication that your item is not very old. Anyone can file a hole into a cowry shell. Try it sometime—it is quite easy. So be careful, because even a filed hole is not positive proof of authenticity. *(See previous photo with old brass hawk bells, p. 13)*

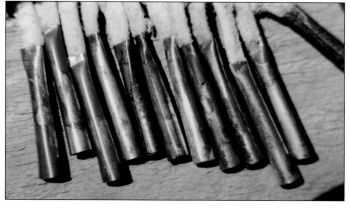

This photo shows the same attachment procedure with a surface patina that has been created by soaking in a solution such as vinegar. If you look carefully, you can seen the spotty markings and uneven coloring of the patina. Most old patinas will be evenly distributed with (maybe) some rust spots here and there.

Sinew is made from the muscular tendons that are located in a deer back next to the tenderloins. It is peeled off, dried, and then broken down into strings that are wetted and twisted into thread. Sinew from elk, buffalo, moose, caribou, and cow can also be made into sinew thread.

(Top to bottom) The small spool is Nymo brand (nylon) thread, which is currently used by many Indian bead workers. (NOTE: Nylon thread was not commercially available until after World War II) The large spool is imitation sinew, which is made from a nylon material that has been heavily waxed. It looks like real sinew but will melt if heat is applied and does

not have the feeling of stiffness that is characteristic of real sinew. In the middle is a slab of genuine deer sinew with the mid-section broken down into individual strings. These are peeled off, one at a time, and twisted into individual threads, as seen at the bottom of this photo. On many old items of Indian manufacture, sinew was used for beading, quilling, and sewing. Sometimes commercial cotton thread and sinew will show up on the same piece, with the beads being strung on the sinew and then sewn down with cotton thread.

Left:
(Left to right) These are new commercially manufactured cones that first became available about 1940. They are usually available in 3/4", 1", and 1-1/4" sizes. They are uniform in size and shape and the top hole is plenty big for stringing on leather thongs. The first one is made from brass, a metal that will seldom be seen among old cones. The second is shiny tin (sometimes aluminum). The second and third cones show different degrees of surface patina that can be induced by soaking in vinegar. Other solutions and heat are sometimes used to create an old looking patina. Sometimes by looking inside a cone you can determine that the outer surface was artificially treated to make it look old. While looking inside the cone, you should also look to see if the buckskin thong or thread has the same patina and cut edges as the outer visible portion. A new cut will be bright and clean without any aging or discoloration. But always remember a good artifaker will also think of this and will probably take the time to apply some sort of patina, thus making it difficult to detect whether or not the buckskin is really old.

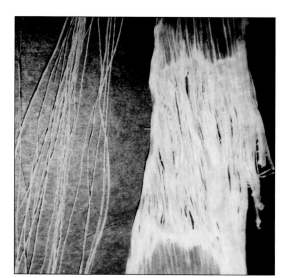

This detail photo shows a slab and twisted threads of deer sinew.

Photo Essay – Old and New Artifact Comparisons

by Carolyn Corey

BLACKFEET WAR SHIRT

Heavy deer hide with painted black stripes and beaded red wool neck panels on both sides. Beaded strips with unique star motif in white and red w. hearts on gr. blue appliqué background. Apx. 78 human hair locks with red wool "firecrackers" and single lt. blue Crow bead hang from shirt sleeve and back shoulder beaded strips. Six white ermine tubes at each shoulder; four cut tubes ornament front.

Chewing Black Bones wore it for a famous Winold Reiss painting seen on far left. The shirt and the Half-Red Half-Yellow Ermine Headdress are known to be Chewing Black Bones "powerful war medicines." He was a famous warrior who in his later years advocated traditional Indian religion. (Winold Reiss also did a painting of Short Face wearing this shirt.)

Text from Raczka, Paul. *Portrait of the Races.* Winold Reiss Exhibition Catalog, Great Falls MT, C. M Russell Museum, 1986.

Painting image from a transparency owned by the Great Northern Railway Co. Foster, Walter. *Indians of the Northwest by Winold Reiss.* Tustin, Calif. Walter Foster Art Books, c.1950.

The new shirt is made to closely resemble the original.

SIOUX QUILLED BAG
Original in Chicago Field Museum. Stylized buffalo tracks motif and red lines are known as protective symbols.

Original Crow pouch at Yellowstone Museum, Billings Airport, MT.

CROW-STYLE FULLY-BEADED POUCH
Trapezoidal-shape; geometrics in white center pink, periwinkle, t. cobalt, black and red w. heart outlined in white. Periwinkle bead edging. Matching buckskin strap. T. red bugle bead loop bottom dangles. Pouch is 3" bottom W x 4.5"L + dangles. Est. 95-150 **SOLD $75(01)**

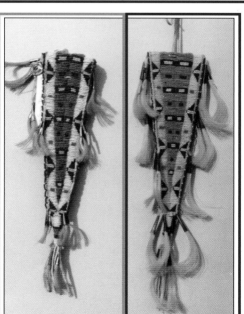

"Enhanced" replica has been made with subtle color variations in the purple, yellow and blue-green quill-wrapped bottom slats; also pale yellow, pale blue and varying red tones in buffalo track designs. Note unique color change between top motifs to purple lines in both copy and original. Quill-wrapped purple, blue, and yellow wrapped thongs with tin cone drops at top of bag. Lane-stitched border in blocks of gr. yellow, gr. blue, t. dk. cobalt divided by single line of rose w. hearts. Top opening is med. blue bead edged. Replica is 8"W x 15"L.

The replica, shown here, and original pipe bag each have opaque white lane-stitched bead motifs repeating the cut beaded apple green color of the pouch along with rose-red w. hearts, cobalt, and lt. blue patterns. Rolled beaded top. Bottom yellow horsehair/tin cone fringes are bead wrapped same colors. 5.5"W x 22"L including bottom tab and fringes.

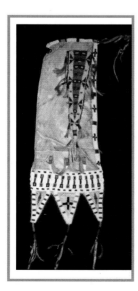

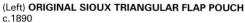

(Left) ORIGINAL SIOUX TRIANGULAR FLAP POUCH c.1890
RARE. Originally tied to a matching pipe bag. Exquisitely beaded flap is gr. white with Sioux green, cobalt, t. rose, gr. yellow and rose w. heart lane-stitched and sinew sewn. Eighteen beautiful yellow horsehair/tin cone dangles (only one is missing the horsehair). Cobalt edge-beaded. 10"L x 2.5"W at top. 2.25"H x 2.75"W pouch has same colors on the side and top borders. Great patina and condition. Est. 1200-1600 **SOLD $1300(02)**
(Right) After we sold this pouch in our 2002 auction, we decided to have a copy made for our collection along with a copy of the original pipe bag, which we did not purchase, due to the high price tag on this item! The copies were made to closely match the original design and bead colors. See flap pouches side by side—we actually prefer the new one that is on the right. The subtlety and uniqueness of the pouch is in the translucency of the white bead background, unusual color of yellow horsehair, and beautiful pastel colors of the cut beaded designs.

The original pipe bag is somewhat wider, but is otherwise a close match to the replica.

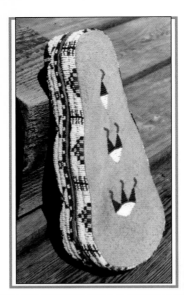

SIOUX-STYLE FULLY-BEADED MINIATURE VIOLIN CASE

Author's collection. The original full-sized violin case (31.5"L) is pictured in *The Flag in American Indian Art.* It was a Christmas gift from a Brule Sioux woman to her German immigrant husband on the Rosebud Reservation in 1899. The modified replica is only 8.75"L and is lane-stitched over buckskin. Czech cut 13° bead colors are t. dk. cobalt, apple green, pale blue, brass with rose-red w. hearts, and gr. yellow.

Herbst, Tony and Joel Kopp. *The Flag in American Indian Art.* Seattle: Univ. of Wash. Press, 1993: 75.

Fig. 177 (⁴⁄₈). Medicine-bag. Height of bag, 7 cm.

ARAPAHO MEDICINE BAG

This replica was made to the specifications as exactingly described by Kroeber in *The Arapaho,* p. 444, where this black and white drawing appears. Red-ochred buckskin with concentric circles of green, yellow, blue, and white. Tabs and top are edge-beaded in t. dk. cobalt alt. with opal. white. There is a hand-carved Catlinite ring tied to the closure thong. The contents of the original bag were pine needles used for incense and a small red pebble and "orange-colored haw." Kroeber states that bags of this type seem to be for "household medicine" rather than those that are more specifically associated with the supernatural.

Kroeber, Alfred L. *The Arapaho.* Lincoln, Univ. of NE Press: 1983.

ORIGINAL PLATEAU PICTORIAL BELT POUCH *Clark Co. Museum, Vancouver, Wash.*

These Flathead Indian-made replicas are appliqué stitched, like the original, with thong closures and calico lined flaps.
(Left) Variation of the same deer motif on flap in Czech cut beads: blue iris and bronze. Chey. pink background with rolled beaded flap in varying blocks of colors. 5.5"L x 5"W. Est. 125-175 **SOLD $125(00)**
(Right) Central area outlined with single row of turquoise. 5.5"L x 5"W. Est. 125-175 **SOLD $95(00)**

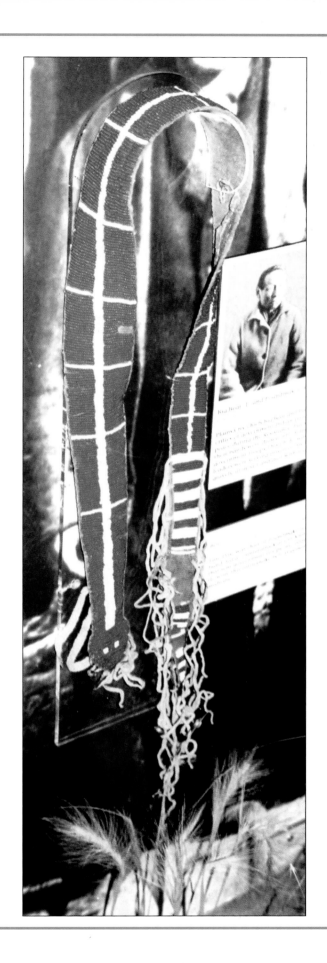

FINE DAY'S MEDICINE SNAKE

Provincial Museum, Edmonton. c.1870. Made by Fine Day's grandmother out of "well-tanned, light weight buffalo hide…using sacred blue and white colors, she stitched on the beads with sinew, adding hawk bells for rattles." Fine Day was one of the bravest war leaders of the Plains Cree. The story of the belt is told by Solomon Bluehorn to Doug Light in 1950: When Fine Day was a young man he was one of six Indians in a horse raiding party. They traveled on foot for several days until they sighted a Blackfoot hunting party returning to their village with fresh buffalo meat. They waited until the following night when the village was all asleep and stole 1-2 horses each and immediately headed home. By noon the next day, Blackfoot pursuers could be seen in a cloud of dust behind them and as they advanced the Cree party raced to the summit of a hill where they killed the horses they had stolen to form a barricade against the oncoming Blackfoot. The Cree were able to shoot many of their enemy but as the numbers grew the Blackfoot surrounded the hill so that the Cree could not escape. By the fourth night, the Cree were dying of thirst. That night, Fine Day had a vision, a spirit in the form of a large rattlesnake—the snake showed him the way down the hill to escape, which he did the following day with his entire war party. Fine Day made good his promise to honor the snake with a sacred bundle. After that, "Fine Day always wore the snake amulet in bandolier fashion. Because of it, he was never wounded or harmed by his enemies because he was protected by the 'Rattle Snake Manitou.'"

Light, Douglas W. *Footprints in the Dust.* No. Battleford, Canada: Turner Warwick Publ., 1987: 296-305. Also see photo of Fine Day's sacred rattle, red stroud breechcloth, and this snake when it was on display in the Fred Light Museum, in Battleford, Saskatchewan on page 344.

*See other unique examples of medicine belts, called "cross belts" (or necklaces by the Blackfoot) in the following article: Raczka, Paul. "Ohkinikski: War Medicines of the Northwest Plains," in *The People of the Buffalo, Vol. 1.* Taylor, Colin & Hugh Dempsey, eds. pp. 130-138. Wyk, Germany: Tatanka Press, 2003.

CREE SNAKE REPLICA

Author's collection. The copy is made from pony trader blue and white pony beads on moose hide with tied buckskin fringes and hawk bell and tin cone "rattles"; the original is made of seed beads on buffalo hide. The copy is 48"L x 2" at widest part.

ORIGINAL PLATEAU LARGE BANDOLIER BAG
Ft. Benton Museum, Montana. Belongs to historian Jack Lepley and was collected on the Blackfeet Reservation in Montana by his family.

PLATEAU-STYLE LARGE BANDOLIER BAG
Author's collection. Fully-appliqué beaded central bag is lt. blue with gr. yellow and t. dk. cobalt; on moose hide. 9" x 6" plus "saved list" drop; brass shoe button trim. Straps are 5"W. white, mustard, and pony trader blue inlaid with red trade wool. Red calico print backed; white muslin bound. Hangs apx. 45"L. Est. 1200-1800

20

I. Indian-Made Artifacts

1. Weaponry & Cases

War Clubs/Dance Wands

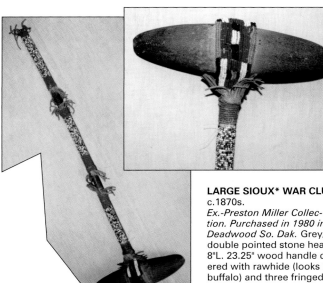

GIANT STONE HEADED SIOUX WAR CLUB c.1860-1880s?
The tag is old and hard to read but appears to say: *"War Club, Brule-Sioux, Dakota, last used by Maste-hiya hiyan, Chippewa Sioux Indian whose American name is John Wells, in Flandreau S. Dakota he took part in the New Ulm Massacre and all depredations in those troublesome times."* Large pecked stone head is 7.5"L. One point is painted black. It is attached with heavy rawhide that goes one third of the way down the wooden handle; sewn with heavy sinew lacing. The center of the 34" handle is decorated with fringed red cloth. Thread wrapped with old seed beads that are mostly "salt and pepper" colors, some are mustard and Crow lt. blue. The last 17" of the handle is plain patinated wood and is terminated with two tubular polychrome beads, red cloth, and dyed red horse hair. This dangle is tacked and glued to the handle. Also there is a hole with brass wire through it, perhaps the wire, glue, and nail were added at a later time. Est. 1400-2000 **SOLD $1400(99)**

LARGE SIOUX* WAR CLUB c.1870s.
Ex.-Preston Miller Collection. Purchased in 1980 in Deadwood So. Dak. Grey/tan double pointed stone head, 8"L. 23.25" wood handle covered with rawhide (looks like buffalo) and three fringed buckskin sections that are wrapped with size 13° seed beads in Sioux green and old-time "salt and pepper" multi-colors. Upon close examination, it appears that some of the beadwork is sinew stitched and some is stitched with old thread. A beaded band (1.5") secures the stone to the handle with unusual designs and colors, including a very old chocolate brown, black, white, greasy Bodmer blue, and Sioux green.

  *This band is very unique and might be an early variation. We think it ranks among the best and most visual we have ever seen. Exc. cond. 25.5"L. Est. 2500-4000 **SOLD $1900(01)**

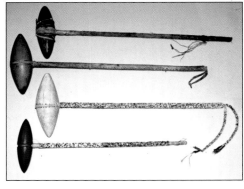

SIOUX STONE HEAD WAR CLUBS
(Top to bottom) c.1870 or earlier.
Highly polished tan/grey double-pointed stone head, 6"L. Rawhide covered and sinew-stitched handle. Overall length is 20.5". There is an interesting and very old thong tied around the head, the purpose unknown. Great old patina, exc. cond. Est. 400-650 **SOLD $450(02)**
c.1870 or earlier. Large 6.5" bauxite stone head that has turned a nice soft brown color from age. There is a slight 3/4" chip off the one point, however, it does not detract from the quality of this fine club. The handle is rawhide covered and sinew stitched with a loop on the end. Overall length is 20". This appears to be the real thing that would be used by a Sioux warrior in battle. Rare, very nice, exc. cond and great patina. Est. 650-950 **SOLD $550(02)**
c.1870. Nicely shaped and polished white bauxite 6.5" double-pointed stone head. Overall length is 19.5" with two 7" bead wrapped tin cone dangles; red hackles on the tips. The beading is sinew sewn with white background and cobalt blue, old time white l. rose and a few gr. yellow mixed into a "salt and pepper" design. There is a buckskin strip with edge beading around the center of the head. This is a truly great war club, exc. cond. and patina. Est. 650-950 **SOLD $650(02)**
This is an old bead-wrapped sinew-sewn handle that didn't have a head. Recently a Catlinite head was attached that was made in Pipestone Minn. about 25 years ago. Head 5.5"L x 17" total L. Est. 150-400 **SOLD $149(02)**

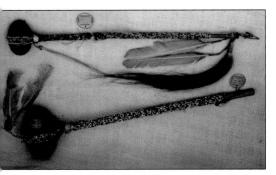

FT. PECK-SIOUX WAR CLUBS c.1870.
Collected on the reservation in Montana by O. Kather of Burlington, Iowa.
(Top) His tag on the club says, *"Boys War Club, Culbertson, Montana. #11."* Rounded hard stone head with full beaded handle with feather and horsehair dangles. The bead colors are "salt and pepper style"—lots of Cheyenne pink, Sioux green, w. lined rose and cobalt. Beads are thread-sewn. 17"L Est. 1000-1500 **SOLD $850(99)**
(Bottom) His tag on the club says, *"War Club, Culbertson, Montana. #10."* Rounded hard stone head with full beaded handle with feather dangles. The stone head has interesting grooves pecked into one end. The bead colors are "salt and pepper style" with Sioux green, white l. rose, cobalt, greasy yellow, etc. Beads are sewn with thread. 19"L. Great old patina and identification tag. Est. 1000-1500 **SOLD $1100(00)**

(Top to bottom): **OLD SIOUX STONE HEAD WAR CLUB** c.1880. The 7"L. double pointed white bauxite head is polished with great old patina. The beading on the handle has an old pumpkin color background with four sections of salt and pepper beading in old colors of white, gr. yellow, Sioux green, white-lined rose, cobalt, and lt. blue, etc. There is a buckskin strip around the center of the head beaded with white and t. red beads. Attached to the strip are two tin cones with pink fluffs. 15"L. Thread sewn. Exc. cond. Est. 500-950 **SOLD $375(04)**

SIOUX (LAKOTA) STONE HEAD WAR CLUB c.1890. Beautifully polished and shaped double pointed light brown stone head. Measures 4.75"L. with a buckskin strip around the center partially beaded with Sioux green and cobalt blue beads. The handle is bead wrapped with white, cobalt and periwinkle blue seed beads. 16.5"L. Sinew sewn. Exc. cond. Est. 450-950 **SOLD $300(04)**

RARE CHEYENNE/SIOUX STYLE BULL TAIL WAR CLUB c.1870. *This outstanding club is the type that was really made to be used.* The 4.5"L. round stone head is grooved and wrapped with wood splints and rawhide. It is painted with red paint in a stripe on one side and crossed stripes on the other side. The handle is covered with sinew-sewn rawhide that ends with the hair of a twisted bull tail that has the tip dyed red. Three sections on the handle are wrapped with fringed buckskin that is wrapped with beads. Beads on the first section are white background with salt and pepper; mixed Sioux green, cobalt, w. lined rose, and gr. yellow beads. The middle section has many shades of blue with unique trans. milky blue beads, and white beads. The end section is wrapped with gr. yellow and Sioux green beads. ALL SINEW SEWN. Great aged patina. Club is 21"L. with the tail additional 17"L. Est. 900-1500 **SOLD $900(04)**

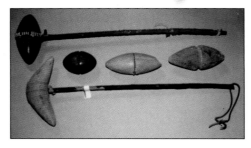

(Top) **SIOUX WAR CLUB** c.1870. Nicely carved and polished brownish grey stone head, 5.5"L. Handle is wrapped with old time wool trade cloth and appears to have once had beads wrapped around it. The stone head has six grooves (a few small nicks on one point) and is held in place with beaded band. 22.5"L. Est. 450-750 **SOLD $450(00)**

(Left to right, center) **SIOUX CATLINITE WAR CLUB HEAD** c.1870. Polished red stone head with groove and drilled hole for handle. Good shape and color. 3.25"L. Est. 250-350 **SOLD $175(00)**

SIOUX GREY BAUXITE WAR CLUB HEAD c.1890? Doubled pointed head with groove and drilled hole for handle. Both points have some pieces flaked off (about 1/2" and 3/4"). Could be re-ground into shape. 5.5"L. Est. 100-200 **SOLD $85(00)**

SIOUX WAR CLUB HEAD c.1880. Rough sand paper-like surface with full groove. Brown color. 6"L. Est. 200-350 **SOLD $150(00)**

(Bottom) **CRESCENT SHAPED STONE HEADED WAR CLUB** c.1870. Grey-brown hard stone has 1" x 1/2" flake missing from surface (1/8" deep and old). Also, a 1-3/4" x 3" oval appears to have been separated from one side and put back. Old choke cherry handle with bark on it. May not be original. Head is 7"L. Club is 20.5 "L. Unusual shape and head appears very old. Est. 350-600 **SOLD $200(00)**

SO. PLAINS RAWHIDE COVERED STONE CLUB c.1870 Could be So. Cheyenne. Unusual configuration flat stone head completely rawhide covered, yellow ochred and simply beaded in white with Sioux green. Dangles now unraveled, probably were bead-wrapped. Buckskin covered and fringed end. This club needs restoration—will be worth a lot more with a little effort. Est. 800-1200 if restored **SOLD $550(01)**

(Top) **LARGE NORTHERN PLAINS WAR CLUB** c.1870s. This is not a tourist war club but a large size club that was made for real use. Large tan colored highly polished bauxite stone double-pointed head with drilled hole for handle. Wooden handle covered with sinew-sewn rawhide. This covering goes completely around the head. Small problem is that one side of this covering tore, long ago. It has been re-attached with two small nails. On real close observation, there appears to be some small spots of old glue applied to hold this repair, which could easily be restored to original condition. Both points of the head have small flakes of stone missing from the time it was used to hit something. Head 7.25". Total 29"L. Est. 500-850 **SOLD $475(05)**

(Bottom) **SIOUX WAR CLUB** c.1900. Double pointed gray/white polished bauxite stone head with horse shoe and heart designs cut into the stone. Also on the top there is a six pointed star and arrow design. These designs are inlaid with black paint; one of the hearts is inlaid with red ochre. The head has a drilled hole for the handle; beaded buckskin band holds head in place. Two small tin cones, one with red horsehair, have been added for decoration. The end of the handle has a 2" attachment of buckskin with 2.25" bead wrapped dangle ending in a tin cone. It appears there were originally two tin cones, one is missing. The beads are t. dk blue, gr. yellow, Sioux green, unusual brick red, and Bodmer blue. This dangle is partially torn loose but could easily be re-attached with a few small stitches of sinew or thread. The buckskin attachment and the wood handle show impressions of once having been wrapped with beads. Stone head 6". Total L 18.5". Est. 200-350 **SOLD $130(05)**

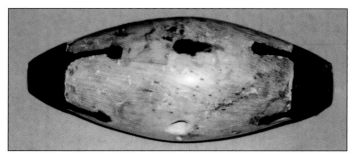

SIOUX WAR CLUB HEAD WITH LEAD INLAY c.1880.
Large white bauxite double-pointed stone head with drilled hole for handle. Both points are decorated with lead in interesting design patterns. One of the lead extensions on the top is in a cross pattern. The lead points are rather flattened as though they were used to hammer something. Fragments of red ochre paint. Point to point 5.5"L. Good patina. Est. 150-350 **SOLD $150(05)**

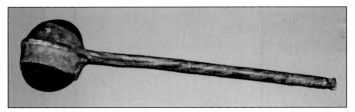

APACHE BULL TAIL WAR CLUB c.1870.
Stone headed club completely covered with sinew-sewn rawhide that includes a black bull tail on the end of the handle. 28"L. including the hair tail. Exc. cond. Est. 400-850 **SOLD $375(04)**

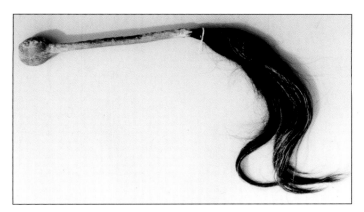

SIOUX MAUL OR CLUB c.1870 (maybe earlier)
Large stone head held in place with wood splint and rawhide (rawhide wrap is 2.5"W). This wrap and the rawhide covering the handle are all one piece, sewn in place with sinew. This is a very early style of construction. Shows a great old patina. 17"L. Est. 600-950 **SOLD $475(99)**

(Top) **SIOUX/YAKIMA STONE HEAD WAR CLUB** c.1870-1900.
The mountain goat effigy stone head is beautifully carved from what appears to be a tan hard bauxite-type stone (5"L). The other side has two red ochre filled grooves. The head is wrapped with buckskin band decorated with red porcupine quilled strips and white bead edging. There is a mass of blue feather fluffs and thongs with tiny carved deer toes hanging from the quilled band. The long handle (21") is wrapped with seed beads and pony beads of the type found on old Yakima tail dresses. and herein lies the Yakima connection of this club. *Since it was collected from the Arrow Trading Post in Toppenish, Washington, in the 1980s, I assume that the handle might have been added by a Yakima Indian.* The handle appears old and has been part of this club for a long time. The seed beads are white; the pony beads are med. blue, white, and white l. rose. Exceptional piece. Exc. cond. Est. 1500-2500 **SOLD $1000(03)**
(Bottom) **TURTLE MOUNTAIN SIOUX BROWN STONE HEADED WAR CLUB** c.1895 or earlier.
Maurice Oliver Collection. (See full provenance on club at bottom.) A book with photos and history of this collection is included. The buckskin and rawhide wrapped handle is completely wrapped with multi-colored seed beads thread-sewn. There is a 1"W. buckskin beaded band around the stone head with two clipped red feathers hanging from leather thongs and a triangular fully beaded tab hanging on the end of the handle. In the photos of the Oliver collection (see following club), this tab had long buckskin fringes that are now gone. The brown stone head is 3.5"L.; entire length is 22.5". Only two rows of beads missing on the tab and two rows on the band that goes around the head; otherwise, the patina and condition are excellent. Est. 1500-2000 **SOLD $850(03)**

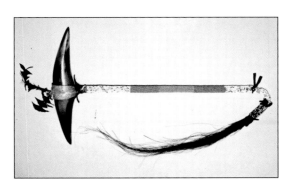

TURTLE MOUNTAIN SIOUX COWHORN CEREMONIAL CLUB c.1895.
This club was collected by Maurice Oliver, who owned the Oliver Drug Store in Oberon, No. Dakota between 1895 and 1920. He amassed a large collection of artifacts from the Indians living on the nearby Turtle Mtn. Reservation. Many were acquired as payment for services and goods from the drug store. After his retirement, about 1920, he moved to Grand Forks, No. Dakota where he often set up exhibits in local department stores. In 1974, I did a book with a history and full page photos of this collection. This club can be located in these photos and guarantees the provenance. The cow horn double-pointed head is well patinated and seems to be lead lined to give it weight. It has two small black feathers cut into a sawtooth pattern hanging from a 1" wide rawhide band to hold the horns in place. The handle is wrapped with cloth that is completely wrapped with white, pumpkin, l. blue and a few green, greasy yellow, t. red and white l. rose beads. There is a black horsehair dangle decorated with green wool felt and beads hanging from the end of the handle. The horns are 9.75", point to point. Overall L. is 28". Exc. patina. Est. 1800-2500 **SOLD $1700(03)**

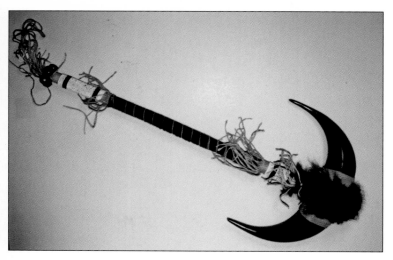

BUFFALO HORN CEREMONIAL CLUB
The horns are from an old club (c.1900) and the handle has been replaced but made to look old. The horns still have the original old cotton cloth nailed to the wood block; the buffalo hair has been replaced. The handle is expertly beaded with sinew in black and white beads with buckskin fringe. The central portion is wrapped with dark blue trade cloth and red ochred buckskin thong. The end has buckskin thongs with four old hawk bells. 22"L. An old one would cost over $1000. Est. 450-650 **SOLD $325(99)**

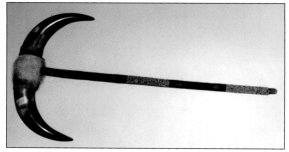

SIOUX? FULLY-BEADED CEREMONIAL CLUB c.1900?
Cow horn attached with hair; leather calico lined. Beautiful intact bead wrapped handle; t. rose, cobalt, pale blue, and dk. Sioux green. Beads have nice natural patina of age. Exc. sturdy cond. 19" total L. 10"W. distance betw. horns. Est. 800-1200

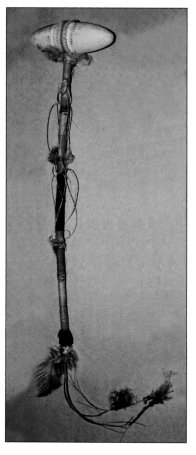

SIOUX WAR CLUB FROM TURTLE MTN. RESERVATION c.1900.
Probably made for child's play or tourist trade. The head is white alabaster and has two grooves with painted red dots. A strip of buckskin and braided horsehair hold it to the handle. The handle is covered with braided horsehair in black, white, and red. Handle also has some green fluffs attached for decoration. This club is very unique and in perfect condition. Horsehair wrapped clubs are rarely found in this good condition. 16"L. Est. 350-500 **SOLD $153(98)**

(Top) **SIOUX WAR CLUB** c.1890
Double pointed 6" head made from dk. grey stone with lead inlays in star patterns and stripes. The stars have a central small square piece of Catlinite. The points of the head are polished smooth and the center is pecked to give a roughened texture. Handle is covered with rawhide that may be buffalo, and is sinew-sewn. Est. 1200-1800 **SOLD $850(97)**

(Bottom) **UNUSUAL SIOUX WAR CLUB.** c.1880.
The head appears to be made from two cow hooves that have been dyed red. The hooves are held in place by a piece of buckskin that has been covered with sewn quillwork with the buckskin edges cut in a sawtooth pattern. 2.75" of the handle is sinew wrapped with salt and pepper beading which has buckskin fringe. Remainder of handle is covered with rawhide that has been dyed (painted?) green. Very minor bug damage to quilling (hardly noticeable). 16.75"L. Exc. cond. Est. 500-950 **SOLD $300(98)**

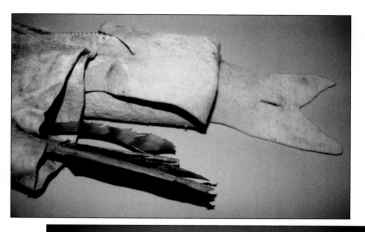

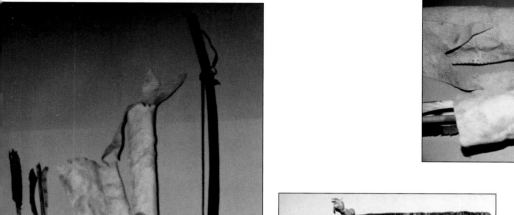

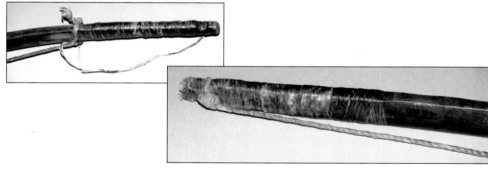

SIOUX BUFFALO HIDE QUIVER, BOW CASE, BOW AND ARROWS c.1860.
This quiver/bow case was made from an old painted buffalo robe. There are black painted robe designs still remaining on the bow case (see detail photo). We believe this case is a very early style with what appears to be a button or toggle hole in one of the forked flaps on the open end of the bow case (see detail photo). We have not found any information telling how this hole was used. However, there is a similar case in the Buffalo Bill Museum in Cody, Wyoming that includes this same style of toggle hole. Judging from the patina and the painted design, this quiver appears quite old. Considering that it is made from the remains of an old buffalo robe that must date back to the 1840s, the case must have been constructed sometime before the 1860s. The bow case is 44.75"L. from the tip of the flaps to the bottom fringe. The double curved sinew backed bow is one of the nicest we have seen. The sinew backing has been blackened. On one end, the wrapped sinew has been covered with a section of intestine. It still has the original twisted sinew string. At one end the string is held in place with an interesting buckskin loop that can be used to pull the string into the nock when stringing the bow. It includes two original arrows but only one still retains the metal trade point. Est. 20,000-25,000 **SOLD $17,000(04)**

CANVAS QUIVER WITH 11 ARROWS c.1920?
Can't tell you much about the origin of these but it could be an Improved Order of Red Men fraternal piece (See companion book, *New Four Winds Guide to American Indian Artifacts,* pp.147-177) or early movie prop, Boy Scouts or even real Indian-made. Nine arrows have iron points. Feathers and points are held fast with cord string wrappings. Hardwood shafts are different sizes and appear to have been hand made. Arrows are from 28" to 30" long. Good cond. Est. 250-350 **SOLD $225(98)**

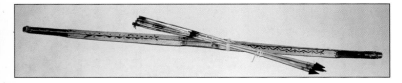

**(Top) RARE PAINTED APACHE BOW
WITH FINE TWISTED SINEW STRING** c.1870.
Has painted zigzag stripes and dots painted on both sides from the hand grip area clear to the nocks. Patina is so dark and old that the color appears to be black. The sinew string is one of the finest we have seen; it has a truly wonderful patina and age. This is a really great old Apache bow. We recently saw a similar bow made and signed by Geronimo, which sold for thousands of dollars. 37"L. Est. 900-1200 **SOLD $850(99)**
(Bottom) SIOUX ARROW WITH METAL TRADE POINT c.1870.
Fine wood shaft with three deep grooves (one goes into squiggly lines about half way down). There is a 1.25" red stripe under the three striped feathers. The 3" metal point with a raised ridge on each side is exceptionally nice. If you look very carefully, you can see that someone applied a little glue under the sinew wrapping at the point and both ends of the feather. Many old time collectors did this so sinew wouldn't unwrap. Minor bug damage to one feather, otherwise excellent condition. 25.25"L. Nice patina. Est. 350-500 **SOLD $350(99)**

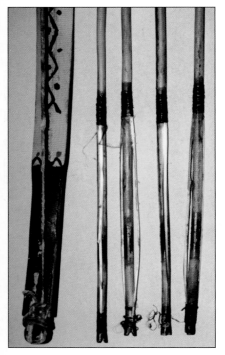

BRULE SIOUX BOW and ARROWS c.1890-1915.
This set was purchased from CHIEF LEADER CHARGE, on the Brule Sioux Reservation, by Ella LeBow between 1940-60. During those years, she was the manager of the Brule Craft Co-op at Rosebud, SD. The bow is 43"L. and strung with a great twisted sinew string. It has painted designs over the entire surface. The colors are yellow, red, orange, green, and black; the designs have a very ceremonial-like appearance. Because it is painted it is hard to tell what kind of wood it is made from—a guess would be Osage Orange. The four arrows are about 23.5"L. and painted yellow below the fletching. Under the feather fletching there are red and blue stripes. The iron points and feathers are attached with sinew. The sinew holding the fletching is painted with red and blue stripes. Each arrow has two feathers with only the stems remaining. Est. 850-1500 **SOLD $900(05)**

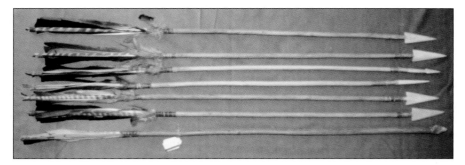

SEVEN BLACKFEET ARROWS
Collected by Harold and Irene Hanneman between 1936 and 1962 when they operated a store in Browning, Mt. on the Blackfeet Reservation. Made from willow sticks, one has a knapped flint point and the rest have interesting variations of carved bone points; all are sinew-wrapped. They all have three feathers with blue fluffs at base and sinew wrapping. Five feathers have painted stripes on feather area. 28.5" to 30.5"L. Feathers loose on one arrow where sinew has come off, otherwise exc. cond. Est. 800-1500 **SOLD $450(98)**

SEVEN BLACKFEET ARROWS
Same provenance as above. Made from willow sticks (six are painted with red ochre) and five have knapped flint points, one with metal point and one point is missing. Points and feathers are sinew-wrapped. Feathers are painted with red and blue stripes. Apx. 30"L. Includes "Certificate of Authenticity," which says they are c.1860-1880 and collected from Fish Wolf Robe. Our belief is more like a 1930s origin. Exc. cond. Est. 750-1200 **SOLD $450(98)**

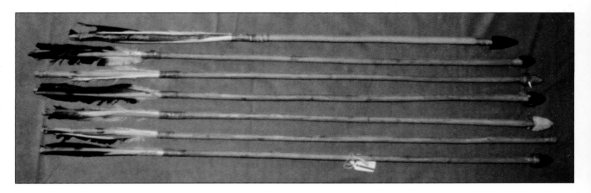

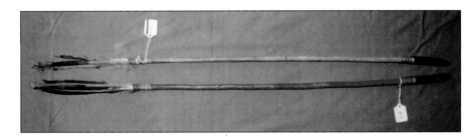

TWO BLACKFEET ARROWS
Same provenance as above. Made from willow sticks and one painted with red ochre. Metal points are 3.5"L. and sinew wrapped. Feathers are sinew wrapped and shaft is painted with red and blue stripes. 32.5"L. Est. 250-450 **SOLD $225(98)**

(Top to bottom) **SINEW BACKED (STRAIGHT STAVE) BOW** Perhaps 20th. c. but it appears just like an old one. Nice layer of sinew and coloring. Sinew is just starting to crackle from age (could be this bow was made thirty, forty or more years ago.) 38"L. Est. 500-850 **SOLD $313(00)**
HOPI OLD BOW Consignor says *"Late 1700 to early 1800s. Sinew-backed short bow with original painting. Found in remodeled house at Walpai, 1st Mesa. AZ."* Now our opinion: Everything the consignor says could be true. This bow is definitely Indian and old. If it was flat instead of oval we would call it a Plains-style bow. The sinew backing and wrapping look the same as on a Plains bow. It is warped sideways and does not have any curve. The patina is excellent; the sinew backing is cracked from age but still tightly glued to the wood; sinew wrapping has correct color patina to be very old. 38.5"L. Est. 600-900 **SOLD $325(00)**
OSAGE ORANGE BOW c.1880 A straight stave bow with nocks that look Eastern in origin. This bow is very nice and has interesting curves around the hand grip area. Exc. patina. 49 .5"L. Est. 300-500 **SOLD $157(00)**
HARDWOOD BOW Pre-1900? Appears to be an old Indian bow, but we can't identify it tribally. It is old dark colored wood with exc. patina; nice curves and notches. 47.75"L. Est. 300-500 **SOLD $188(00)**

(Top to bottom) **OLD PLAINS INDIAN ARROW WITH METAL TRADE POINT** c.1870. This is a Sioux style arrow with two squiggly lines incised into the wood shaft. The point and dark feathers are attached with sinew. All three feathers are intact. One feather has some bug damage and is not attached on one end. The sinew area around the point has been colored with a grey pigment. 1.25"point, 26"L. Exc. cond. with great patina. Est. 250-350 **SOLD $200(01)**

SAME. c.1870.

This is another Sioux style arrow with straight lines incised into the shaft. The feathers and metal point are wrapped with sinew that has a great old patina. One feather is missing and the two remaining ones have been glued to the shaft long ago. Even though we don't like to see this old glue we can give the guy credit because the feathers are still there and the glue hardly shows. The area of the shaft under the feathers still has red paint and a very dk. blue? center stripe. Has a beautiful sharp iron point 2.5"L. Arrow is 26"L. Est. 300-450 **SOLD $250(01)**

SAME. c.1870.

The feathers and iron trade point are sinew-wrapped. The wrapping around the nock end of the feathers is missing and they are being held in place by an old thread. The area under the feathers is painted with red and blue stripes. The point is 1.5"L. Arrow is 26.75"L. Est. 300-450 **SOLD $205(01)**

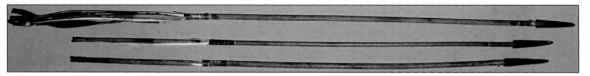

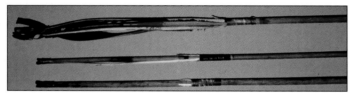

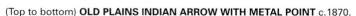

(Top to bottom) **ORIGINAL PLAINS ARROW WITH METAL TRADE POINT** c.1870 or earlier.

2.5" long iron point lightly covered with rust and attached with sinew wrapping. Point is a little loose but still firmly attached. Fletchings are gone except for the fragments that are under the sinew wrapping. Has a great carved nock and two worn lightly squiggled "blood grooves." Length is just short of 24". Original arrow with excellent patina. Est. 200-400 **SOLD $150(05)**

SAME. c.1870 or earlier.

Great 2.25" long iron point attached with sinew wrapping. Feather fletching is fragmented (see photo) but the sinew that held it is still there. Red, yellow, and blue painted stripes with some purplish coloring on some of the sinew. A great feature on this arrow is the so called "blood grooves." There are three of them; one has neat squiggly lines for 3.25". Entire length is just a hair over 24". Est. 200-400 **SOLD $150(05)**

SAME. c.1880 or earlier.

Great 2.25" long iron point attached with sinew. The sinew holding the point is painted red, a few wraps are missing (see picture). All the feather fletchings are still intact and sinew wrapped. The shaft is straight and decorated with some unusual painted designs. 28"L. with great old patina. Est. 350-500 **SOLD $277(05)**

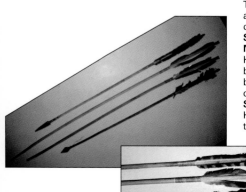

(Top to bottom) **OLD PLAINS INDIAN ARROW WITH METAL POINT** c.1870. This is a Sioux style arrow with incised (squiggly lines) wood shaft. The point and three striped feathers are attached with sinew. The shaft has red and green stripes painted in the feather area. Nice patina and in exc. cond. 2.5" point and 15.5"L. It is unusual to find an arrow with all the feathers still intact. Est. 500-700 **SOLD $500(99)**

NEZ PERCE ARROW c.1870.

Has three feather attached with sinew. About 2" of the tip is broken off. Appears as though the slit that held the metal point broke. With an extra point, this could easily be restored into a complete arrow. 32"L. Est. 200-350 **SOLD $200(99)**

SAME. c.1870.

Has short 1/8" notch in tip (see next arrow for style of point this arrow had). The wood around the tip appears worn, like it might have been shot a few times without a point. Three feathers show slight bug damage but are almost complete. Again, with a point this could easily be restored into a complete arrow. 29"L. Est. 200-350 **SOLD $100(99)**

SAME. c.1870. Complete with unusually shaped metal trade point. Some wrappings of sinew are missing but there is still enough to hold both feathers and point in place. The area under the three feathers is painted red and one unique feather has the outer edge painted red. Slight bug damage to one feather. Nice dark patina. Point is 1"L. Arrow is 23.5"L. Est. 350-500 **SOLD $225(99)**

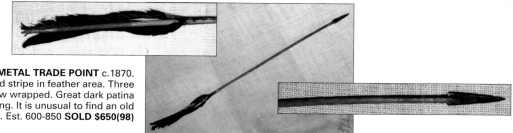

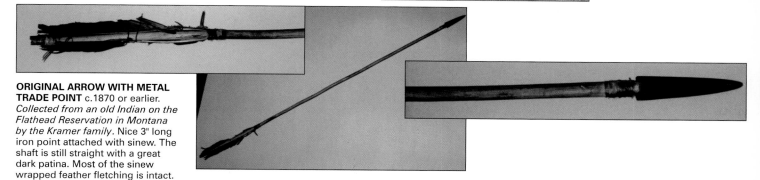

OLD SIOUX WAR ARROW WITH METAL TRADE POINT c.1870. Fine wood shaft with red painted stripe in feather area. Three feathers and metal point are sinew wrapped. Great dark patina and in exc. cond. 2" point and 26" long. It is unusual to find an old arrow with feathers still intact. Est. 600-850 **SOLD $650(98)**

ORIGINAL ARROW WITH METAL TRADE POINT c.1870 or earlier. *Collected from an old Indian on the Flathead Reservation in Montana by the Kramer family.* Nice 3" long iron point attached with sinew. The shaft is still straight with a great dark patina. Most of the sinew wrapped feather fletching is intact. This is an unusually long arrow measuring 31". The overall patina is as good as it gets. Great example. Est. 350-550 **SOLD $375(04)**

OLD PLAINS STYLE TOMAHAWK c.1880s? The one certain thing we can say about this piece is that it is old. The patina is great. The head is made from sheet metal that has been cut and folded around the handle. The fold area is decorated with stamped lines and it is held in place by two tacks. The handle is painted red (good age appearance) and decorated with brass tacks (steel shanks). The handle is wrapped with beaver fur and has minor bug damage or use wear. Dangling from the handle is an old porcupine quilled ornament on rawhide slats with horsehair (and one purple fluff still left). It resembles a Sioux style Wapeneki (hair ornament). Colors are orange, purple, green, and red. This lot also includes a second tomahawk handle minus the head. It is decorated with tacks, thimble, beads and silk ribbon. Est. 1000-2000 **SOLD $1300(00)**

CHEYENNE ARROWS WITH METAL TRADE POINTS c.1880? 3" iron points are sinew wrap attached. Feather fletching is in good shape; faint paint colors show at notched end. Incised "squiggly" lines, nice dk. patina. Apx. 24"L. Est. EACH 450-750 **SOLD $500-650 Each (98)**

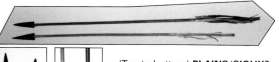

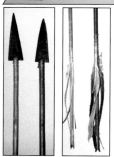

(Top to bottom) **PLAINS/SIOUX? ARROW WITH IRON POINT** c.1870. This is a great arrow and maybe just a bit nicer than the next one. It has a very nice iron point. The feathers are still intact and wrapped with sinew. The nock is very correct and handsome. The wood and sinew have a nice dark patina. This is a terrific early arrow and desirable example. 27.5"L. Est. 600-850 **SOLD $550(03)** **SAME** c.1870. Another great arrow with sinew wrapped point and feathers. The feathers are a bit disintegrated but the quills are still intact. The nocks are carved correctly and the iron point is a classic style of the type being used in the mid to late 1800s. 25"L. Great patina. Est. 450-650 **SOLD $325(03)**

BLACKFEET FORGED SPEAR c.19th C. *Collected on the Blackfeet Res. in Mont.* 12"L. blade on carved wooden spear, total L. apx. 6' Est. 800-1500 **SOLD $800(00)** *Holding spear is the buyer Putt Thompson, trader from the Crow Res. He is making a rare cameo appearance at the Great Falls Mont. Russell Show.*

Preston Miller Knife Sheath Collection

SIOUX LONG FULLY-BEADED KNIFE SHEATH c.1875
RARE. "This is the first one [knife case] that I've seen made from a tail; the curled hair makes it a longhorn...not a horse. The bilaterally-symmetrical cut of the case is a Northern Teton characteristic. This is basically a 'rectangular' knife case like several photographed by D. F. Barry among Sitting Bull's crew in the early 1880s." (Mike Cowdrey. Pers. comm. 5/06). This unique piece is backed by a complete bull tail, which is 46"L. The front panel is beaded in periwinkle blue vertical lane-stitch with t. dk. cobalt, red w. heart, gr. yellow and apple green chevron, squares and horse track motifs. See close-up photos for upper panel that holds the knife. This knife case portion is 9.5"L. Beaded triangular panel 27"L. Tiny pairs of tin cones ornament the sides. All sinew-sewn. Est. 8500-12,000

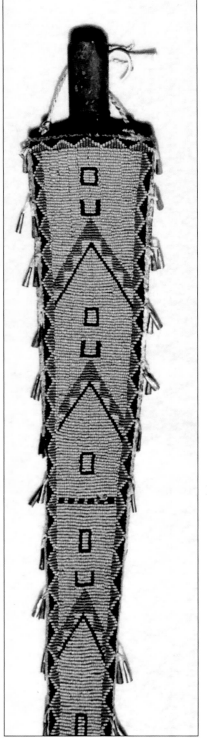

SIOUX FULLY-BEADED KNIFE SHEATH c.1890
Periwinkle with detailed lane-stitched patterns in rose. w. heart, dk. cobalt, gr. yellow, and Sioux green. Buckskin covered rawhide. Top is Sioux green bead edged. Quill-wrapped handle and extensions either side are pale yellow, rose-red, white, and blue with tiny tine cone trim. All sinew-sewn. 7"L. Est. 900-1200

SIOUX FULLY-BEADED KNIFE SHEATH c.1890
Gr. yellow bkgrd. with typical Sioux lane-stitched concentric box motif and diagonal stripes in t. cobalt, rose w. heart, and Sioux green. Tiny tin cone dyed horsehair fringes and side trim. T. cobalt blue rolled top. All sinew-sewn. Buckskin covered rawhide. Twisted buckskin hanger. 9"L. Est. 1500-2000

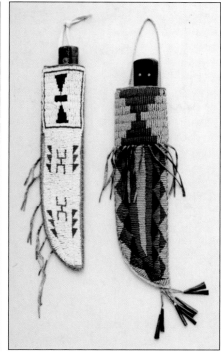

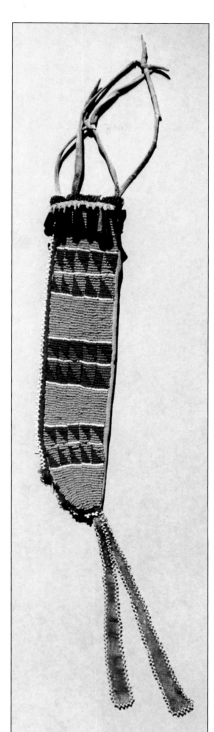

SIOUX KNIFE SHEATHS

(Left to right) c.1870 *RARE* two piece construction rawhide sheath (see photo of back) with buckskin fully-beaded panel added to front. White bkgrd. with simple geometrics in rose w. heart, cobalt blue; top has inverted triangle motifs in tiny size 16°-18° forest green, t. rose, and black cuts. Six quill-wrapped side thongs in alt. red and white. Rose w. heart single line border. Sinew-sewn. 10"L. Est. 1500-2000

Traded from Dick Pohrt in Flint Mich. In 1974. c.1885-1890 Rose w. heart and periwinkle with cobalt blue and Sioux green. Central buckskin fringes and buckskin tin cone extensions on bottom. Sinew-sewn. 9.5"L. Est. 1200-1800

CROW FULLY-BEADED KNIFE SHEATH c.1870 Vertical lane-stitched "slanting diamond" pattern lt. blue, cobalt with white horizontal lines. Central row of diamonds in pumpkin top and bottom diamonds are Crow pink. Red wool welted side with white bead edging. Top flap triangles are t. bottle green, rose w. heart, and Crow pale blue fringed with tin cones. 9.5"L + 6"L. red-ochred pale Crow blue bead edged buckskin drops. Est.1200-2000

(Left to right) **CREE ABSTRACT FLORAL BEADED KNIFE SHEATH** c.1880? Contour beaded stylized symmetrical floral motif on top is t. forest green, Chey. pink, t. rose, t. yellow, and t. gold outlined in t. dk. cobalt on gr. white ground. Lane-stitched sides and top single line border in rose w. hearts. Tin cone fringes with red wool dangles. Buckskin over rawhide. Harness leather belt strap with copper rivet on back. 9"L. Est. 900-1500

TAHLTAN VOLUTE KNIFE AND SHEATH c.1870 Moose or elkhide with cotton twill top, bound with red and white patterned calico; sides bound with heavy cotton. Beadwork in characteristic haphazard linear patterns in white, t. white, t. bottle green, and t. pink. Central zigzag line has single alt. bead colors. Metal strip bottom reinforcement. 11"L. Hand-forged iron knife with volute shaped handle wrapped with cotton muslin strips. 14.5"L. Est. 1500-2500

(Left to right) **FLATHEAD (SALISH) TACK KNIFE SHEATH**

Was on display at Log Cabin Bar in Arlee Montana for many years. Originally belonged to Joe LaMoose. Very heavy harness leather with square shanked brass tacks. Much use has produced a shiny natural patina that, along with the horse design scratched into the back (see close-up), makes this a valuable sheath. Preston has made and sold copies of this case for over thirty years in his trading post catalog. Because he uses a template to mark the tack positions, the resulting copies are easily recognizable. 12.75"L. Est. 3000-5000

LARGE BLACKFEET? TACK KNIFE SHEATH
c.1890

Made from heavy harness leather with steel-shanked tacks. The tacking process is especially interesting because after being bent the shanks were cut short with a chisel. The top third section shows tack shanks that were bent but not chiseled. There are incised lines cut into the leather between each row of tacks. Shows lots of patina from much use and includes the original knife. 13.5"L.. Est. 2500-4000

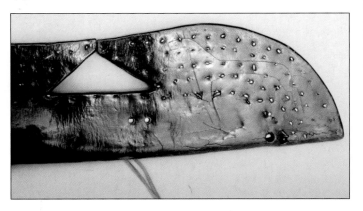

BEADED AND NICKEL SILVER BUTTON DECORATED KNIFE SHEATH
c.1870

Purchased at the Kalispell Gun Show in 1974 from Byron Higbee of Halsey, Oregon. Diagonal stripe pattern in white, t. cobalt, bottle green, gr. yellow, and rose w. heart. Back of case has four point star and the name *"L. W. Owen"* etched into the heavy harness leather. Shows years of patina and is uniquely formed to the knife that is unquestionably original to the case. Buttons are fastened by leather thong. It is held together with two copper rivets and fine brass wire pins. 9.75"L. Heavy antler handled hand-forged knife. 10"L. Est. 3000-5000

Knife Sheaths/Rifle Cases

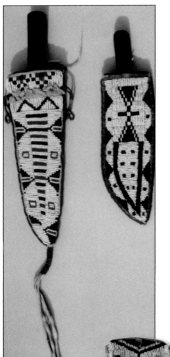

(Left) ARAPAHO FULLY-BEADED KNIFE SHEATH with knife c.1890 Pred. white with cobalt and rose w. heart in classic stripe, box, and triangle motifs. Delicately edge-beaded with gr. blue; lane-stitched and sinew-sewn. Side prs. of loop dangles on sides are gr. blue, rose w. heart, and t. gold. Bead wrapped bottom dangle (6.5"L) is gr. blue and rose w. heart. Buckskin back. Completely intact. Pristine cond. 8.5"L. Est. 700-950 **SOLD $510(99)**

(Right) SIOUX FULLY-BEADED KNIFE SHEATH with knife. c.1880 Pred. white with t. forest green and t. rose motifs. T. rose edge-beaded. Sinew-sewn and lane-stitched. Rawhide case has buckskin covered front. Perfect cond. Sheath 7.5"L. Est. 600-950 **SOLD $500(99)**

SMALL NEZ PERCE BEADED KNIFE SHEATH and KNIFE c.1890? *Collected in Idaho.* Beautiful early appliqué-stitched design motifs, diff. each side. 1) White with central rose w. heart and two surrounding dk. cobalt designs. 2) Stripes in alt. gr. yellow, white, dk. cobalt, and rose w. heart, Interesting rolled beaded vertical edge in t. gr. pink/white varied beads. 6"L incl. 1.25" bottom buckskin fringes. 1.5"W. Dark age patina. Ivory handled 7"L. knife (not shown) has stamped illegible maker and *"patent March 5, 1811."* Exc. cond. Est. 500-950 **SOLD $500(04)**

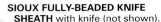

SIOUX FULLY-BEADED KNIFE SHEATH with knife (not shown). c.1880 Beaded in white with rose w. heart, apple green, t. dk. cobalt, and periwinkle. Rawhide case with buckskin front. 9"L + 3.5"L beaded bottom drop with red fluffs and tin cone dangles. Unrestored piece has two to three green beads missing and several in white edge beadwork, otherwise exc. cond and convincing old patina. Est. 950-1600 **SOLD $900(99)**

CHIPPEWA FULLY-BEADED KNIFE SHEATH c.1880 Appliqué beaded front has gr. white background with typical gorgeous floral motifs in pastels: rose w. heart, Crow pink, pale blue, t. gold, gr. blue, dk. cobalt, t. forest green, t. dk. rose with t. amethyst stem. Black velvet back and binding. Polished cotton lining. 12.75"L x 4" top opening. Perfect cond. Est. 750-1500 **SOLD $800(04)**

SIOUX FULLY-BEADED KNIFE SHEATH c.1890 *Marlon Krause Collection.* White bkgrd. with t. dk. cobalt, apple green, and gr. red-orange triangle and cross motifs; all sinew-sewn and lane-stitched. Edge-beaded in same colors with white and dk. cobalt bead hanger. Also hole punched in back long ago for twisted wire and buckskin hanger. Rawhide front covered with buckskin. Rolled beaded thong drop, same colors with red fluff remnants. Old worn 7"L. butcher knife inside. 8"L x 3"W. Est. 550-900 **SOLD $500(05)**

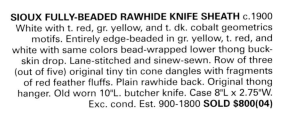

SIOUX FULLY-BEADED RAWHIDE KNIFE SHEATH c.1900 White with t. red, gr. yellow, and t. dk. cobalt geometrics motifs. Entirely edge-beaded in gr. yellow, t. red, and white with same colors bead-wrapped lower thong buckskin drop. Lane-stitched and sinew-sewn. Row of three (out of five) original tiny tin cone dangles with fragments of red feather fluffs. Plain rawhide back. Original thong hanger. Old worn 10"L. butcher knife. Case 8"L x 2.75"W. Exc. cond. Est. 900-1800 **SOLD $800(04)**

PLAINS FULLY-QUILLED OLD-TIME KNIFE SHEATH *Made from an original war shirt neck flap from the Richard Pohrt Collection.* Sewn zig-zag quillwork in beautiful unfaded yellow, with olive green and red central strip bordered in dk. brown. Masterfully made into a sheath with braided buckskin strap and 7" thong drops with white oval trade beads; four quill-wrapped drops in pale yellow. 9"L top is 4"W. Est. 500-800 **SOLD $600(02)**

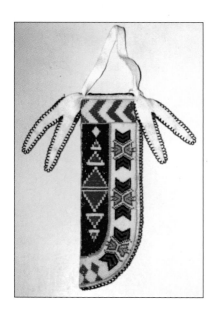

MONTANA CREE BEADED KNIFE SHEATH
Tag reads *"March 24, 1974 Emma Chiefstick, Rocky Boy Res."* Fully-beaded both sides in exquisite cut bead appliqué geometric patterns: cobalt, milky-white, rich red, and lime green. White buckskin handle with drops edge-beaded in fancy red/cobalt. Same edge-beaded along side and top. Rawhide insert. Fully-lined with dk. blue cotton. Sheath 10"L x 3"W. Est. 500-850 **SOLD $500(03)**

BLACKFEET WARRIOR'S KNIFE SHEATH, METAL TWEEZERS, and SEWING KIT.
RARE c.1870. Collected from a family near Heart Butte on the Blackfeet Reservation in Montana. They are descendants of Hugh Monroe, the famous half-breed scout, trapper, and Blackfeet interpreter. James Willard Schultz's book titled "Rising Wolf, The White Blackfoot" is the story of his life. The sheath is made from old boot or saddle leather held together with seven copper rivets. It has a belt slit and the brand *"BX"* incised into the leather. The butcher knife is original to the sheath and has *"Sheffield, England"* stamped in the blade. It is rare to find sheaths with their original knives, equally rare are the metal tweezers made and used by Indians to pull whiskers. Contrary to popular belief, Indian men did have light facial hair growth. The reason it never grew into a beard was that they were constantly pulling it out with handmade tweezers like this one, which is expertly made by an Indian and even now pulls hair effectively. 3"L. The cloth sewing kit contains a buckskin pouch full of red ochre trade paint. Warriors carried pouches like this to paint their faces before going into battle, or during sacred ceremonies when red paint was used to represent mother earth. Rolled cloth sewing bags like this were also used to carry needles, thread, thimbles, and other things necessary to keep mocs and clothing in repair during war parties or around the tipi camp. Measures 4" x 10" unfolded and still has old needles, thread, and a thimble inside; pearl button closure. Knife sheath, 9"L. Knife is 11.75"L. A rare and hard to find collectible. Exc. cond. and patina. Est. 1500-2500 **SOLD $1480(01)**

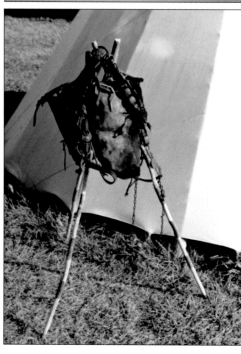

FLATHEAD WARRIOR'S HUNTING GEAR c. 1890.
This set was found in an old log cabin in the mountains near Schmidt Lookout, w. of Camas Prairie betw. Perma and Hot Springs on the Flathead Res. Montana. This is a super rare complete set of items that an early Indian hunter would have had with him when he set out on horseback to kill game or enemies. The contents are as follows: A) Rawhide knife case (17"L.) with two old knives. B) Laced rawhide bag (8.5"L x 8"W.) filled with ulu-style knife, celluloid harness ring, small saw, etc. C.) Large saddle leather bag, hand made and similar to U.S. Cavalry saddle bag. Contents: Chatillions spring balanced scale, iron shoe last, silver inlaid bit, two prs. of Indian tanned Plateau-style mocs (one pair well worn, the other in better shape), two hammers (one made from stone and the other half an iron dumbbell). D) three weathered and rusted bridle bits. Very rare one-of-a kind collection with excellent documentation. Est. 1500-2000 **SOLD $1100(98)**

CANADIAN METIS RIFLE CASE c.1875
Preston Miller Collection. Northern Regions of Western Canada. Smoked moosehide characteristically richly embellished with silk ribbon appliqué work with single line beaded designs and narrow braid. Leather fringe trim is quill-wrapped and separated by brass facet seed beads. Back seam is navy ribbon bound and characteristically trimmed with multi-colored wool yarn tassels and Crow beads with quill-wrapped thongs. Excellent condition. 49"L. Est. 5000-8000

Most of these style rifle cases are floral beaded as the one seen in *Metis*, Julia D. Harrison, Glenbow-Alberta Institute, Canada Exhibition Catalog, 1985: p. 51. Mittens are often seen with similar silk ribbon trim as the pair from No. Alberta seen in *American Indian Art Magazine*, Vol. 11, #2, Spring 1986, same author and exhibit from Glenbow Museum, p. 55.

2. Horse Gear

Saddles & Saddle Parts

NEZ PERCE RAWHIDE COVERED SADDLE c.1870
Wooden saddle covered with rawhide and sinew-stitched. Some of the original rigging intact, including one of the two saddle pads and two girthing rings attached to rawhide straps. Dk. patina of age. 17"L x 13"W x 10"H. Est. 500-750 **SOLD $450(99)**

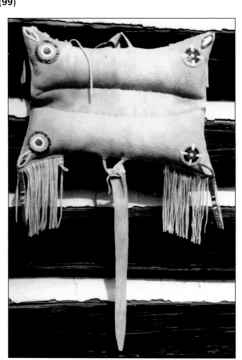

ASSINIBOINE QUILLED PAD SADDLE c.1960
Made by the late Juanita Tucker (famous Indian doll maker), Ft. Belknap Res. Montana. Beautiful smoked hide with sewn quilled rosettes, ovals, and drops. Quillwork is all "zig-zag" technique with green, yellow, white, and red dyed quills. Never used. Minor bug damage to the quills (maybe 5-10%) gives it an old look, otherwise exc. cond. Quills are unfaded. 18"L x 13"W +5.5" drops. Est. 500-800 **SOLD $550(03)**

INTERMONTANE STIRRUP and BEADED PANEL c.1880
Collected on the Flathead Res. Brass tacked sinew-sewn rawhide covered wooden stirrup. Appliqué-stitched panel is lt. blue with rose w. heart, cobalt, gr. yellow, and apple green (half of the green beads are missing). Red wool braid bound with one third white edge-beading intact. Panel needs restoration. Est. 500-800 **SOLD $450(99)**

NEZ PERCE RAWHIDE COVERED RIDING SADDLES c.1860
The following three superb saddles were purchased from an Indian family on the Nez Perce Reservation in Idaho. This is the type of saddle used during the Nez Perce War in 1877.
(Left to right) Both forks are carved from wood. This style is rare and early, as indicated by the rounded protrusions on the ends of both forks. Covered with sinew-sewn rawhide and in perfect cond. It is very rare to find one of these saddles with no tears or loose stitching. Great patina and cond. 17"L x 10"W. x 9.5"H. Est. 900-1800 **SOLD $650(98)**
Both forks are carved from antler. Has most of the original leather rigging and a canvas belly band. Shows lots of use with exc. patina. Nice early complete saddle. 18"L x 12"W. x 9.5"H. Est. 850-1500 **SOLD $625(98)**
Front and back forks are carved from antler—entire saddle is covered with sinew-sewn rawhide. This saddle has an unusual rawhide attachment on one of the forks, probably used to attach a riding sling as seen on the earliest saddles. Great patina and cond. 16"L x 12"W x 11"H. Est. 800-1500 **SOLD $850(98)**

Saddle Blankets, Saddle Bags, Bridles, etc.

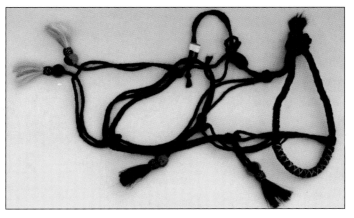

METIS BRAIDED HORSEHAIR HACKAMORE
Made by an old horse wrangler named Renee at Gang Ranch, the largest privately owned ranch in Canada BC, early 1900s. Natural dark brown braided horsehair. Four tassel trim: wool multi-color yarn balls and Turk's head with natural dk. horsehair fringe. Est. 250-400 **SOLD $175(00)**

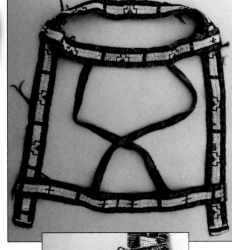

NEZ PERCE BRAIDED HORSEHAIR LEAD ROPE
Steve Shawley Collection. Nat. tan and brown horiz. stripes. Est. 250-400 **SOLD $200(99)**

SIOUX FULLY-BEADED BRIDLE
c.1870
RARE. Beautiful early design and (apx. 13°) seed bead colors: white central stripe with apple green and cobalt triangular border motifs; rose w. heart crosses and brass facet vertical stripes. (1.5"W). Inside criss-cross strips (5/8"W) have diagonal alt. stripes in luscious gr. robin's egg blue and rose w. hearts. All buckskin strips edged with tiny brass facets, 75% intact. Sinew-sewn. Two tiny tin cones with rose feather fluffs still intact. Back shows use. Exc. cond. for its age and wear, still supple and useable. Est. 1800-3000 **SOLD $1950(2000)**

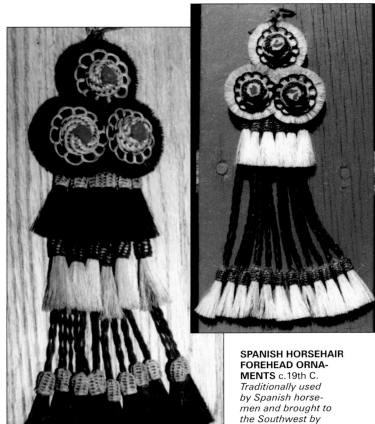

SPANISH HORSEHAIR FOREHEAD ORNAMENTS c.19th C.
Traditionally used by Spanish horsemen and brought to the Southwest by their descendents. Natural undyed black and white horsehair braided drops, with tassels and rosettes—all of horsehair. Each of three rosettes has red cloth overlay. A. Predominantly black. B. Predominantly white. Nice age patina. 9"L. Est. 300-500 each **SOLD $225 each(00)**

PLATEAU BEADED HEADSTALL c.1890-1910
Probably Nez Perce. Superb size 13° and smaller cut beaded stylized pastel floral and star patterns on dk. blue wool. *"JULY 4"* lettering is gr. yellow; other motifs are t. rose, Crow pink, pale blue, lt. green, and white. All outlined with 3/8" brass sequins. Six unusual large (5/8") brass sequins attached with lt. blue beads. Pink binding faded but intact. Back lined with pastel calico pattern. Back shows use. 17"W x 14"L. Est. 1500-2500 **SOLD $1600(03)**

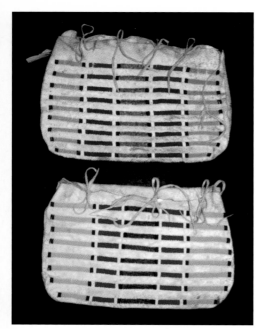

CROW SADDLE BAGS
c.1890.
Beaded lines are lt. blue, red w. heart, t. green with white, and cobalt. Each bag slightly varying shades of colors, i.e., pale blue, gr. red, and t. bottle green. 14"W x 9"H. Heavy supple buckskin; beautiful light patina. Est. 2000-2800 **SOLD $1700(99)**

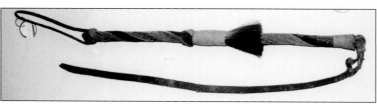

HALF-HITCHED HORSEHAIR QUIRT c.1890?
From Montana State Prison at Deer Lodge. Spiral stripes are black, red, and faded green. Natural dk. horsehair fringes secured with natural braided wrapped horsehair. Braided strap. Latigo whip. All original. Shows age. Exc. cond. Hangs apx. 40"L. Est. 350-450 **SOLD $250(00)**

Ellen Big Sam and martingale with another Flathead woman. c.1910. Flathead Reservation, Montana.

FLATHEAD FULLY-BEADED MARTINGALE c.1900
Preston Miller Collection. Made by Ellen Big Sam, Salish, Flathead Reservation. She was "an expert and prolific beader known for her abstract floral designs." White appliqué beaded background (tiny size 13º and 14º) seed beads; typical Flathead contoured stylized flower pattern in delicate pastels of C. pink, t. cranberry red, t. pink, t. forest green, apple green, periwinkle, silver cuts, gr. yellow, and black. Panels are black velvet bound, bottom tabs and border are red trade wool decorated with 5/8" brass rimmed mirrors. Hawk bell and one remaining sleigh bell bottom trim. Calico backing shows use. 45"L x 17"W. *Purchased from Old Barn Auction, Ohio listed as Blackfeet. We paid high dollar because we had several photos of her on horseback with this martingale and we collect her beadwork.* Est. 3500-4500 **$4000(04)**
See vest, gloves and leggings from the Preston Miller collection made by her in Sacred Encounters, *Jacqueline Peterson, U. of Okla, Press, Norman: 1993, p. 152.*

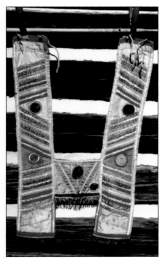
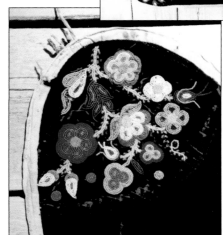

PLATEAU HORSE COLLARS c.1890
(Left) Red, white, and green silk ribbons trimmed with real brass sequins sewn with seed bead centers. Red and blue Fox braid bound. Background is dk. green wool (as seen through some of the silk, which is raveling). Celluloid backed mirrors. Top portion has wide purple silk ribbon. Four top eyelets delicately hand-sewn. Backed with indigo and white calico. 36"L x 21". Est. 400-500 **SOLD $325(02)**
(Right) Completely covered with real silk ribbon in shades of pastel rose, greens, purple, pinks, orange and gold with strips of tiny clear celluloid sequins bordered with clear seed beads. Six aged mirrors (brass with paper back)—incredible patina! Back is dk. blue twill; shows age. Real silver metallic fringe along bottom. Four hand-sewn eyelets for leather thongs at top. A few pieces of silk starting to ravel, otherwise VG cond. 34"L x 20"W. Est. 450-650 **SOLD $550(02)**

CHIPPEWA-CREE BEADED VELVET SADDLE BLANKET c.1880
Usually worn under a pad saddle. All four corners embellished with lavish floral motifs. Corner fabric appears to be silk velvet, central body rayon velvet. Backed with muslin and bound with faded calico. Holes from missing fringe all around. Shows use; silk velvet nap worn in spots; body has interesting patch; lining shows dark patina of use. Apx. 40" x 30". Est. 1500-2000 **SOLD $1200(99)**
See Amer. Ind. Art Mag., Winter 1998, p. 65 for photos of similar blanket and Riel Rebellion soldier using one.

NEZ PERCE BEADED SADDLE DRAPE c.1940
Collected from a Umatilla family in Oregon. Beautiful white elk hide with appliquéd beaded panels and strip: lt. blue bkgrd. with yellow, red, black, and white geometric pattern is 9.5" x 11". Strip is lt. gr. blue with tri-cut geometric pattern in copper and t. rose outlined in black and red. 2.5"W. x 37"L. (4) 13"L trade bead drops; red facets with black and lt. blue ponies, and old cowries. Heavy canvas lining shows some use. 108"L x 14"W. Pristine hide and beadwork. Est. 1800-2500 **SOLD $1600(01)**

APACHE SADDLE BAG c.1900
Unusual and very attractive all-over cotton appliqué diamond pattern; black, red, white, and pink. Canvas backed. Heavy twisted cotton fringes hang 12"L. 15" center opening forming bag. 15"W x 84" (42" folded). Several tears in back easily patched. Clean; nice mellow fading of bright colors. Est. 700-900 **SOLD $850(03)**
See similar bag illustrated in *Western Apache Material Culture* by A. Ferg, Color Illus. #3, Ariz. State Museum.

3. Ethnographic Pieces

Hide Scrapers

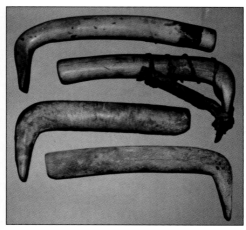

(Top to bottom) **SIOUX ELK HORN HIDE SCRAP-ER** c.1860.
Early style with a 3"L. extension for the blade. Also the patina looks to be very old. There is a strip near the back area that appears to have been burned or dyed long ago. Exc. cond. 14"L. Est. 350-500 **SOLD $300(99)**
SAME. c.1860.
Has metal blade, covered with rawhide, still laced to the horn. This is the hard to find large bent iron blade. There are four groups of lines etched into the sides of the horn.

Some people believe these indicate the number of hides scraped. Has four tack holes in end; two of these still have the square shanks of the brass tacks in place. This would indicate the scraper is quite old. There is also a drilled thong hole in the end. Great old patina. 12-1/2"L. Est. 750-900 **SOLD $550(99)**
SAME. c.1860.
Great old scraper with an extra long blade attachment extension. Has over 61 lines cut into the sides. Patina shows lots of use and age. 11.5"L. Est. 500-600 **SOLD $650(02)**
SAME. c. pre-1860.
Has early style long blade extension. Patina indicates this scraper has spent some time laying in the ground or exposed to the elements. Almost appears to be petrified. It has a series of interesting holes drilled like a design in the back end. 12"L. Est. 400-600 **SOLD $175(99)**

TWO OLD FLATHEAD INDIAN HIDE TANNING TOOLS c.1890.
These belonged to Louise Conko. The hair and flesh scraper was made from a scythe blade and the hide stretcher was made from a horse harness blinder. These tools are great examples of the Indians' clever use of worn out items to create something that would be useful. Relics like these are a thing of the past. Est. 100-200 **SOLD $85(01)**

(Top) **PLATEAU HIDE STRETCHER** c.19th C.
From Warm Springs Reservation, Oregon.
Wooden handle with forged iron blade that is riveted and tied into place. Nicely aged patina. 21.5"L. Est. 150-300 **SOLD $85(00)**
(Bottom) **WOODEN HIDE FLESHER** 19th C.
Consignor says "beamer type from Isleta Pueblo." Iron blade with filing to form a sharp, saw-toothed edge. Handle is made from a curved piece of wood. Great old patina. Apx. 15"L x 3.5"W. Est. 75-150 **SOLD $75(00)**

Miscellaneous Tools

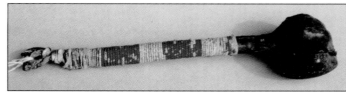

MANDAN/HIDATSA QUILLED STONE MAUL c.1870 or earlier.
Used to crush chokecherries, dried meat, etc.* The handle and stone head are covered with buffalo hide. Sinew-sewn. Red, white, and yellow quill-wrapped softened rawhide strips are wrapped around handle. Some quills are missing or worn out from use and age. 14"L. Unrestored, exc. patina and condition considering the age of the item. Est. 600-900 **SOLD $600(06) on eBay**
   *See *The Way to Independence,* Carolyn Gilman, Minn. Hist. Soc. Press, 1987: p. 64, photo and historical information.

PEMMICAN POUNDER c.1860s
Prob. Sioux or Cheyenne. Nicely shaped stone and handle covered with rawhide. The end of handle appears to have been chewed by a small animal; no distraction as it enhances authenticity. 4"H x 10"L. Est. 300-450 **SOLD $265(00)** See *No. American Indian Artifacts,* Lars Hothem 5th ed. p. 272.

FLATHEAD BITTEROOT DIGGER c.1880.
Found in an old log building on the Flathead reservation in Mont. These were used years ago to pop the bitterroot out of the ground for drying and eating. Hand forged iron digger with weathered wooden handle. 18.5"L. with 7" wood handle. Nice old patina. Est. 85-150 **SOLD $45(99)**

Wood & Horn Bowls/Spoons

WASCO/WISH-RAM SHEEP HORN BOWL and LADLE c.1820. *RARE. Columbia River artifact. Usually found only in museums and occasionally in Indian homes, along the Col. R. basin, where they are prized as family heirlooms.* Bowl has typical incised bands of interlocking triangles; flanges have three rectangular holes. These unique pieces were formed by extensive work of steaming and re-shaping to form a wider and flatter configuration. Ladle is plain with single hole. Flanges 1) broken piece apx. 1/2" and 2) apx. 1" end broken. Exceptional dark patina on both. Bowl: 8"W x 6"L x 4.5"H. Ladle: 7" x 5"W. Est. 2500-5000 **SOLD $1800(99)**

Soft Gold, Ore. Hist. Society: 1982, pp. 58-59. Also see *American Indian Art*, Norm Feder: 1971, p. 96.

PLATEAU BURL WOOD MORTAR c.1850. *From Warm Springs Reservation, Oregon.* Beautiful polished patina (from use) and nice hand hold "ears" protruding from rim. 10" diam x 11.5"H. Very nice and rare. Est. 500-750 **SOLD $425(98)**

OLD HORN SPOON c.1880 or earlier. Brown to black horn that could be mtn. sheep or cow. Expertly made. There are the remains of a tag sticking on the handle that says *"Iroquois Horn Spoon."* If so, this would make it quite rare. Only one or two spots of slight worm damage. Apx.10"L. Est. 200-350 **SOLD $105(02)**

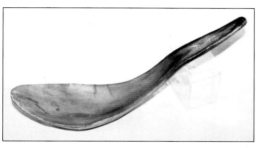

MOUNTAIN SHEEP HORN SPOON c.1860.
Rare, finely made and shaped spoon showing good age and native use. Has a few worm holes that are hardly noticeable. Very nice, exc. cond., 12.25"L. Est. 300-450 **SOLD $275(02)**

PLATEAU OLD BURL MORTAR and PESTLE c.1860?
Yakima Reservation, Wash. RARE. This one has carved side handles and apx. 2" sq. rim piece broken out. Shows Indian use by smoothed edges and pounded interior. Incredible patina. 10"H x apx. 10"top diam. The phallic pestle is perfectly shaped; 12"L x 2.25" diam. Est. 600-900 set **SOLD $337(03)**

SIOUX QUILLED BUFFALO HORN SPOON c.1870
Red quill braided wrapped handle and alt. red and white quilled wrapped looped drops with faded red horsehair in tin cones. Spoon has superficial crack line on the top surface only—adds to wonderful patina of entire piece. 11"L x 4"W. 7" suspensions. Exc., all-original cond. Est. 750-950 **SOLD $850(00)**

Ceremonial Items: Necklaces, Fire Tongs, and Buffalo Stones

BLACKFEET MEDICINE NECKLACE
c.1890.
Collected by Bonnie Wise of Browning, Montana. She was one of the early collectors of old Indian material on the Blackfeet Reservation. She said it belonged to Home Gun, a famous Blackfeet Indian warrior. It has a 3.75" brass disc with stamped foliate designs, ermine stripes, and two brass hawk bells hanging on a buckskin thong. 15.5"L. with remnants of red medicine paint stain. Rare, exc. cond. Est. 500-750 **SOLD $500(02)**

BLACKFEET SUNDANCE NECKLACE
c.1900
Heavily red-ochred. Central horse-hair lock with black basket beads and old dentalium shell laced with thong. Hangs apx. 15"L. Est. 350-500 **SOLD $225(99)**

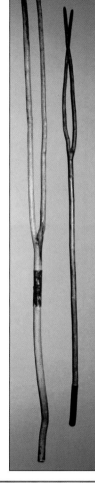

(Right) BLACKFEET CHOKECHERRY FIRE TONGS c.1880.
RARE. Collected by Paul Janetski of Great Falls, Mt. and displayed in the West Yellowstone Museum for over thirty years. These tongs were used to lift hot coals from the fire to light medicine pipes and smudges. Most were originally part of important medicine bundles. Tips are burned black from lifting hot coals and the surface has a reddish tint from being rubbed with red medicine paint. There is a small section of decorative bark on the handle end. These are very rare and seldom seen for sale. 43.5"L. with great patina. Exc. cond. Est. 300-500
(Left) BLACKFEET MEDICINE DRUM BEATER c.1880.
RARE. Collected by Paul Janetski of Great Falls, Mt. and displayed in the West Yellowstone Museum for over thirty years. This type of beater was used to beat the flat folded rawhide drum that is a part of the Beaver Bundle Medicine. The sound is said to resemble the beating of a beaver's tail on the water. Probably made from chokecherry wood with a section of bark remaining on the handle for decoration. These are very rarely available for sale. 48.5"L. with great patina. Exc. cond. Est. 300-500

BLACKFEET SUN DANCE NECKLACE
c.19th C.
Belonged to Walks in the Air, son of Sitting Calf. Includes documentation. There are several Winold Reiss paintings showing examples of these necklaces worn on important Blackfeet leaders. Heavily red-ochred buckskin thong with sinew attached hair lock; laced lt. blue padre beads and dentalium shell. Exc. cond. Est. 500-750 **SOLD $550(00)**

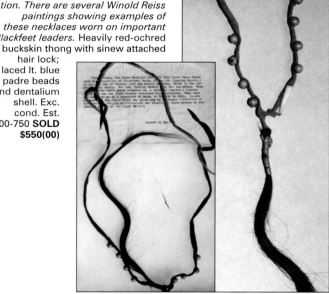

BLACKFEET SUNDANCE NECKLACE and MEDICINE STONES NECKLACE 19th C.
Chas. Conrad Mansion, Kalispell Montana. Found here in 1984. Heavily red-ochred buckskin. Sundance necklace has hair lock and smooth dentalium shell with laced blue Russian facets. Hangs apx. 12"L. Two hanging stone pendants hang from separate buckskin suspensions on buckskin medicine necklace. Hangs apx. 13"L. Est. 900-1500 **SOLD $950(01)**

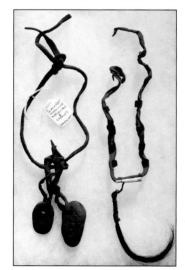

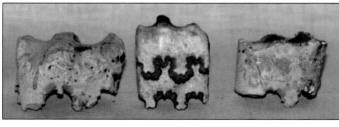

BUFFALO MEDICINE STONE FOSSILS Pre-historic.
These are ancient Ammonite fossils that the Blackfeet Indians call an "Iniskim." They are often individually owned and worn about the neck as good luck medicine charms. They have also been found in important bundles, as they were used to call buffalo herds in the old days. Prices vary according to their rarity and likeness to a real buffalo. Read the story of the buffalo stones as told by Mike Swims Under p. 307, also p. 319 buffalo stones in a medicine bundle. Adolf Hungry-Wolf *The Blackfoot Papers-Vol. II, Pikunni Ceremonial Life,* Skookumchuck, B.C., *Good Medicine Fdn., 2006*
(Left to right) 2.25"L. Est. 60-200 **SOLD $125(03)**
SAME. A rare double Iniskim which looks like mating buffaloes. 1.5"L. Est. 150-250 **SOLD $80(03)**
SAME. 2.75"L. Est. 50-125 **SOLD $50(03)**

Masks

EARLY IROQUOIS CORN HUSK MASK
Tag reads *"Women's Mask used in Harvest Dance. Collected by C.W. Andras. Cattarangus Reservation, New York Seneca 1917."* Beautiful patina, in rare exc. shape. 12"L x 10"W. Est. 900-1500 **SOLD $750(98)**

RARE FULL SIZE BUFFALO HEAD MASK
Consignor says 1930s but it looks more recent to us. Made from a real buffalo head. *Buffalo masks like this were worn in the Buffalo Dance of the Mandans. Bodmer did paintings of such dancers in the 1830s. They were also used on horses. This one appears as though it could be used either way.* Hide seems to be semi-tanned rawhide. Real buffalo horns with small decorative holes running full length. Est. 550-950 **SOLD $440(00)**

4. Pipes

See also Czech-made replica pipes and stems, p. 169.

Frequently asked questions about pipes and pipe smoking:

Are all pipes ceremonial? The T-shaped pipe, also called the Plains pipe, was often used as a ceremonial or sacred pipe—for prayer and ceremonies but also for trade agreements, healing, peace or war discussions, even to settle land disputes; the pipe was used to solemnize the occasion. Not all pipes are ceremonial. Generally, elbow-shaped pipes are for personal smoking and were the most common type used in the 18th and 19th centuries.

What is Catlinite? A special red pipestone, also called the sacred stone by Indians, has been quarried in S. W. Minnesota for more than three hundred years. The legend is that after a great battle "the…blood of the slain to go into the ground and become red pipestone." This vicinity has been considered sacred ground and a place of peace since that time. Various Indian tribes, i.e., Iowa and Oto, frequented the region until the Dakota forced these tribes out and took over the quarrying here by 1700. It became an important trade item for the Dakota people. In 1937, the Federal Government acquired ownership of the quarries to help regulate and preserve the "art of pipe making." Today, Dakota pipe makers are employed and several are fourth generation pipe makers. It is called Catlinite in honor of the artist George Catlin who visited here in 1836.

Pipestone Indian Shrine Assoc. brochure, National Park Service, Pipestone, Minn., C. 2000.

Pipes on the Plains, by Rbt. A Murray, Pipestone Indian Shrine Assoc., Nat. Park Service, U. S. Dept. of Interior, 1993.

Indians Quarrying Pipestone at Pipestone Quarries c.1890 postcard. Penciled message on the back says, "These are Indians getting out that stone like the knife I gave you. They make thousands of different things to sell…" *Preston Miller Collection.*

(Top) **SIOUX CATLINITE KNIFE** c.1890-1910.
Collectors often overlook these as being of recent make. (See preceding postcard message about buying a knife c.1890). There are several in the Univ. of Pa. Museum collection that were collected by Amos Gottschall in the 1880s. This one is a very unique design and made from dark red stone. Beautifully made and highly polished. 11.5"L. Est. 250-400
(Bottom) **SIOUX CATLINITE BOWIE KNIFE** c.1890-1910.
Star designs etched into the handle with *"U.S. Made by Sioux Indian"* etched into the blade. A great piece of multi colored red pipestone. It was broken in half but has been expertly repaired and you would never see the damage without looking very carefully. 15"L. Est. 350-600

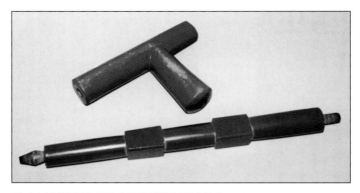

(Top) **LARGE OLD RED CATLINITE PIPE BOWL** c.1880.
Collected from Nez Perce Indians around 1926. Small tapered tobacco hole, which is typical of early pipes. Highly polished with great patina. Hexagon shaped tip and domed bowl top. 6.25"L x 4.25"H. Exc. cond. Est. 250-400 **SOLD $250(05)**
(Bottom) **LARGE OLD RED CATLINITE PIPE STEM** c.1880.
Collected from Nez Perce Indians by Robert Wait around 1926. Nice dark red Catlinite with round and square carving. Interesting wooden pieces in either end. 13.5"L. Exc. cond. Est. 200-300 **SOLD $75(05)**

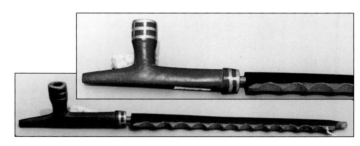

CHIPPEWA LEAD INLAID RED CATLINITE PIPE AND STEM c.1880.
Collected in Minn. Interesting T-bowl shape with excellent intricate lead inlay pattern. The stem is carved and painted with green and mustard yellow paint. Bowl is 7.5"L x 3.5"H. Stem is 17"L. Exc. cond. Est. 750-1200 **SOLD $800(04)**

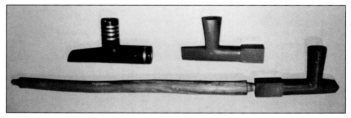

(Left to right) **BLACK STEATITE PIPE WITH LEAD INLAY** Contemporary. Well-made and ready to smoke. 6"L x 3.25"H. Est. 150-250 **SOLD $125(00)**
CATLINITE PIPE
Many auctions would tell you this pipe is from 1880. But the holes just don't look that old. Maybe someone re-shaped them? It is a very nice pipe including an old stem. 5.5"L x 3-1/8"H. Est. 150-250 **SOLD $160(00)**
SIOUX CATLINITE T-SHAPED PIPE WITH ASH? STEM Pre-1900
From an old trading post. Nice patina from use, dark smudges on bowl. Rich bowl color-incised rings are only decoration. Faint *"25.00"* pencil mark on ash stem. 18"L. Bowl apx. 5.5"L x 3.25"H. Est. 300-450 **SOLD $325(00)**

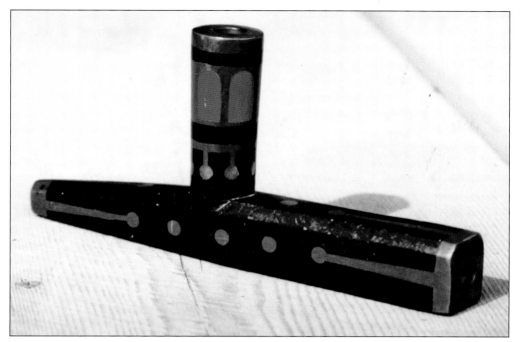

SIOUX INLAID BLACK STEATITE PIPE BOWL c.1880. *Dennis Lessard Collection from So. Dakota.* Beautifully contrasting inlay of six pieces of Catlinite with lead around the bowl. This is one of the best pipes of this style we have seen. 4-1/8"H x 9"L. Exc. cond. Est. 1800-2400 **SOLD $1600(99)**

(Top) **CATLINITE PIPE BOWL** c.1870? L-shaped bowl with tapered stem hole. 3"H x 4.5"L. Est. 300-450 **SOLD $250(01)**

(Bottom) **CATLINITE PIPE WITH MATCHING STEM** c.1890? Elaborately carved stem and bowl. Even though it is old it has never been smoked. Mint cond. Bowl is 6"L x 3"H. Total length is 15.75". Est. 450-650 **SOLD $350(01)**

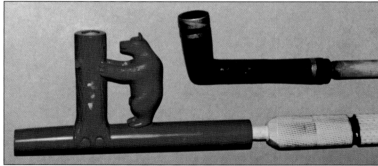

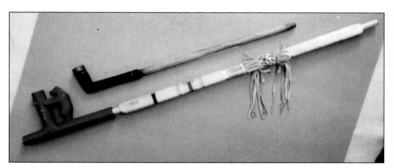

(Top) **BLACK STEATITE L-SHAPED PIPE WITH LEAD INLAY** c.1860. Consignor says it is Blackfeet. *Most likely this is a personal smoking pipe.* Stamped brass ring around bowl. Beautiful patina and polish from use. Tapered bowl is lined with caked tobacco from lots of use. Has old style tapered stem hole. Has round wooden stem. L-shaped bowls are *RARE* and early. Bowl is 2.5"H x 5"L. Est. 1000-1500

(Bottom) **CATLINITE PIPE WITH BEAR EFFIGY BOWL** Contemporary *Made by Myron Taylor (Chaska), famous Chippewa/Sioux 3rd generation pipe maker.* The bear is taking honey from a tree. The stem has unique burnt designs with colored grooves depicting the four directions: East-red, the sun rises and the beginnings of life; North-white, cold winds of winter and hardships and discomforts; South-yellow, warm winds of summer and good things of life; West-black, the sun sets and life ends. This is an outstanding and highly polished pipe with its original stem. Bowl is 4.25"H x 7.75"L. Total length with stem is 31". Est. 750-1200 **SOLD $563(98)**

See *Lost and Found Traditions* by Ralph Coe, Seattle: Univ. of WA, 1986, p. 122.

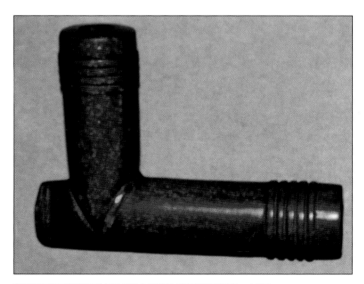

INTRICATELY CARVED CATLINITE ELBOW PIPE c. 1880. Beautiful speckled red Catlinite encircled with raised ridges at both holes. Tobacco hole is blackened but not caked with tobacco. 4.5"L x 3.5"H Est. 450-700 **SOLD $500(98)**

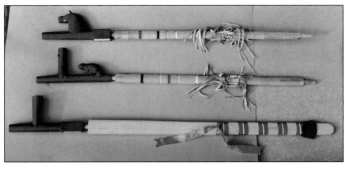

OLD CATLINITE V-SHAPED PIPE and STEM c.1880.
Both the stem and bowl are made from Catlinite and highly etched with designs, including arrow designs. Notice the wonderfully carved stem. Made from a rich dark red Catlinite. Bowl is 5.25"L and stem is 7.5"L. Est. 450-650 **SOLD $300(02)**

(Top to bottom) **SIOUX CATLINITE HORSE EFFIGY PIPE** Contemporary *Made by Myron Taylor (Chaska), famous Chippewa/Sioux 3rd generation pipe maker*.* Bowl is unsigned. The stem has unique burnt designs with colored grooves depicting the four directions. See previous pipe for stem description. Bowl is 3.75"H x 7.75"L. Total length with stem is 31.5". Est. 750-900 **SOLD $500(99)**
      *See *Coe*, p. 122.

SIOUX CATLINITE BEAVER EFFIGY PIPE c.1990.
Same provenance as above. The bowl is made from speckled red Catlinite, signed by *"Chaska"* and depicts a beaver looking towards a tree (pipe bowl), which has its teeth marks carved in it. Expertly carved, a true work of art. Bowl is 4"H x 8"L. Total length with stem is 32". Est. 750-900 **SOLD $500(99)**

BRULE SIOUX CATLINITE PIPE c.1960.
Made by Joel Feather of Mission, So. Dak. This is a ceremonial pipe. Expertly carved and shaped dark red Catlinite bowl with quill-wrapped stem with Mallard duck skin trim and orange silk ribbon. Porcupine quill wrapping is red and white. Bowl is 4"H x 8"L. Total length is 36.25". Est. 600-850 **SOLD $500(99)**

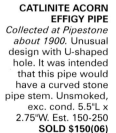

LARGE CATLINITE EAGLE HEAD PIPE WITH TACKED STEM Contemporary.
Superb carved bowl is 4.5"L x 2.75"H. 21" stem has twelve brass tacks for decoration. Est. 175-350 **SOLD $200(02)**

CATLINITE PIPE WITH FISH EFFIGY STEM c.1890.
Dark red Catlinite bowl and stem. The bowl is etched with foliate and block designs. The stem is beautifully carved and etched to look like a fish. This is an outstanding and unusual pipe. Bowl is 6.5"L. and stem is 9"L. Includes a specially made metal stand for display. Est. 950-1500 **SOLD $750(99)**

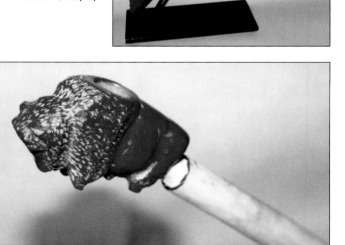

CATLINITE ACORN EFFIGY PIPE
Collected at Pipestone about 1900. Unusual design with U-shaped hole. It was intended that this pipe would have a curved stone pipe stem. Unsmoked, exc. cond. 5.5"L x 2.75"W. Est. 150-250 **SOLD $150(06)**

BUFFALO EFFIGY PIPE
Age is unknown but it is probably a newer pipe because it shows no signs of having been smoked. Buffalo shaped bowl is exceptional in design and polish. The tobacco hole is tapered and grooved, indicating it was not done with a modern drill. Stem appears to be more recent. Bowl is 2.5"L. and stem is 11.5"L. Est. 200-350 **SOLD $150(02)**

WOODEN INDIAN FACE WITH GLASS EYES EFFIGY PIPE c.1800s.
This is a non-Indian made pipe. Absolutely beautifully carved and patinated pipe. Wood is a beautifully polished brown and hair is black. This is one of the nicest pipes of this type that we have seen. Includes a new bamboo stem. 3.75"H. Exc. cond. Est. 150-250

LARGE BLACKFEET PIPE WITH SPIRAL STEM Contemporary
This black stone pipe was made by Gary Middle Rider, the grandson of Chief Middle Rider. It is like the pipes used in medicine pipe ceremonies. According to Adolf Hungry Wolf, the black pipestone was as sacred to the Blackfeet as Catlinite was to the Sioux. He says that only black locally-made pipes were used in Blackfeet ceremonies. * This style of pipe is often called "Micmac," although is has wide distribution to the Plains and Southeast. The bowl is 3.5"L and 3.75"H. with a 21"stem (not shown). Est. 350-450 **SOLD $350(04)**
**Blackfeet Craftworker's Book,* 1977: p. 67.

VERY SMALL CATLINITE PIPE Contemporary.
This is a size probably used for a woman's personal smoking. Small 1" x 1" bowl with little leaves carved in relief. Total length only 5". Est. 50-100 **SOLD $30(01)**

(Top to bottom) **BLACKFEET BLACK STEATITE PIPE WITH FILE BURNED STEM** Contemporary
Made by Preston Miller. This is a personal smoking style. Bowl is 3.5"H.X 2.5"L. Stem is 10"L. Exc. cond. Est. 100-175 **SOLD $100(03)**
SIOUX T-SHAPED CATLINITE PIPE WITH INLAID STEM 20th C.
Bowl is beautiful red Catlinite and wood stem is inlaid with what looks like Catlinite. This is the only one I have ever seen made like this. Bowl is 4.25"L x 3.75"H. Total 18"L. Exc. unsmoked cond. Est. 250-350 **SOLD $250(03)**

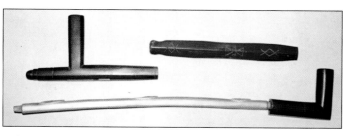

BLACKFEET BLACK STEATITE PIPE WITH STEM c.1880?
This was traded to us from the Blackfeet Reservation in Montana. Bowl is L-shaped and nicely carved. No tobacco residue in the bowl. The ash stem is spiral carved and painted red, green, and black. Bowl is 3.5"L x 2.75"H and overall length is 19". Est. 300-500 **SOLD $350(01)**

(Left to right) **OLD CATLINITE T-PIPE BOWL** c.1880.
Large but finely shaped bowl with engraved lines and eight-sided bowl. The base is six-sided with interesting knobs on the end. Nice dark red stone with speckles on one side. Heavily smoked. 9"L x 5.75"H. Very nice with a good "feel" to it. Est. 350-500 **SOLD $350(02)**
OLD CATLINITE PIPE STEM with interesting designs engraved into the top surface. c.1880.
Dark red Catlinite with great patina. 10.5"L x 1.25"W. 1" thick stem. Stone stems are scarce. Est. 200-300 **SOLD $225(02)**
CATLINITE ELBOW-SHAPED BOWL WITH FIGURAL WOOD STEM 20th C.
Nice dark red bowl that has a remarkable smooth polish. The lightly curved stem is ash with three animal heads carved into it. Each head has the eyes inlaid with beads. Bowl is 4.5"L x 3.5"H. Stem is 17.5"L. Est. 295-400 **SOLD $350(04)**

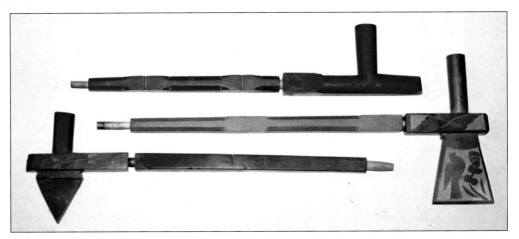

(Top to bottom) **OLD CAT-LINITE T-SHAPED BOWL WITH STEM** c.1890. Bowl is made from nice dark red, lightly speckled stone and highly polished. The stem is a little lighter solid red stone, 10.5"L. This bowl was smoked and is 7"L. x 3.75"H. Exc. cond. Est. 395-650 **OLD CATLINITE TOMA-HAWK-SHAPED BOWL WITH STEM** c.1890. *"In the later 1700s, the French and English, realizing the esteem which Indians held the pipe, began to manufacture metal hatchet pipes."* Stone reproductions out of Catlinite were made starting in the early 19th century. This is a really fine example of this style of pipe. The bowl and especially the blade are etched with foliate and bird designs. The stem is Catlinite and has foliate designs as well. Bowl is 4"L x 7.75"H. Stem is 15"L. Unsmoked. Est. 350-500 **SOLD $300(02)** *Pipestone Indian Shrine Assoc. brochure, 2000.
SAME c.1900.
Interesting dagger-shaped blade made from nice dark red Catlinite with etched designs on both sides. The other side (not shown) has beautiful floral designs. The stone stem was broken in the middle but has been expertly repaired so that it is barely noticeable. Has been smoked. Bowl is 4.75"L x 5.5"H. with a 12.5" stem. Est. 200-400

PIPE TOMAHAWK-SHAPED CATLINITE PIPE c.1900.
Probably Sioux. Made from dark red Catlinite with old looking patina. Nicely carved with designs and grooves. The blade was broken off and glued back (not noticeable). Smoke and stem hole are blackened from use. 6.5 "L. Est. 300-425

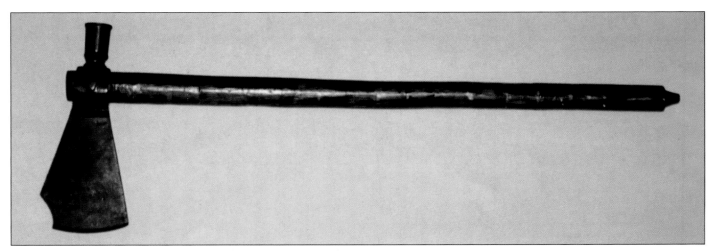

CAST IRON PIPE TOMAHAWK c.1870.
Plains-style Indian tomahawk with 22"L. file burned handle. The head is 8"L. and has a 1" nick broken from one corner. Appears to have been broken a long time ago. It has a bit of shine to both the handle and the head that might be from being covered with some sort of preservative a long time ago, possibly shellac or varnish. The head slides off the handle but could be easily tightened with a wedge of buckskin. Est. 1000-1600 **SOLD $1350(04)**

The following three pipes are definitely not new, but the age and tribal attributions are not known.

LARGE GREY/BROWNISH STONE FROG EFFIGY PIPE
The patina is very good and old looking. 7"L. Exc. cond. Est. 85-250 **SOLD $89(03)**

(Left to right) **BLACK STONE FROG EFFIGY PIPE**
Unique, intricately carved design with nice patina. 3"L x 3.25"H. Exc. cond. Est. 75-150 **SOLD $65(03)**
BLACK STEATITE PIPE WITH SNAKE EFFIGY wrapped around bowl and laying on top of stem. Nicely carved with good, old looking polished patina. 4.5"L. x 3.5"H. Est. 85-250 **SOLD $85(03)**

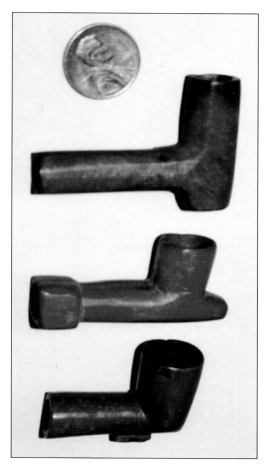

NEZ PERCE CATLINITE PIPES
The following three pipes were purchased from an Indian family. These are probably personal, not ceremonial, pipes. They appear old and were in the family for many years.
(Top to bottom) **A)** Unusually shaped nice red Catlinite, polished and shows use. 2"L x 1.25"H. Est. 150-250 **SOLD $100(00)**
B) Unused, but it is old. Finely made with thin bowl. In fact, it is so thin there is a very small hole worn through on the one side. Perhaps this is why it was never smoked. 2"L x 5/8"H. Est. 100-200 **SOLD $60(00)**
C) This is probably the best one, shows lots of use and looks really old. It is a typical Nez Perce old style pipe design. 1.5"L x 1"H. Est. 300-450 **SOLD $150(00)**

OLD INDIAN-MADE PIPES
(Top to bottom) **A)** Very old gray stone pipe bowl from Minn. with a collection *"#1049"* written on the outside of the bowl in black ink. 2"L. Exc. cond. Est. 125- 275
B) Ancient Catlinite platform pipe from Minn. The bowl is broken and has a collection *"#1004"* written with black ink. 3.25"L x 2"H. Exc. collectible from the old, maybe prehistoric, times. Est. 95-200
C) Cree gray/blackstone bowl, highly polished and caked with tobacco, showing many years of heavy use. 2.75"L x 2"H. Exc. cond. Est. 175-300 **SOLD $175(05)**

5. Boat Models
Canoes & Kayaks

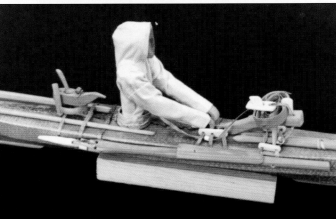

DOGRIB KAYAK-STYLE MINIATURE BARK CANOE c.1880.
Exquisitely detailed model made from wood slats, bark and spruce root lacing. 32"L. from tip to tip. There is only one 3/4" split in the bark on one gun whale cover. This is one of the best examples of a bark canoe that we have seen. Patina, size, condition, and workmanship are excellent. Est. 450-600 **SOLD $500(04)**

LARGE CHIPPEWA BIRCH BARK CANOE c.1900.
Expertly made and root laced. Hardwood gunwales and ribs expertly fitted and laced and tacked into place. It is in mint perfect cond. 24.5"L. Est. 350-500 **SOLD $450(04)**

MAKAH CANOE MODEL c.1890.
Classic form carved from cedar with fine old blue painted design. 4.5"W x 21.25"L. Exc. cond. Est. 250-350

SAME. c.1890.
Classic form with interesting red and black painted designs and dog? head carved into bow. 4.75"W x 18.25"L. Nice old look and exc. cond. Est. 250-350

ESKIMO KAYAK W/ FIGURE and HUNTING TOOLS c.1900.
Wood figure is wearing white cotton parka; harpoons, etc. are carved from wood and bone. Hide covered kayak and sinew sewn. Paddles are missing. 24.5"L. Exc. cond. Est. 650-900

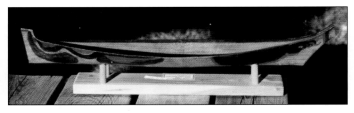

NOOTKA CANOE MODEL ON STAND c.1920
Char. yellow cedar; painted crudely in red and black interior and exterior with bird motif. Varnished. Good old patina. Bottom inked (under varnish) *"Nootka 1920-30"*. 23.5"L 3.5"H. Professionally-made stand of natural cedar 16" x 2.5". Est. 250-350 **SOLD $201(00)**

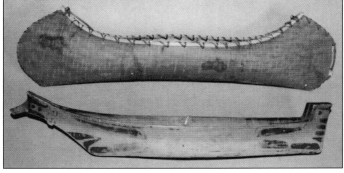

(Top) BIRCH BARK CANOE Contemporary.
This style was made by Indians for the tourist market. These are very common but hard to find in good condition. 18"L. Est. 15-25
(Bottom) MAKAH WOODEN CANOE c.1900?
Prob. yellow cedar with faded cobalt painted N.W. Coast motifs. Characteristic stylized animal head prow. This is a nice one, all one piece, good patina. Drilled hole side center. 16"L. 3.75"W. Est. 250-450 **SOLD $300(00)**

II. Trade Goods

1. Hudson's Bay Company Collectibles

By Preston E. Miller

In 1670, England's King Charles II granted a charter to "The Governor and Company of Adventurers Trading into Hudson's Bay." Thus the Hudson's Bay Company (HBC) was able to control nearly three million square miles of Canadian Territory for over three hundred years. Forts and trading posts were established for the purpose of gathering fur pelts to be shipped to European consumers. Trappers of Scotch and French descent and Indians brought their furs to the Company and exchanged them for trade goods. Guns, brandy, textiles, knives, axes, tobacco, and other goods were bartered for furs, of which the beaver was most important. The hair of the beaver hide was shaved off and matted into a felt by European hatters to make beaver head gear, which was considered most stylish in European fashions. Millions of beaver were trapped and made into top hats and hundreds of useful items were developed to trade for the hides. The following examples are some of the items that were developed by the HBC and other traders to entice Indians to trap that "Pug-Nosed Rodent with the Lustrous Coat."

I have also included some items that were made and marketed by the Hudson's Bay Company after the fur trade era. Since the company operated Northern Stores and department stores well into the 20th century, there are many items available. Because of the company's unique and long history, HBC collectibles continue to be of growing interest.

See. p. 14, Newman, Peter, *Empire Of The Bay*, Ontario, Penguin Books, Canada LTD., 1989.

COAT OF ARMS
Prints dating back to 1679 indicate that the coat of arms and motto of the Hudson's Bay Company were adopted soon after the 1670 Charter was granted by King Charles II. It shows up on many items that were traded through the Company stores. The coat of arms has four beavers in the center with a fox sitting on a trader's hat at the top and two elk adding support on each side. The beavers denoted the main objects of trade. The sly fox sitting on the medieval trader's hat was symbolic of the individual trader's ability, and the supporting elk symbolized male dominance and power. At the bottom is the motto *"Pro Pelle Cutem,"* which explains that the company wanted beaver skins, "cutem," for the sake of the fleece, "Pro Pelle," which would be used to make felt top hats. Shown here is an illustration from the front cover of a book called *The Great Company*, by Beckles Willson, c.1900.

TOP HATS
The soft undercoat of the beaver fur was well suited to the making of top hats because the microscopic barbs on the hairs caused them to cling together, forming a strong felt. The felt was then shaped into hats. This old carte de visite photo shows Wm. Segee, a sure enough dude, wearing his stylish top hat while posing with a clay trade pipe in his mouth.

CREE TRADE HATS
Big Bear and members of his band decked out for a trading session at Fort Pitt, along the Saskatchewan River, in the summer of 1884 or 1885. It was customary for Indians to dress up in their special finery while trading at the fort. Top hats decorated with colorful plumes and ribbons were part of their special attire.

Postcards & Stereoscope Cards

What is a Hudson's Bay Company postcard? This is a good question. Since most dealers do not have a category heading for the company I will supply a description. First, I would include any card with the Hudson's Bay Company name or postmark. Also, I would include any card that shows goods, services, equipment, people, or locations that are somehow related to the company. With all those possibilities you would think there should be a large amount of cards available, but up to now the numbers seem limited. Here are some examples I have collected. Mostly they show stores and trading posts. Most cards are still reasonably priced.

Northern Stores photograph from Central News Photo Service of N.Y. This 8" x 10" photograph is included because it shows a dog team with a cariole sled that has the letters HBC and company coat of arms painted on the side. Est. 25-50

"Fort Garry 1872, now Winnipeg, Man. No. 3489." Published by the B. C. Printing & Litho, Vancouver, B. C. Since I paid $32.50 for my example I will say this rather desirable card should have an estimate of $30 to $40.

Cowboys and Indians standing in front of an HBC trading post. Other versions include Calgary as location. Est. 30-55

"Fort Garry Gate & Dog Train, Winnipeg." C. S. Co. Ltd., Winnipeg. Various versions of this card are available in color and black-white. Est. 3-10

"Hudson's Bay Store, Bear Island, Timagami, Ont. Photos by Canadian National Railways." Postmarked Aug. 2, 1931. Est. 15-25

"Hudson's Bay Post at Fort Chippewyan," by Valentine, Winnipeg. Est. 10-20

"Hudson's Bay Co. Store, Yorkton, Sask." Notice company delivery wagon with coat of arms sitting alongside the store. Est. 25-40

Calgary Store postcard marked Sept. 16, 1931. Cards showing department stores in larger Canadian cities are numerous. Est. 5-20

Stereoscope card titled "796. Hudson's Bay Co's Post – Rat Portage." Back of the card identifies the photographer as F. Jay Haynes for the Canadian Pacific Railway. Est. 125-175

No title on this card but other examples taken at the same time identify this as "Pembina half-breeds on a trading tour, a distance of six hundred miles to St. Paul, where they exchange their furs for merchandise." Published by Upton of Minneapolis and St. Anthony. Est. 125-175

"Hudson's Bay Trappers, Ft. Wm," by Taylor's Gallery, Saint Paul. Est. 100-150

"Hudson's Bay Co's Fort Built 1853."
Image of the Bastion at Nanaimo,
B.C. Est. 30-60

Catalogs

Hudson's Bay Company catalog No. 61 for years 1911 to 1912. Measures 9.25" x 13.25" with 129 pages. Most items are illustrated and this is an excellent source for identifying merchandise. Est. 75-150

"Mail Service Bulletin" for Nov. 1922. This is a catalog of Hudson's Bay standardized merchandise, which had been manufactured specifically for sale at HBC store in order that the benefits could be passed on to their customers. Very interesting concept for 1922. Measures 6.75" x 10.25" with 40 pages. Est. 50-125

Tokens, Medals, and Buttons

Northwest Company tokens. The Northwest Company of Montreal was the first company to issue a "Beaver Token." Tokens of brass and copper were issued in 1820. It is ironic that during 1820 the N.W. Co. was taken over by The Hudson's Bay Co. and the tokens were outdated. However, they proved very popular with the Indians, who used them as ornamental medallions. Most specimens are found with drilled holes to enable them to be strung on necklaces or sewn onto clothing. Most of the known examples were found along the Columbia River in Washington and Oregon. They are very rare. The token on the left is brass and was found under the floor of a fallen down cabin along the Abiquz River near Silverton, Oregon. The one on the right appears to be copper and was found by Leroy Gienger on his Modoc Point Ranch in Klamath County, Oregon. They are 1-1/8" dia. with a value of $800 to $1500.

Set of brass tokens introduced by the Hudson's Bay Co. sometime between 1854 and 1857. In exchange for their furs, Indians and trappers were given tokens that they could then spend in the HUDSON'S BAY COMPANY STORE. These early tokens have the coat of arms on one side and the value marks on the opposite side. They were based on the value marks of one beaver, half beaver, quarter beaver, and one eighth beaver. The letters "H.B." stand for the company and the "E.M." stands for the East Main District in which they were first issued. The letters "NB" should have been "MB" which stood for "Made Beaver." Est. 200-500 each.

Set of aluminum tokens that were issued in Eskimo country in 1946. They were based on monetary values of 5¢ to $1.00. One large square token was worth one Arctic Fox skin. Est. 35-50 ea. Square token Est. 50-100.

Aluminum tokens for use in St. Lawrence-Labrador District. Issued in 1, 5, 10, and 20 M.B. (Made Beaver) about 1918 or 1919. There are two versions; one is stamped on both sides and the other has one side blank (see 20 M.B. token in photo). Est. 25-60 ea.

Aluminum tokens for use in Yorkton District. Based on monetary values of 5¢ to $1.00. Est. 25-60 ea.

Long Service medal with leather covered case. The awarding of silver medals was started in 1920 as part of the 250th Anniversary Celebrations. This is a silver medal awarded to D.W. Garrett in 1940 for fifteen years faithful service. Est. 300-400

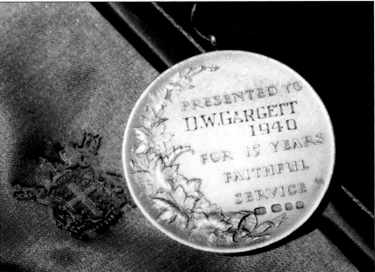

Hudson's Bay paper currency. "In addition to the metal tokens, the York Factory issued paper currency in denominations of 1 shilling, 5 shilling, and 1 pound notes beginning in the 1820s and extending through the 1840s. These were large notes, 4-3/4" x 9-3/8" and known as 'the Hudson Bay Blankets.' They were issued primarily for the use of persons employed by the York Factory in work other than fur trading. It is recorded that they passed as regular paper currency throughout the territory of Rupert Land, now largely the Province of Manitoba, throughout west central Canada and as far south and west in the United States territory as St. Paul, Minnesota and San Francisco, California."* They were elaborately engraved notes payable in 60 days after sight at Hudson Bay House in London. Condition and signatures help determine their value. Est. 500-1500.

*Curto, James J. *Indian and Post Trader Tokens*, paper presented at the 1951 A.N.A. Convention, Grosse Point, Mich. 1951, reprinted from *The Numismatist*.

This bronze medal and a book were distributed in 1920 in commemoration of the 250th Anniversary of the Hudson's Bay Co. The book was titled *The Hudson's Bay Company, 1670-1920,* and was by Sir William Schooling, K.B.E. Medal est. 100-200; Book est. 40-85 (not pictured)

Long Service medal with additional five years silver bar attachment. It was awarded to Miss M.E.R. Warren in 1937 for fifteen years service. Est. 200-300 without case.

Enameled buttons were issued to each holder of a Long Service medal. The button is worn on the coat lapel when the wearing of the medal would be inconvenient. Lapel button on right is unidentified. Est. 15-50 ea.

George Simpson commemorative medals were presented by the HBC governor at a special pageant held at Fort St. James in 1928.

HBC belt buckle. This is a rare nickel buckle that was distributed on a canvas cartridge belt by the Hudson's Bay Co. about 1880 to 1910. The buckle is embossed with the Company coat of arms, name, and *"Incorporated 1670"* date. Value is $400 to $600

10K gold Long Service ring. Est. 125-200

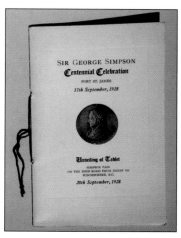

Small brass *"Hudson's Bay Coy. Winnipeg"* button of type used on work clothes. 15 mm. dia. Est. 20-40

Centennial celebration booklets containing historical information and photographs were prepared to celebrate the unveiling of the Sir George Simpson memorial at Simpson Pass on the High Road from Banff to Windermere, B.C. on Sept. 20, 1928. Est. 25-50

Small cast brass button with embossed coat of arms. 15 mm. dia. Includes certificate of authenticity documenting that it was found in 1961 at the mouth of Crab Creek on the Columbia River. It was found with other items including a Phoenix button, several early military buttons, and numerous copper and glass beads. Probably dates from late 1700s to early 1800s. Back is embossed with *"BEST QUALITY."* Est. 300-500

Two early cast HBC buttons found at Brandon House, an HBC post of the 1790s in Manitoba, Canada on the Assiniboine River. Ex. Ronald Watson collection. Larger one, approx. 20 mm., appears to be brass and the smaller one, approx. 16 mm., is pewter. This also was made in a larger size and shows an Indian shooting a flintlock gun at a running fox. Markings on backs are difficult to read but appear to be from Firmin, an English manufacturer. Est. 200-400 each.

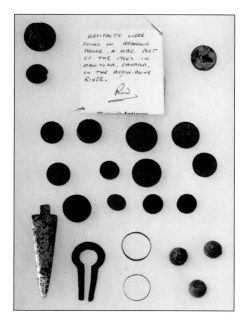

Other buttons and artifacts found at Brandon House.

Brass Hudson's Bay Company uniform button with coat of arms. Back is stamped *"Firmin & Sons – London."* Also available in smaller size. Est. 75-150

Solid brass button with embossed Sitting Fox on a trader's hat emblem surrounded by the Latin motto *"Pro – Pelle – Cutem."* (See coat of arms description at beginning of the HBC section.) Back has *"Firmin & Sons L –Strand – London."* Est. 75-150

Assomption Sashes

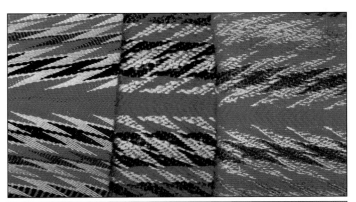

Hudson's Bay Company brightly colored wool sashes were worn by Canadian fur traders along with their Great Coats, beaver hats, and other finery to impress the natives. These sashes were known as Ceintures Fléchées, or Arrow Sashes, because the earliest examples had designs resembling arrows. Most were made just northeast of Montreal at L'Assomption and because of this they are often called Assomption Sashes. By the 1820s they became a standard accessory for many Indians and half-breeds. The earliest examples, starting in the late 1700s, were made from very "fine hard wool" using the finger weaving method. By 1885, in order to cut costs, The Hudson's Bay Co. began importing mechanically woven sashes from England. The sash on the left is an early "hard wool" sash dating from the early 1800s. It is 6" wide and 10 feet 10" long including the fringe.

Value is $1000 to $2000. The example on the right is of the loom woven type that became popular in the later 1800s. It is 9" wide and 11 feet 6" long, including the fringe. Value is $800 to $1500.

Three Assomption sashes showing different widths and weaves.

Kettles

HBC lidded copper kettles were introduced by The Hudson's Bay Co. about 1780 and continued to be sold into the early 1900s. They were especially popular with Indian customers and were far superior to wood, bark, or pottery vessels. They were made in varying sizes that could be fitted or nested inside one another to conserve space while being transported. The size is often stamped into the lid. In this photo the largest is 3 quarts and the smallest is 1 quart. These are difficult to find and most desirable when complete with the lids. They come in five sizes of 1, 1-1/2, 2, and 3 quarts, plus 1 gallon. They are made from copper sheet and insides are tinned. These kettles were one of the earliest articles made for the trade and were also used by the company men. Values range from $600 to $1500 depending on size and condition.

Nested brass and copper kettles like these, with hand made handle lugs riveted to the sides, were made in graduated sizes. They could be nested together for transporting. Kettles like these were already being traded in the 17th and 18th centuries. Later kettles have cast metal handle lugs. Value is $75 to $250. Large kettle on the left was originally owned by the Big Bear family of Plains Cree Indians. It was obtained from Big Bear's youngest son, Horsechild, who was twelve years old when he and his father surrendered to the Northwest Mounted Police in July of 1885. It was collected from the family by Doug Light, who as a young boy was visiting the reserve with his father when he found this kettle laying in the bushes near the Big Bear home on the Cree Reserve near Battleford. He asked the family how much they wanted for the old kettle. They told him to just take it because they had newer better ones and didn't need that old dented one anymore.

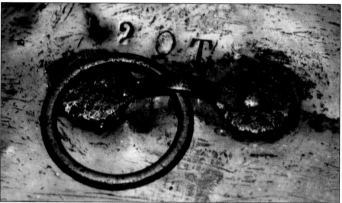

Pottery Jugs

Pottery jugs were made for the Hudson's Bay Company in various sizes, with the company name applied as part of the surface glaze. This photo shows some of the sizes and logos. The small 5-1/2" jug on the left was made at the Medalta Pottery Co. near Medicine Hat, Alberta and was still being sold at the Calgary store in the 1960s for $10.00. The 12-1/2" jug on the right also has the company coat of arms in the glaze but it is a much older version. It probably dates to around 1900 and has the word *"IMPE-RIAL"* in the glaze. Price values for the larger jugs are quite variable. Est. 300-800.

A 2 quart trade kettle showing details of the lid ring and handle bungs. These are important identifying features to be inspected when authenticating a kettle. Modern replicators have not yet produced these parts accurately.

Two modern HBC kettles that have been made in the past ten years for re-enactors and buck skinners. Be careful as these are sometimes aged and being sold as old. Est. small 65, large 95

Jugs with *Nelson, B.C.* logos in 9-1/2" and 14" sizes. Est. for 9-1/2", 350-450; Est. for 14", 450-650

Jug with paper label was a refillable vinegar jug. The owner could send it back for refills without being charged for the jug. Est. 100-200. The large 11-1/2" and small 10" Winnipeg jugs usually sell for between $250 and $450.

Rarer and older #2 size *Nelson, B.C.* jug with logo pressed into the surface and colored blue. Because this jug is scarce, the crack has little effect on its value. Est. 500-1000

(Left)Very rare Red Wing jug with HBC coat of arms logo and the word *Imperial* in the glaze. Also includes the 5 gallon and Red Wing markings. 19-1/2" high. Est. 1200-1900.
(Right) Jug with brown glaze top and *H B Co* pressed into the surface. Very old and could date to before 1850. 18" high. Est. 900-1500

Tins

Tobacco, tea, and coffee were often packaged in lithographed metal containers. Most of these date after the 1880s and well into the 1900s. They are colorful and highly sought after by collectors. Condition and rarity determine the value. Scratched and rusted tins are worth less. Every collector searches for examples in the very best condition.

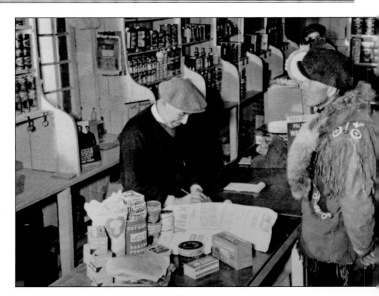

Isaiah Clark, a full blooded Cree, getting supplies from Joe Keeper, the store clerk at Norway House in Manitoba. The supplies on the counter include an *Imperial Mixture Tobacco* tin, *Fort Garry Baking Powder,* and a box of *Fort Garry Tea.* Notice the large slab of bacon. This photo is from the Dec. 1943 issue of *The Beaver* magazine.

HBC tobacco ad from 1922.

Small tobacco tins. After 1892, the Hudson's Bay Company packaged its popular *"Imperial Mixture"* smoking tobacco in a variety of red tin containers. The paper tax seals on three of these are dated 1908 and 1915. The two largest tins in the bottom center are 2-7/8" high. In excellent condition they sell for $75 to $150.

Various sizes and shapes are available.

Fort Garry Coffee and tea ad from Dec. 1932 issue of *The Beaver* magazine.

This photo shows three large HBC tobacco tins. (Left to right) The round 1 lb. *"Imperial Mixture"* tin is 6" high and dated 1915 on the paper seal. The next two are 1/2 lb. tins. The one on the right is dated 1915 and has illustrations of a Hudson's Bay Transport Steamer on one side and the Winnepeg Store (which was the HBC Canadian "Headquarters") on the other. Value $100 to $200.

Red cut plug and blue Fort Garry pocket tins. Cut plug Est. 35-60; Ft. Garry Est. 75-150

Two sizes of Fort Garry tobacco tins. The detailed and interesting lithography makes them highly desirable. Est. 75-200

Two versions of the 1/2 lb. Fort Garry tobacco tins. Both are very desirable. 4-3/4" high. Est. 200-350

Hudson's Bay Company tea tins were made with red, green, and blue background colors. The lids are attached with a wire pin. The front shows the HBC coat of arms, back is the quality number of the tea, sides show Jack Canuck – Fort Garry and The Girl of the Golden West. These photos show all sides.

Fort Garry smoking tobacco cloth bag. 4-1/2" high. Est. 175-250

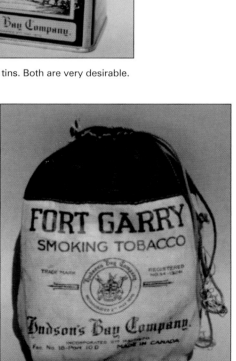

Four sizes and three colors of HBC tea tins are available. A complete set would contain four of each color. 5-1/2" Est. 100-250; 6-1/2" Est. 200-300; 8-1/2" Est. 300-500; 9-1/2" Est. 400-600

Different sizes, colors and quality numbers of tea tins.

These two large Fort Garry coffee tins are among the most beautiful and collectible of the Hudson's Bay Company types. The blue *"Fort Garry Brand Pure Coffee"* 5 lb. tin was distributed by the wholesale branch in Winnipeg. It is 10" high and includes a wire handle. Values range between $450 to $650. The red Fort Garry tin is also from the wholesale division in Winnipeg, Man. and Vancouver, B.C. On the back it has a nice lithograph of the HBC flag and stands 8-3/4" high. Value would be $400 to $550. Both examples have beautiful lithos of Indian and trader activities outside the walls of Fort Garry. If you look carefully, you can see three Indians in front of their tipi smoking calumets (stone pipes).

Very rare and early HBC *"SEASONS TEA"* tin. 11-1/2" high x 8-3/4" square. Missing the lid. This is the only example I have seen. I am guessing that it dates before 1890. Est. 1000-1500. These same litho designs show up on smaller tins with a green background. I have two sizes, but the condition was too poor to include photos.

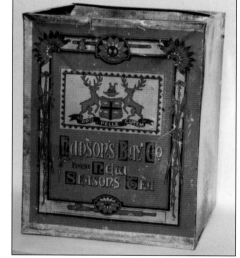

Large coffee tin from the Wholesale Department of the Winnipeg and Vancouver stores. It is 13-3/4" high. Est. 75-150

Three variations of one pound Fort Garry coffee tins. Est. 40-75 each

Cardboard and paper tea and coffee containers. Est. 15-25 each

Hudson's Bay Company pin box and three spice tins. Pin box est. 20-40; Spice tins est. 50-100 each

Bottles

There are many variations of HBC bottles. They include grocery store products, medicine bottles, and the more popular bottles for wines and spirits.

The first bottle is *"Hudson's Bay Co's 'Special' Best Procurable Old Highland Whiskey."* It is green glass with a paper label. This bottle is illustrated in the HBC 1910-11 catalog. 9-3/4" high with a value of $75 to $125. The second is clear glass with the company coat of arms embossed on one side and a nice Sitting Fox and trader's hat on the other. The paper label is missing. It has an aluminum screw cap and the year 1938 embossed into the bottom. 9" high, Est. 25-75. Number three is a dark brown whiskey bottle with the HBC coat of arms embossed into the glass. It has a cork stopper and dates from about 1930. 8" high, Est. 20-50. Number four is embossed with *"Hudson's Bay Co., Incorporated 1670"* and has acquired a purple tint from age and exposure to sunlight. It is 11-3/4" high with a value of $150 to $250. The fifth bottle is full of whiskey. Est. 35-65

Assortment of HBC whiskey bottles. Est. 15-75

Hudson's Bay Company rum bottles. Est. 20-75

Full bottle of *"1670 SCOTCH WHISKEY,"* still wrapped in its original tissue paper. Corked cap. Est. 75-125

Collection of embossed glass medicine type bottles. They are embossed with the HBC name and/or coat of arms. Often they have acquired a bluish tint from exposure to sunlight. Mostly pre-1900. Est. 50-150 each

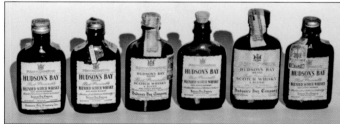

A collection of miniature whiskey and rum bottles. Most of these date from the 1930s to 1960s. They are often found unopened. Est. 10-25

Bottles and cardboard containers with paper labels containing the HBC coat of arms logo. Because the labels are fragile, these are rather hard to find. Est. 25-75

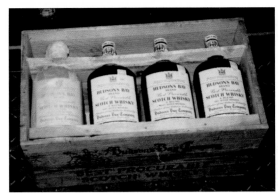

Hudson's Bay Company wooden folding box. Folds flat for compact storage. 13"L x 10"W x 11.5"H. Pat'd June 28, 1898, June 16, 1931 by *Hubbard Folding Box Co.* of Minn. Est. 250-350

Full case of twelve cork top and unopened Hudson's Bay Company *"BEST PROCURABLE"* Scotch Whiskey bottles. All but three are still wrapped in original tissue paper. Probably c.1930s or 40s. I purchased these on eBay from a seller in Florida. Est. 800-1500

Cardboard box for shipping twelve one pound coffee tins. c.1930s or 40s. 15.5"L x 10-1/2"W x 7.5"H. Est. 100-175

Wooden box for *"1670 BRAND SCOTCH WHISKEY."* 14"L x 13"W x 9.5"H. Est. 75-175

Two wooden boxes for HBC rum. 17"L x 11.75"W x 9"H. These also come in red print. Est. 100-175 each

Hudson's Bay Company storage hamper with original metal closing clasp for a lock. Coat of arms is stenciled on the lid. These were made in red and green colors. Green is more scarce. c.1890-1915. Est. 350-500

China

HBC china includes those pieces that are clearly marked to show that they were produced especially for the company. In pre-department store times, there were few, if any, china pieces so marked. After 1870, the company was busy building urban shopping stores in most large Canadian cities with china departments and deluxe restaurants. The chinaware departments mostly sold pieces for use in the home but only a limited number of dining sets received special HBC markings. The restaurants were another story, as the company went to great efforts to give customers an experience that would be long remembered. Because of this we have large varieties of marked china and silverware for today's collector.

The age of department stores also created the souvenir market. The company continued to promote its historical fur trade connections by producing china pieces that people could take home as remembrances of those earlier times. They produced cups, plates, pitchers, pots, etc. using historical events and places for the designs.

China with green coat of arms logo and *"W. H. GRINDLEY & CO OF ENGLAND"* markings on the back. Est. 50-100 each

China with five green stripes and the HBC letters in black is the most common pattern. It is available in most all shapes that would be used for restaurant servings. Most examples were made by *"RIDGWAY OF ENGLAND"* and *"SOVEREIGN POTTERIES OF CANADA."* Plates, est. 6-20; cups and saucers, est. 50-100; bowls, est. 15-35

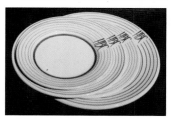

White plates with HBC logo. *"RIDGEWAY"* marking on the back. Est. same as green striped pattern.

China with blue stripes and coat of arms logo and *"COPELAND ENGLAND FOR A. T. WILEY & Co. LTD. OF MONTREAL"* markings on the back. Large plate, est. 40-75; butter dish, est. 25-40

Deluxe oval dish with blue and gold stripes and blue coat of arms logo. Marking on back is *"T. G. GREEN & Co LTD, CHURCH GRESLEY, ENGLAND."* Est. 65-150

Fort Garry pottery tea pot with *"MADE IN JAPAN"* embossed on bottom. Unlike most souvenir pieces, these pots often show signs of having been used to brew a cup of tea. 3.75" high. Est. 85-195

Examples of Hudson's Bay company marked china for household use. These cups and saucers are marked *"LIMOGES CHINA-FRANCE."* Cups and saucers, est. 25-50

"FT. GARRY GATE, WINNIPEG" cup. Marked *"WHEELOCK, DRESDEN, GERMANY"* on bottom. 2" high. Est. 35-75

"OLD FORT GARRY GATEWAY, WINNIPEG" tea cup. Marked *"SHELLEY CHINA, ENGLAND"* on bottom. 2.75" high. Est. 25-65

"H.B.CO FORT, FORT FRANCES" pot with handle. No mark. 1.75" high. Est. 15-40

"H. B. Co's FORT EDMONTON, 1892" flower vase. 4.75" high. Est. 25-50

"OLD HUDSON BAY CO. FORT & N.V.C. CO. SHIPPING, NANAIMO, B.C." cup. No mark. 2-3/8" high. Est. 25-65

"OLD FORT GARRY GATE, WINNIPEG" plate. 9.5" dia. Est. 40-75

"PARLIAMENT BUILDINGS AND OLD HUD-SON'S BAY CO. FORT, EDMONTON, ALTA" cream pitcher. Marked "VICTORIA, AUSTRIA" with a crown on the bottom. 2.75" high. Est. 25-65

Wall hanger saucer, 5" dia. Est. 25-65

Bowl with handles, 5" dia. Est. 40-85

"CANADIAN DOG TRAIN AND REMAINS OF OLD FORT GARRY WINNIPEG" plate. 6" dia. Est. 35-65

"THE DEATH OF THOMAS SCOTT BEFORE THE WALLS OF FORT GARRY, MARCH 4TH 1870" plate. 7" dia. "MADE IN GERMANY" mark on back. Est. 40-75

"OLD HUDSON BAY CO, FORT & N.V.C. CO, SHIPPING NANAIMO, B.C." plate. 7" dia. Est. 40-75

"HUDSON'S BAY Co's STORE, CALGARY, ALTA." Plates in red and green. 10" dia. WEDGEWOOD, ETRUSIA, ENGLAND" marking on back. Est. 45-95 each

"THE BASTION, NANAIMO, B.C." plate. 8.5" dia. On back, "BUILT A.D.1853 AS A PROTECTION FROM MARAUDING INDIANS." Est. 40-75

Crystal glass goblet, "MADE BY ROYAL BRIERLEY OF ENGLAND TO COMMEMORATE THE 300th ANNIVERSARY OF THE HUDSON'S BAY COMPANY" in 1970. "LIMITED EDITION, No. 13 OF 400" on bottom. 5.5" high with box. Est. 35-75

"OLD HUDSON BAY Co's BLOCADE HOUSE, SAULT STE. MARIE, ONT." Plate 7 3/8" dia. "VICTORIA, AUSTRIA" with crown mark on back. Est. 40-75

HBC glass flask with coat of arms etched into the glass. 6.5" high. Est. 40-75

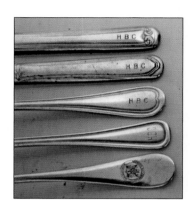

HBC silverware. Makers' marks include *"McGLASHAN STAINLESS"; "WM. A. RODGERS HOTEL PLATE, ONEIDA LTD."; "QUEEN'S PLATE, MADE IN CANADA"; "RODGERS XII & INTERNATIONALS CO."* Est. 5-15 each

Wedgewood bottle with coat of arms. 4" high. Est. 75-125

Commemorative spoon with original box. Marked *"STERLING-BM Co, MADE IN CANADA."* Est. 10-25

Silverware

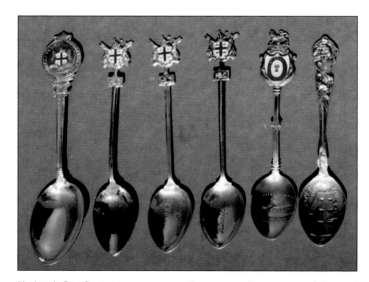

Hudson's Bay Company commemorative spoons. Numerous varieties and commemorations are available. Average length is 4.5". Est. 5-20

Boxed set of engraved spoons issued in 1970 to celebrate the HBC's 300th anniversary. Made by *"COMMEMORATIVE PRODUCTS LTD. OF OTTAWA."* Est. 20-35

Trade Knives and Axes

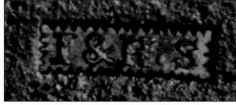

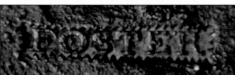

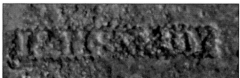

Corresponding dagger blade makers' marks that match previous photo. (Top to bottom) #1 *"JUKES COULSON & CO"*. #2 *"JUKES COULSON & CO, SHEFFIELD"*. #3 *"I & H.S."* and *"FOSTER"*. #4 *"JUKES COULSON &CO"*. #5 *"I & H SORBY"*.

DAGGER BLADES. Five dagger blades traded by the Hudson's Bay Company. Indians could make their own handles or use them on lances or war clubs. (Left to right) #1 is stamped *"JUKES COULSON & CO."* and was found in Montana. #2 is stamped *"JUKES COULSON & CO., SHEFIELD"* and was found at a flea market in Washington state. #3 has the initials *"I & HS"* within a jagged cartouche stamped into the tang. This stamp was used by John and Henry Sorby of Sheffield sometime after 1827. The name *"FOSTER"* appears within a similar cartouche on the opposite side. It was collected in Montana. #4 is stamped *"JUKES COULSON & CO,"* which was a Sheffield cutler who used this stamp between 1774 and 1867. It was found along a creek north of Joplin, Montana by William Meldrum about 1916. 12.5" long. #5 is stamped *"I & H SORBY"* within a jagged cartouche. The cross bars were cut off and an iron tube was slipped over the tang to improvise a handle. The tang was pounded flat at the end of the tube to hold the handle in place. It was found in a bucket of garden tools on a farm on the Nez Perce Reservation near Lewiston, Idaho. Each of these dagger blades has a value of 500-1200

Example of dag with Indian made handle. See *"CHIEF KWAH'S REVENGE"* in Sept. 1943 issue of *The Beaver* magazine for the rest of the story.

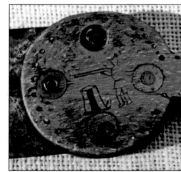

DAGGER KNIFE made by *"BALDWIN AND HILL"* of New York. The name is controversial as the only blacksmith in New York city directories with a similar name is *"BALDWIN AND HEYL"* from 1869 to 1871. Some have the maker's name stamped into the blade and some do not. This example does not have a visible stamp and is perhaps an earlier version. These are rare and always have the Indian shooting his muzzle loader over a tree stump burned into the handle. 14.75" long. Est. 8,000-12,000

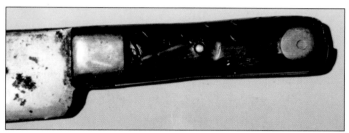

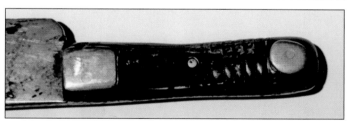

"HUDSON'S BAY COMPANY CAMP KNIFE" with the blade stamped *"Unwin & Rodgers, Sheffield."* This company was established about 1833, and among other things, advertised *"Indian Hunting Knives."* This style knife is sometimes called a *"Buffalo Knife,"* however, the term *"Camp Knife"* seems more fitting because the blade is made from heavy steel that can be used to split wood, chop bones, and do many other camp chores. The handle is made with black horn scales that are held in place with a brass plate and two brass rivets. This knife was collected from Assiniboine Indians on the Ft. Belknap reservation in Montana. The handle has horse tracks and notches carved into it and shows much wear from long hard use. 13.5" long. Est. 5,000-8,000

SCALPING KNIVES. In early fur trade inventories, knives of this type are referred to as *"Scalpers."* Early references date back to the French & Indian War Period and continue until the mid 1800s, when the term "skinning knife" becomes more common. The shape of the blades are always similar, as are the three holes for riveting the diamond shaped wooden handle. (Top to bottom) #1 is stamped *"P.C.J. & Co., CAST STEEL."* This is the trade mark for *"PIERRE CHOTEAU JR. & COMPANY,"* which was a major trading firm operating out of St. Louis beginning in 1838 through to the 1860s. The handle is not original to the knife but has been in use for a long time. This knife was found in a junk knife box at a Billings, Mt. second hand store in 1998 for $5.00. #2 Blade is stamped "P.C.J. & Co." and it still has its unique diamond shaped wooden handle. It has *"T.I. 1849"* carved into the handle and is 12" long. #3 has "Cross and F" mark stamped into the blade. This was the mark of Hiram Cutler, who made knives for the American Fur Co. in the 1830s. It also has the original diamond shaped handle. *Ex-Thain White coll.* #4 has a "Cross and L" mark stamped into the blade. This mark was first registered in Sheffield in 1750 and was used by both the Hudson's Bay Co. and the Northwest Company. #5 was made by *"JUKES COULSON & CO."* of Sheffield, England who was a prominent supplier to the HBC and was first listed as an iron merchant in 1767. This knife was found along the Teton River in Montana by Ernest White in 1906. It is 9" long. The scarcity of these knives makes it difficult to establish a set value. Our estimate would be that blades should sell from $200 to $800 and examples with handles from $500 to $2000.

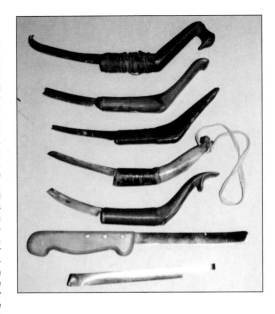

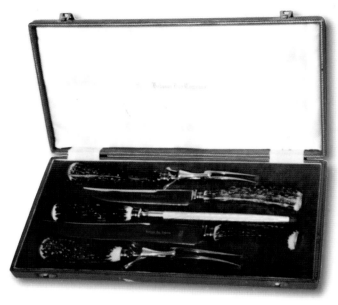

The crooked knife (also canoe knife) is unique to the American Indian trade. It was used by Indians and Eskimo craftsmen to make canoes, paddles, ax handles, wooden spoons, bowls, cups, snowshoe frames, etc. Natives traded for the blades and fitted them to handles. Auguste Choteau, an early fur trader, submitted a bill for a crooked knife in 1806. Many blades were made by natives and blacksmiths at forts and trading posts throughout the north country. The top knife was collected by Sheriff Boots Combs of Eureka, Montana from Kootenai Indians during the last Sun Dance at Tobacco Plains. The curved blade is forged from a file and attached to a wooden handle with rawhide lacing. The end of the handle thumb rest is decorated with a carved birds head. (10.25" long, value $800 to $1500) The next four knives have straight blades for carving. Two blades are attached with wrapped brass wire and the fourth one has an antler handle. (Value is from $300 to $600 each) The sixth and largest knife has "Hudson's Bay Co." etched on the blade and was still being sold by the HBC in the 1970s. (11.5" long, value $50 to $100) The bottom curved blade was made in Sheffield and was still being sold by the HBC in the 1960s.

CARVING SET. Hudson's Bay Company five-piece antler handled carving set in red satin and velvet-lined box. 16"L x 8"W x 1-1/2"H. Knives have HBC and Sheffield markings. Probably from 1930s or 40s. Est. 75-150

Iron trade axes were among the earliest and most popular items traded to Indians and trappers. Large felling axes and smaller belt or "squaw axes" in many sizes were made in large quantities by French, English, and American makers. Iron axes were traded to most all Indian Nations starting in the 1600s. (Top to bottom, L. to R.) The belt axe at the top is unique because it still has its original handle. It was collected from Sioux Indians in South Dakota. The axe is 4.75" long, with a value of $200 to $350. The first axe in the second row is triple stamped with the "I.S." and crown stamp of John Sorby, a maker in Sheffield, England who began manufacturing edged tools about 1790. (The first axe in the close-up photo shows the stamp more clearly.) (7" long, value $200 to $400). Next is a large felling axe with the "I. & H. SORBY" stamp that was first adopted in 1827 when his son Henry joined the family firm. (See second axe in close-up photo.) (9.5" long, value $150 to $250) Of the next two belt axes, the top one shows much use and is shortened from continued sharpening. It has no maker's marks and was collected in South Dakota. It is interesting because it shows so much use. (4" long, value $75 to $150) Under it is an unusual brass belt axe that was found protruding from the banks of the Missouri River just south of Linton, N. Dakota, along with the remains of an old tacked knife case and belt. (4.5" long, value $100 to $200). The first axe on the bottom was found near the old Catholic Mission on the Flathead Reservation in St. Ignatius, Mont. It has a deep stamp that appears to be an upside down "J" and a "B". (5.75" long, value $125 to $200) Next is an axe that was de-accessioned from a museum in Spokane, Wa.; the provenance is "found in 1886 on the battleground of a massacre of those at Ft. Kearny in 1866." It probably dates much earlier and had already seen much use before it was lost in 1866. This little bit of history makes it a very interesting specimen. (5.25" long, value $150 to $250) The third belt axe was found along Kiona Creek near Packwood, Wa. near the site of an early trading post. It is very interesting because the letters "I.D." are deeply stamped into the blade. "I.D." was the early mark applied by the U.S. Indian Department, the forerunner of the modern Bureau of Indian Affairs. (5" long, value $200 to $400). The fourth axe was dug by Emil Repac of Red Lodge, Mont. at the site of old Fort Manuel Lisa near the confluence of the Yellowstone and Big Horn Rivers in Montana. This trading fort was established by Manuel Lisa in 1807. (8" long, value $200 to $400)

BREAD KNIVES. Blades have HBC coat of arms etchings. Bottom one has *"JOSEPH FENTON & SONS, CUTLERS, SHEFFIELD"* stamped into the blade. 14.5" long. Est. 25-65

Trade Guns

As early as 1620, the French began to distribute guns to Indians. By 1761, the name "Northwest Gun" was used to refer to the most popular trade gun style. These usually had .60 caliber smooth bore barrels. They are most easily distinguished by their unique brass dragon-shaped side plate. Other things to look for are the oversized trigger guard that was developed to satisfy the need northern Indians had to fire their guns in sub-zero temperatures without removing their buckskin mittens. This need was also responsible for the development of one finger mittens. Use of brass tacks driven into the wooden stock for decoration is another distinguishing characteristic. A "Tombstone Fox" stamped into the lock, facing left, with the upstanding tail is exactly like the one on the company coat of arms. It is inset into a rectangular cartouche shaped like a plain grave marker with the letters "E.B." just below the fox. A similar fox, facing right, within a circle cartouche was used by the North West Company until it merged with the HBC in 1821.

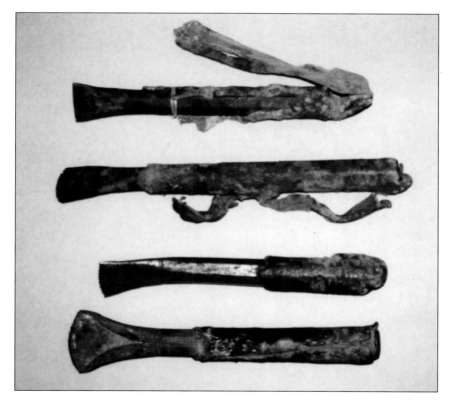

TRADE GUN BARREL FLESHERS. Long after Northwest guns served their usefulness as a hunter's or warrior's weapon, their remains were turned into useful objects. These four fleshing tools were forged from old gun barrels. (Top to bottom) #1 Belonged to Mrs. Little Dog of the Montana Blackfeet and still has its original leather wrist thongs. #2 Collected from Sioux Indians in South Dakota. #3 Came from Agnus Vanderburg on the Flathead Reservation in Montana. #4 Was found in a second hand store in Missoula, Montana. All of these date before 1880 and have values of 200-500.

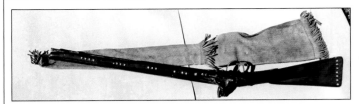

(Left to right) The first gun has *"PARKER FIELD & CO, 1860"* stamped into the lock plate. Numerous unused holes in the lock plate indicate that it was converted from a flintlock mechanism to a cap lock. The second gun has *"BARNETT, LONDON, 1871"* stamped into the lock plate. It was collected in the 1950s from Indians in Alaska who were still using it for hunting. Both are approx. 4 feet long. Est. 3500-5000 each

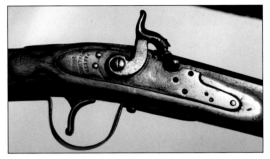

PARKER FIELD 1860 lock plate.

PARKER FIELD 1860 brass dragon.

"Barnett" flintlock dated 1871. It has a *"Tombstone Fox"* stamped on both the lock plate and barrel. The barrel was shortened by its Indian owner to make it more suitable for use on horseback and in forested areas. This gun has a notarized certificate from the great grandson of Conrad Kohrs, a famous historical rancher and trader from Deer Lodge, Mt., stating that "it was picked up on the plains S.W. of Fort Benton by C.K. cowboys shortly after the Custer Massacre in 1876." It shows many signs of Indian usage including brass tacks in the stock for decoration, carved notches in the stock, hand chiseled front and rear sights on the barrel, stock worn through to the ramrod where it lay across a saddle while riding, and light chisel marks toward top front of the barrel to cut down glare from the sun. It includes a sinew-sewn moose hide scabbard. It is 3 feet + 2.5" inches long. Value $4500 to $6000

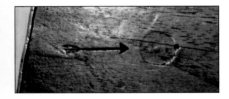

PARKER FIELD 1860 running fox stamp and arrow in stock.

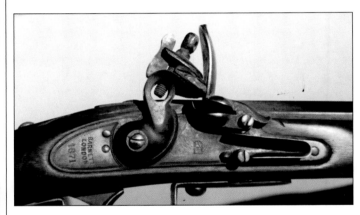

PARKER FIELD 1860 Indian face etched into the putt plate.

BARNETT LONDON 1871 lock plate.

BARNETT LONDON 1871 sitting fox, tombstone mark on lock plate.

BARNETT, LONDON 1871 lock plate.

BARNETT, LONDON 1871 brass dragon.

BARNETT LONDON 1871 brass dragon and notches in stock.

BARNETT LONDON 1871 barrel markings.

BARNETT 1870 fusil in relic condition. It has been shortened by cutting off some of the barrel and the butt end of the stock. This enabled the owner to fire it with one hand while on horseback or to hide it under his wearing blanket. Shortened guns are sometimes called "blanket guns." 27.25"L. Est. 4000-8000

BARNETT LONDON 1871 chiseled back sight on barrel.

BARNETT 1870 fusil lock plate.

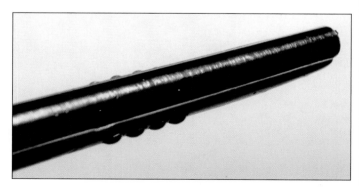

BARNETT LONDON 1871 chisel marks and sight on front of barrel.

(Left to right) CHIEF'S GRADE PRESENTATION TRADE GUN. As the name indicates, these were developed for trade or as gifts to Indian notables and chiefs. #1 has a flint lock. The trigger guard and side plate are engraved with an Indian shield, bow, and crossed arrows. The most identifying feature of a chief's grade gun is the silver medallion inset into the stock at the wrist area. It shows the embossed bust of an Indian with head feathers and a bow and quiver full of arrows. These guns are quite rare and most date before 1850. 4' + 4" long. Est. 9000-12000. #2 is a percussion type with the name of the maker, "KETLAND," stamped into the lock. There is a boar's head surrounded by a hunting horn on the lock and on the brass butt plate. The brass trigger guard and side plate are engraved with an Indian shield, bow, and crossed arrows. The silver Indian bust is inset into the stock at the wrist area. It still has its original metal ramrod. 4' +2" long. Est. 6000-9000

HUDSON'S BAY COMPANY SHOTGUNS. (Left to right) #1 is "THE IMPERIAL No 5" double barreled cartridge firing breech loading shotgun. Both locks are stamped "HUDSON'S BAY COMPANY" with lots of engraving, Damascus barrels and a Vulcanite butt plate. 3' +10.5" long. Est. 800-1200. #2 is double barreled cap lock shotgun made by "I. HOLLIS & SONS" of London. Both locks are marked "HUDSON'S BAY COMPANY MADE IN ENGLAND." Because of the "made in England" mark, we must assume this gun was made after 1890. Shotguns were still being sold at HBC stores into the early 1900s. This one was collected in Alaska. 3' + 9.5" long. Est. 900-1500.

CHIEF'S GRADE flint lock and percussion locks.

HBC SHOTGUN breech loading lock.

HBC SHOTGUN cap lock.

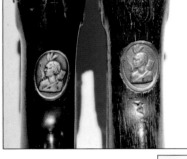

CHIEF'S GRADE silver medallions.

CHIEF'S GRADE brass side plate.

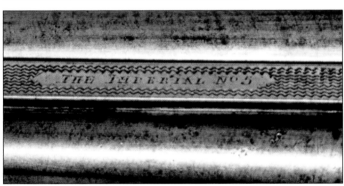

THE IMPERIAL No 5 barrel marking.

CHIEF'S GRADE brass trigger guard.

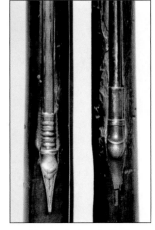

CHIEF'S GRADE ramrod ferrules.

I. HOLLIS & SONS barrel marking.

Steel Strikers

Strikers date to the very beginning of the fur trade. Many shapes and sizes were made by blacksmiths on the frontier or imported from cutlery companies in England. For Indians and trappers they provided an easier way of starting a fire in the days before matches were available. Striking the steel against a piece of flint causes sparks to fly. The sparks were caught in tinder and ignited by blowing on them. With practice, you can even light your tobacco pipe with a steel striker.

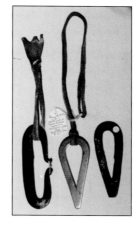

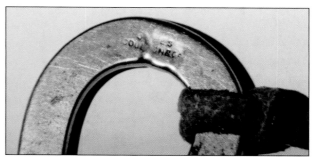

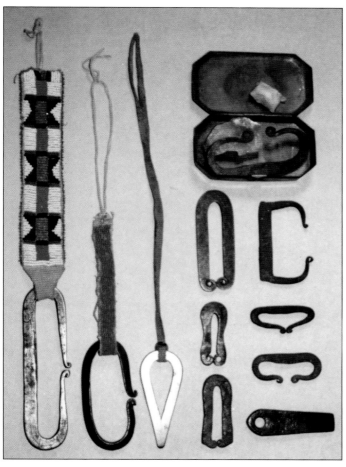

The large striker hanging from a beaded belt tab is Blackfeet and was purchased at a Sotheby's auction in 1972 for $80. It is over 100 years old. The striker part is 6" long. Value is $800 to $1500. The second striker was collected from the Montana Blackfeet and is forged from a triangular shaped file stamped with the word *"Disston."* It has a beaded buckskin belt tab and dates to about 1880. The steel is 4" long with a value of $400 to $900. The third example is tear drop shaped steel collected from Nora Spanish on the Montana Blackfeet Reservation in 1973. It has a *"Jukes Coulson & Co."* stamp and was made by this Sheffield cutlery company between 1774 and 1867. This style was traded by The Hudson's Bay Co. Marked strikers are quite rare. It is 3.75" long with a value of $600 to $1000. At the top right is a brass tinder box, which was used to keep the striker and tinder dry. Under it is a striker shaped like a letter "D" that was found by Jim Dressler along the Menominee River in Michigan. It is very early and could date from the 1700s. It is 3.5" long with a value of $200 to $400. The rest are Spanish style strikers made for trade in the southwest and Mexico. Values range from $100 to $250 each.

(Left to right) #1 Large striker made from a file. Collected in Montana by Paul Janetski and displayed for many years in the West Yellowstone Museum. 4.25" long. Est. 450-600. #2 Tear drop shaped striker collected from Blackfeet Indians. It has a *"JUKES COULSON & CO."* stamp showing lots of wear from years of dangling on a buckskin carrying thong. J. Coulson was a knife making company in Sheffield, England between 1774 and 1867. Very rare. 3.25" long. Est.600-1000. #3 Early striker stamped *"WALDEN CAST STEEL".* It was found on a hill overlooking a buffalo pound site south of Plentywood Montana in the 1950s. 3.75" long. Est. 450-600

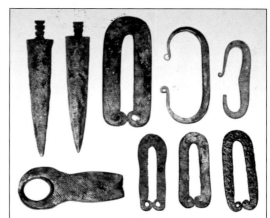

Assortment of early strikers and two metal trade arrow points. Strikers, est. 50-100 each; arrow points, est. 100-200 each.

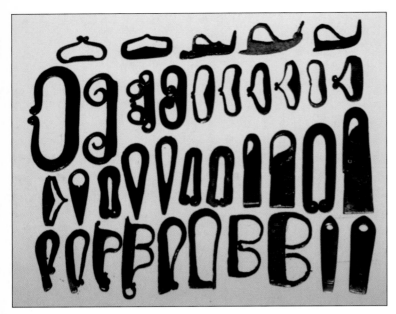

Steel strikers have a long history of use. Some examples date back to the 16th century. Many have been uncovered around medieval European castles. This photo shows some of the many styles available from European and North American sites. Est. 35-300 each

ZIPPO LIGHTERS with HBC coat of arms logos are available from numerous HBC locations. Est. 35-85

Miscellaneous HBC Collectibles

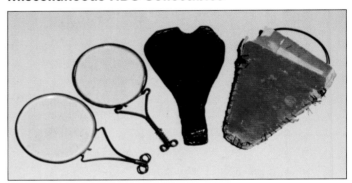

MAGNIFYING or BURNING GLASSES like these date back to 1750. They could be used for reading or starting fires. They were a popular trade item into the middle 1800s. They have brass or copper frames around a rock crystal lens. Many came with leather, wood, or paper carrying cases. 3.5"L. Est. 200 to 400

HUDSON'S BAY COMPANY MATCHES. Wooden matches in HBC marked boxes were still being sold in the 1960s.

MAGNIFYING OR BURNING GLASS with folding buffalo horn frame. It has the initials *"E.B."* and the date *"1764"* etched on one side of the frame. 2" x 2.5"; Est. 300-550

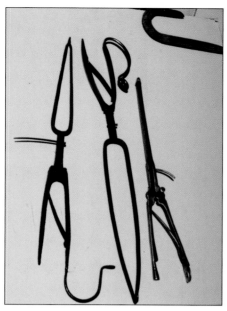

PIPE TONGS were made specifically for picking up small coals to light tobacco pipes. Various knobs and flattened ends with holes were used to tamp the tobacco and create a draw of air to keep the tobacco burning. They were especially popular in taverns and meeting halls. Often brass lidded pots were kept handy on the table from which to lift a hot coal. The one in the middle is 21.5"L., c.1750-1800. It came from a five generation family estate in Joliette, a small city north of Montreal, Canada. Est. 700-1500 each

Pair of aluminum shoe stretchers with HBC coat of arms logos. Est. 35-75

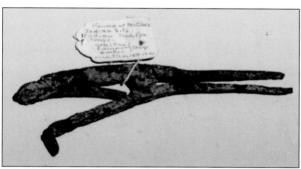

This small pipe tong was found at a Seneca Indian site south of Rochester, N.Y. and dates from 1690 to 1720. It includes a striker, tamper and ember tongs. 6" long. Est. 350-500

THE BEAVER MAGAZINE. In 1920, Vol. 1 #1 of *The Beaver* was issued as an in house magazine for employees of the HBC. By Dec. 1924, it was being printed with a color cover and by Sept. 1933 a larger format and the subtitle "A MAGAZINE OF THE NORTH" was adopted to promote distribution outside the sphere of the HBC. Today, copies are collected for their outstanding photos and scores of historically important articles concerning the history of the company, Indians, Eskimos, and the Canadian fur trade. In 1994, the magazine was acquired from the HBC by Canada's National History Society and currently prints articles about all areas of Canadian history.

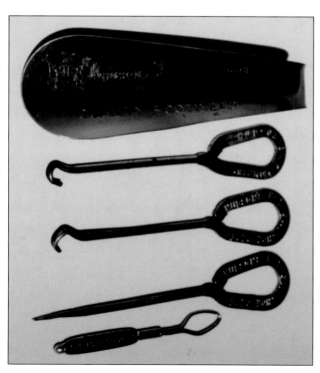

Hudson's Bay Company metal shoe horn and button hooks. One of the button hooks has been straightened for use as an awl. Est. 20-50 each

Sept. 1927 issue.

Dec. 1932 issue.

Beaver House souvenir booklet, printed for visitors to the headquarters of the Hudson's Bay Company in London. Contains a photo illustrated history of the company. c.1950. Est. 15-25

Mar. 1942 issue.

Historical Exhibit of The Hudson's Bay Company, souvenir booklet. Colorful cover with many photographs of objects in the exhibit. Est. 15-35

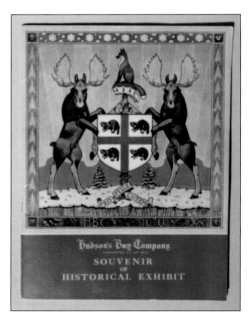

The Beaver as it appears today.

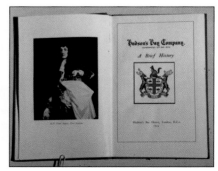

A Brief History of The Hudson's Bay Company, printed by Hudson's Bay House in 1934. Hard back book with 68 pp. of history and photographs. Est. 20-35

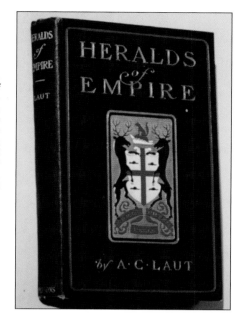

Heralds Of Empire, Being the Story of One Ramsay Stanhope, Lieutenant to Pierre Radisson in the Northern Fur Trade, by A.C.Laut, c. 1902. Hard back with beautiful cover and 372 pp. of historical information. Est. 25-50

CALENDARS. Yearly calendars were given away by the HBC. They contain prints of paintings portraying important events in the history of the Hudson's Bay Company. They average 18" x 31" and are colorful and frameable. Examples in excellent condition are very desirable. Est. 75-150

Lower Fort Garry–A History of the Stone Fort, by Robert Watson. Published by the HBC in 1928. Hardback with 69 pp. of photos and information. Est. 20-65

1929 Calendar, "RED RIVER CARTS LEAVING FORT GARRY 1863."

The Fort Garry Historical Pageant, photo souvenir booklet printed for the 250th Anniversary Celebration at Winnipeg in May 1920. Est. 25-75

1932 Calendar, "GOVERNOR GEORGE SIMPSON WELCOMED BY JAMES DOUGLAS AT FORT ST. JAMES IN 1828."

The Hudson's Bay Record Society, printed 33 volumes of original HBC journals, letters, and records. These hard back limited editions were sent to members and subscribing institutions. Lots of information that is not easily available elsewhere. Prices vary according to the material. Most copies fall between est. 75-150

1942 Calendar, "R.M.
BALLANTYNE AT
TADOUSSAC, 1846."

CIGAR BOXES AND CIGARS that were still being sold in The Bay in the
1970s. Empty boxes, est. 35-75; full boxes, est. 125-200

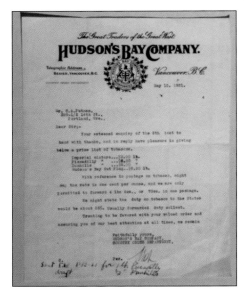

HBC LETTER listing
tobacco prices.
Dated May 10, 1921.
Est. 20-40

1956 Calendar,
"TRADING
CEREMONY AT YORK
FACTORY."

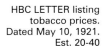

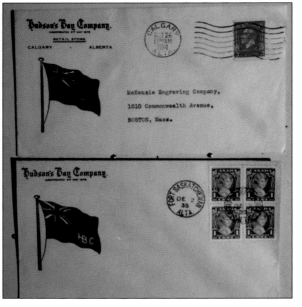

HBC CIGAR BOX. The outside
has been decorated with incised carving and stained dark
brown. Est. 75-150

HBC FLAG ENVELOPES dated 1934 and 1935. Many different
postmarks and dates are available. Est. 5-50 each

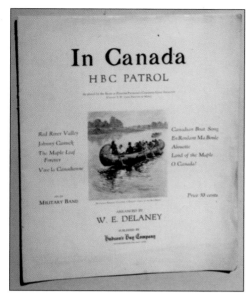

"IN CANADA, HBC PATROL" sheet music "as played by the band of Princess Patricia's Light Infantry." c.1929 by Hudson's Bay Company. Est. 30-60

HBC PRINTER'S INK BLOCKS. Est. 25-50

1913 MODEL T HBC toy delivery truck. Die cast metal toy made by Ertl in 1988. Several other years and models are available. Est. 20-50

INDIAN BEADED ROSETTES with HBC designs. These are scarce but interesting. The coat of arms rosette was made by Madeleine McIvor in the 1950s. She was the Cree wife of the last store manager at York Factory before it closed in 1959. Est. 75-250 each

HBC POCKET KNIFE. *"La Ronge, Sask."* printed on other side. 3"L. with two blades. Marked *"IXL, George Wostenholm, Sheffield, England."* Est. 40-84

Boxed HBC playing cards by *"John Waddington Ltd., Leeds & London."* Est. 50-100

HUDSON'S COM-PANY SCALE manufac-tured by *"Pelouze Scale & Mfg. Co. of Chicago."* Patent dates from 1898 to 1903. Company coat of arms is printed in gold on both sides. 8.5"H. Est. 250-350

HBC REVOLVING NEEDLE CASE, contains 100 needles. Listed in 1911-1912 fall HBC catalog at 10¢ per case. 2.25" long. Est. 75-150

HBC 6 inch wooden ruler. Est. 20-40

Boxed set of six HBC handcrafted beverage coasters. 4" x 4". Est. 15-30

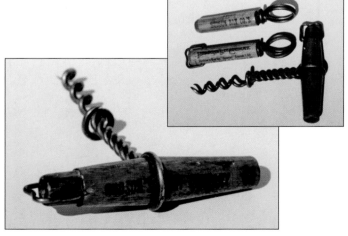

HBC complimentary CORK SCREW and BOTTLE OPENERS. One of the bottle openers is marked "WRC DECAPITATOR, PAT. MAR. 1, 1918." Openers are 4.75"L. Est. 75-150

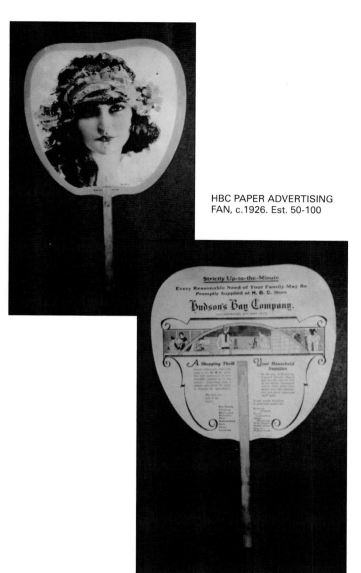

HBC PAPER ADVERTISING
FAN, c.1926. Est. 50-100

References for this section:

Gilman, Carolyn. *Where Two Worlds Meet.* St. Paul, Minnesota Historical Society, 1982.

Gooding, James. *Trade Guns of the Hudson's Bay Company.* Alexandria Bay, New York, Museum Restoration Society, 2003.

Hanson, James A. *Fur Trade Cutlery Sketchbook.* Crawford: The Fur Press, 1994.

Hanson, James A. *Spirits In The Art.* Kansas City: The Lowell Press, Inc., 1994.

Hanson, Charles E. *The Northwest Gun.* Lincoln, Nebraska: State Historical Society, 1956.

McGregor, Doug. Personal communication, 1998.

Newman, Peter. *Empire of the Bay.* Toronto, Canada: Madison Press Books, 1989.

Pietrangelo, Dominic. *Illustrated Spectacles of the American Revolution 1650-1850.* Glendale Hts. IL: D. S. P. Publ., 1994.

Plummer, Dan. *Colonial Wrought Iron.* Ocean Pines, MD: Skipdale Press, 1999.

Russell, Carl P. *Firearms, Traps & Tools of the Mountain Men.* New York: Alfred A. Knopf, Inc., 1967.

Wheeler, Robert C. *A Toast to the Fur Trade.* St. Paul: Wheeler Productions, 1985.

Hudson's Bay Co. Catalog, 1910-1911. Winnipeg, Canada: Watson & Dwyer Publ., 1977.

The author is interested in buying and selling trade items, or exchanging information. Contact Preston Miller, Box 580, St. Ignatius, Mt. 59865, Ph. 406-745-4336.

2. Trade Beads

About 400 years ago, explorers and traders brought glass beads to America. Most of these beads were being made in European countries with strong glass producing traditions, i.e., Italy, Bohemia (now known as the Czech Republic), and others. These glass beads gradually replaced the shells, bones, stones, and quills the Indian people had been using to ornament their bodies, clothing, containers, sacred objects, etc. The Europeans soon discovered Indians might give a horse, beaver skin, or other valuable object or service for certain glass beads. Thus, the term "trade beads" came into being.

Meanwhile, beads were also being traded to other countries. Millions of beads were traded into Africa, where they became status symbols to denote individual and family wealth. These African beads caught the attention of American "hippies" in the 1960s and were soon being imported to the U.S. by the tons. The values quickly rose as Africans began gathering these beads and bringing them to America, where willing buyers were anxious to trade for cash. Today collectors, artists, bead clubs, Native Americans, etc. have created a demand for beads that has caused prices to continually rise.

A portion of the author's HBC collection.

Many of the beads in this section come from the African trade and are strung on grass. In today's market, beads traded directly to American Indians are less common. Genuine American Indian trade beads are scarce, but both African and American Indian trade beads are commanding respectable prices.

TRADE BEADS

ARE MEASURED IN MILLIMETERS
1" = 25.4 mm   1/16" = apx. 1.5 mm

ACTUAL SIZE
Beads graduated from 10 to 1 mm in size

We have chosen to illustrate primarily those African trade beads that have a counterpart in the North American Indian trade. Beads exported from Africa are most easily identified by the native grasses on which they are often strung; because these beads are often more than 100 years old they sometimes show considerable wear and darkened patina.

Chevrons and Striped Beads

Chevrons are probably the most popular and collectible bead. The name refers to the star-like chevron pattern that forms around the hole at either end. The most popular version is composed of multiple layers of white, red, and cobalt blue glass. The earliest and most collectible types were first made around the year 1500 and can be identified by their seven layers of colored glass. Often the first inner layer and the third layer are trans. green glass. Later examples usually have six layers of white, red, and cobalt. They are still being made today, both in Italy and by glass artisans in America. Many variations in size and colors are available; some are larger than a chicken egg.

Large chevrons were not prominent in the early North American Indian trade. Some examples about the size of a cherry have been recorded as being found at North American sites. A collector should check the provenance very carefully if he is told his purchase has come via the American Indian trade.

Small pea size examples have been excavated from 16th and 17th century sites in New York and Pennsylvania. (See more information under Green Chevrons, p. 89.) These are made from "pinched" glass tubes that give the layers a rounded shape following the curve of the bead. The chevrons found in the African trade are usually chopped or cut and tumbled glass, which produces layers that follow a straight line making the chevron pattern easily visible. (See African trade blue chevron strand, p. 89.)

S. S. Haldeman writes about two chevron "rosetta"* pattern beads having been found on a site in So. Calif. before 1879. See photo in his 1879 "Report Upon U. S. Geological Surveys," Vol. VII, Archaeology plate XIII, Gvt. Printing Office, Washington, D.C.

See also Dubin, Lois Sherr. *History of Beads.* New York: Harry N. Abrams Publ., (1987): 116-117. Concise edition (1995): 44-45.

*Rosetta means star in Italian.

Large Chevrons

LARGE GREEN 7 LAYERED CHEVRONS MADE FROM OLD VENETIAN GLASS CANES
c.1850-1910?
We obtained these from an African bead trader, who said they were newly cut and faceted beads made from very old chevron glass canes. They are absolutely beautiful and one of the rarest old beads available. The outer color is a dark green followed by white, brick red, white, milky white, white, and clear glass. The largest one averages 26mm. diam. x 41mm. L. 24 beads in graduated sizes. 36" loop. Exc. cond. Est. 900-1500 **SOLD $900(05)**

LARGE OLD 6 LAYER CHEVRONS Pre-20th C. Cobalt, brick, and white layers. Size variations from 12-34 mm L. TRADING POST PRICES **(06):** $55 each for those without tags; far right, $125; front left, $45

LARGE OLD 6 LAYER CHEVRONS 20th C. Cobalt, brick, and white layers. Size variations from 17 to 25 mm. TRADING POST PRICES
$20 each (06).
Similar size, color, and shape chevrons excavated at a Wisc. site dating from 1650-1770. See *Beads: Their Use by Upper Great Lakes Indians,* 1977:51.

Small Chevrons and Striped Beads

(Top) GREEN CHEVRONS
By the 1600s and 1700s, forms of this bead were being traded to tribes on the Eastern coast of America and Canada. They are made from a white core with brick red, white, and green glass layers that are drawn in glass tubes. These are heated and pinched into individual beads. This process gives the bead its stripes and bulbous shape with chevron patterns on both ends. Small green and blue chevrons were excavated from sites along the Susquehanna River, Lancaster County, Penna.

See Francis Jr., Peter. *Beads of the World.* West Chester, PA: Schiffer Publishing Ltd., 1999: 57.

Picard, John and Ruth. *Chevrons and Nueva Cadiz Beads, Vol. VII.* Carmel, Calif.: 1993: 105-110.

Fenstermaker, Gerald B. *Early Susquehanna Bead Chart 1550, Vol. III.* Lancaster, PA., 1974.

(Center) STRIPED OVAL BEAD
An early bead probably dating to the 1700s, made in many color combinations. Identical beads were used in the North American trade. 7 x 12 mm TRADING POST PRICES **$2 ea. (06)**

(Bottom) LARGE STRIPED BEAD
Early style similar to ones traded to North America from 1600-1700. Brick red wire wound core covered with layer of white to which red and blue stripes have been applied. Apx. 12 x 15 mm. TRADING POST PRICES **$5 ea. (06)**

See Francis, pp.54 and 64.

Fenstermaker, *Early Susquehanna Bead Chart 1550, Vol. III.*

(Left) EARLY CHEVRONS FROM A NORTH AMERICAN SITE 17th C.
Five chevrons from Keller and Manor sites, Lancaster Co., PA. By comparison, the curved beads found in early No. American sites are bulbous or round as shown by this photo. Apx. 6 mm. L.
(Right) AFRICAN TRADE BEADS Late 19th C.?
Note that these six beads on the right are blocky with ends straight or crudely ground to reveal star pattern. Apx. 7-9 mm L.

4-10mm size chevrons were found at numerous 18th century and early 19th century Canadian historic sites, forts, and Indian sites. Outside layer colors were red, navy, or "palm green." Shapes were round, tubular, and flat (tabular).

"Classification Occasional Papers in Archaeology and History No. 1," Ottawa, National Historic Sites Service: 1970.

This small size was also documented at a Great Lakes site: see photo* of a round blue chevron and a blue chevron tube bead with rounded ends, sizes 7-10 mm, found at the Rock Is., Wisc. Site, occupied from 1650-1770.

Beads: Their Use By Upper Great Lakes Indians. Exhibition Catalog: Grand Rapids Public Museum Publ. #3, 1977: 51.

BLUE-GREY CHEVRONS
We have no record of this bead being found at an early No. American site, but it is a beautiful and collectible bead style dating back many years. Note the many variations of stripe patterns. Apx. 6 to 9mm. TRADING POST PRICES **$2-4 ea. (06)**

SMALL BLUE CHEVRONS
African trade beads in sizes similar to those found on No. American sites. However, only semi-rounded beads, straight ends or tubes with ends ground to show layers are on this strand. Straight end tubes were also found on No. American sites. Sizes: 5-8 mm W. x 5-10 mm L. Apx. 22" string. TRADING POST PRICE **$175(06)**

(Top) CROSS TRAILS BEADS
These were an early pre-1800 style popular with Plains Indians during the 1860-1885 period. Wire-wound oval bead with red, white, and blue stripes applied to surface creating a cross-shaped pattern. Apx. 8 x 12 mm. TRADING POST PRICES **$4 ea(06)**
(Bottom) DUTCH (DELFT) BEADS
Dates back to the 1600s; found at a Great Lakes fort occupied from 1700-1781. White oval beads with blue spiral stripes. 9 x 12mm TRADING POST PRICES **$4 ea(06)**

See *Beads: Their Use by Upper Great Lakes Indians.* Exhibition Catalog, Grand Rapids Public Museum, MI., 1977: 52.

WHITE CROSS TRAILS WITH COBALT EYES
This bead often shows up on Plains Indian artifacts. We see them on early bear claw necklaces and Crow medicine stones. The lines are pink. Aver. 10 mm x 10 mm. TRADING POST PRICE **$4 ea(06)**

GOOSEBERRY BEADS
Found on Indian sites as early as the 17th century. (Excavated at a Great Lakes fort site occupied 1700-1781.*) This popular bead was made from drawn clear glass with white stripes. 3 to 5mm-24" loop. TRADING POST PRICE **$35(06)**
*See *Beads: Their Use by Upper Great Lakes Indians,* p. 51.

ORIGINAL KILO PACKAGE OF WHITE CROSS TRAILS BEADS
Purchased from Dennis Lessard, when he lived in Mission So. Dak. in 1971. He found this old package in a NYC warehouse. Contains beads strung and sold by the bunch, as shown. Brown paper wrapped, stamped "Made in Italy." Tied with string holding a single bead used as an example.

Lamp-Wound Venetian Fancy Beads

References for this section:

Francis Jr., Peter. *Beads of the World.* Atglen, PA.: Schiffer Publishing, Ltd., 1999.
Jargstorf, Sibylle. *Glass Beads from Europe.* Atglen, PA.: Schiffer Publishing, Ltd., 1995.
——. *Glass in Jewelry.* Atglen, PA: Schiffer Publishing Ltd., 1998.
Miller, Preston E., and Carolyn Corey. *The Four Winds Guide to Indian Trade Goods and Replicas.* Atglen, PA: Schiffer Publishing, Ltd., 1998.
van der Sleen, W.G.N. *A Handbook on Beads.* York, Penna.: Liberty Cap Books, 1973.
Woodward, Arthur. *Denominators of the Fur Trade.* Pasadena, CA.: Westernlore Press, 1970.
——. *Indian Trade Goods.* Portland, Oregon: Historical Society, 1965.

See photos of the lampworking process in Jargstorf 1998, pp. 66-67. Each bead is hand-made, one at a time, with the result that each one is unique. Many varieties of these early "fancy" beads were traded from the Plains to the Pacific Coast from 1800-1860. (Woodward 1965, p. 39)

(Left to right) **WHITE CROSS TRAILS WITH COBALT EYES** c.1820. 27" loop strung on grass. Exc. cond. Est. 70-150 **SOLD $100(05)**
YELLOW CROSS TRAILS c.1840. *Popular Plains Indian bead.* Red, white, and blue stripes. Aver. 8 x 12 mm. on 29" loop. Est. 30-75 **SOLD $35(05)**
WHITE CROSS TRAILS c.1840. Same as above. On 27" loop strung on grass. Est. 20-65 **SOLD $20(05)**

(Left to right) **OVAL MILK-WHITE WITH BLUE STRIPE** Aver. 8 x 15mm. 27" loop strung on grass. Est. 15-30 **SOLD $20(05)**
DELFT (DUTCH) WHITE WITH BLUE DIAGONAL STRIPES c.1840. Aver. 9 x 12mm. 32" loop on grass. Est. 85-150
BLACK FEATHER BEADS c.1850. *RARE. Black is the rarest color in which this bead was made.* This is a great string with hardly any broken or chipped examples. Aver. 8 x 18mm. on 26.5" loop, strung on grass. Est. 175-250

FEATHER or COMBED BEADS
A lamp-wound bead with white and blue stripes that are combed into a feathery design. 9 x 22mm. TRADING POST PRICES **(06)**: RUBY RED **$10 ea**; BLACK or GREEN **$15 ea** Less common.
van der Sleen, pp. 42-47.
Francis, pp. 64 and 69.

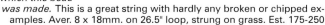

(Top to bottom) **WHITE CROSS TRAILS WITH CO-BALT EYES BEADS** c.1820. The lines are a pink color. Avg. 10mm x 10mm. 27" loop strung on grass. Exc. cond. Est. 50-100 **SOLD $50(99)**

TRADE BEAD NECKLACE. c.1840. *RARE* Includes 22 black beads with white designs know as "6's", 29 striped beads, and 8 others all with designs that date back into the 1700s in the N. Amer. trade. Average size bead 11mm x 13mm on a 28" loop. Exc. cond. Est. 225-350

BLACK FEATHER BEADS c.1840. *RARE These are usually red; it is very hard to find a whole string of black ones.* The feathering is mostly red and white. These are exceptionally nice with only a few chipped or broken beads. Avg. 7mm x 19mm. Loop is 27" and strung on grass. Exc. cond. Est. 175-300

ROUND TRANS. COBALT BLUE BEADS with white foliate trailed designs. *This bead shows up on N. Amer. Indian sites dating back into the 1700s*.* Very rare to find a full string of these. Avg. 8mm. W and L. 34" loop strung on grass. Exc. cond. Est. 250-400 **SOLD $225(99)** *See *Beads: Their Use by Upper Great Lakes Indians,* p. 52.

FROSTED CLEAR GLASS VENETIAN FANCY BEADS 20th C. Beautiful oval beads with stylized floral designs in cobalt, red, yellow, and white. 38 beads strung on grass. Each bead measures apx. 23mm x 17mm. 36" loop. Exc. cond. Est. 85-150

LARGE "AMBASSADOR"* BEADS 19th C. Apx. 26-30 mm. each. Black with lt. blue over white end stripes; multi-colored circles and dots. Slashes of aventurine, gold-toned metallic lines (see definition following). TRADING POST PRICES **$25-30 ea(06)**

Fancy lampworked large floral bead on display at Rocky Mountain House National Historic Park Museum, Alberta. Early 19th C. The forts built by the Hudson's Bay Co. and Northwest Company at this location were occupied between 1799-1861. They were excavated during archaeological digs on the site between 1962-1977. A similar bead is found on the earliest known Venetian bead sample card, which is on display at a museum in Vienna, Austria. There are a large variety of trailed flower-like bead patterns on this card, which is from the Venetian manufacturer Giorgio B. Barbaria, given to the Hapsburg monarch, Franz 1st in 1815. (Jargstorf, 1995 pp. 60-61) Written evidence suggests that lampworked beads with stylized floral patterns such as this were made by Muranese/Venetian lampworkers "since at least the last third of the 18th century." (Ibid, p. 150) Distribution of fancy beads to North American tribes was from the Plains to the West Coast during the period 1800-1860. (Woodward 1965, p. 39) NOTE the remarkable resemblance to the preceding contemporary Venetian floral beads. This gives an idea of the difficulty of bead dating when the same style has been made for over two hundred years.

The **aventurine** process was invented in Murano in 1644 and beads were made with this decoration as early as the 17th century. Aventurine is called "goldstone," although there is no gold used—the flecks are copper. However, it did not become really popular on beads until the 1820s when new glass colors were "re-created" and now made in "large scale production." (Jargstorf 1998. "Aventurine Jewelry," pp. 125-134)

*IMPORTANT NOTE: There are dubious origins of the nomenclature *"Lewis and Clark," "Ambassadors,"* etc., as there is no record of these beads on the Lewis and Clark expedition.
See Francis, p. 120, *"Some Bead Fallacies."*
See Picard, *Fancy Beads Vol. III.*

(Top to bottom) **FROSTED CLEAR GLASS VENETIAN FANCY BEADS** 20th C. Beautiful oval beads with simple floral designs in cobalt, red, yellow, and white. Each bead measures apx. 23mm x 17mm. Exc. cond. TRADING POST PRICE **$10 ea(06)**

LARGE FLORAL FANCY BEADS 20th C.? Black with white, blue, red, and yellow. apx. 25 mm. Pristine cond. TRADING POST PRICE **$25 ea(06)**

(Left) **PAIR OF *"LEWIS and CLARK"** TRADE BEADS** Black with red, white, and blue trailed design. 6 x 25-29 mm L. TRADING POST PRICE **$50 pr (96)**
(Right) PAIR OF *"AMBASSADOR"** TRADE BEADS Black with lt. blue stripes each end. 32 x 13 mm. TRADING POST PRICE **$60pr (06)**

(Left to right) **TRADE BEAD NECKLACE WITH "LEWIS and CLARK BEAD"** 19th C.
The L. and C bead. is 12 x 27mm. *There is no evidence to support the idea that any fancy lampworked beads were carried on the L and C expedition.* Other beads include red and black eye beads, T. red 6 sided oval tubes, black oval polychromes with yellow, red and blue designs, etc. 32.5" loop ready to wear. Est. 80-150 **SOLD $95(05)**
TRADE BEAD NECKLACE WITH BLACK and WHITE "#6's" 19th C.
Number 6 beads are what the African bead traders call them. They are rather rare and this is a nice collection of them. Other beads include a cobalt blue bead with red, white, and blue spiral stripes. Also a bunch of multi-colored chevrons. Aver. 13mm. diam. on 27.5" loop. Est. 195-300
RARE STRING OF LARGE "GHOST BEADS"
These are probably contemporary, even though some people insist they are old. The design resembles a ghost like figure. They are black with shades of milky white patterns. Aver. 15 x 15mm. 32" loop strung on grass. Exc. cond. Est. 85-175 **SOLD $126(05)**

White Hearts and Eye Beads

WHITE HEART, white lined, or white center all refer to a style of bead with a white interior, also known as CORNALINE D'ALEPPO. A rose-red outer layer was made in imitation of the red agate carnelian (French word is cornaline); Aleppo is a city in Syria, well-known as a trade center, where carnelian was traded. The term CORNALINE D'ALEPPO is usually reserved for larger necklace beads. In North America, they are sometimes called HUDSON'S BAY BEADS, or "under whites" by the Blackfeet, prior to the 19th century.

The earliest examples are made by melting two layers of glass over a wire rod that produced a hole when cooled and slipped off. This method can be identified by the visible spiral lines that are produced when the glass is wrapped around the wire. Nearly all of the early white center beads made for North America were made in this manner. Later, probably after 1890, most were made by the drawn glass method, in which long glass tubes were cut into bead size, heated, then tumbled in sand to round off the sharp edges. This method produced a more uniform bead in size and shape. Most modern white hearts are produced in this way; however, in the last decade wire-wound examples have been produced in India distinguished from earlier Venetian counterpart by a more blocky and less rounded shape (see following photo example).

(Left to right) **WHITE CENTER WIRE-WOUND BEADS** Contemp. This bead is now being made in India and is included here because the style (and rose-red color) closely resembles those popular in the American Indian trade from 1800-1870. Rose-red, 4 x 6 mm, 29" loop (apx. 170 beads) **$15(06)** TRADING POST PRICE Rose-red, 6 x 13 mm, 29" loop (apx. 113 beads) **$20(06)**
WIRE-WOUND ROSE WITH WHITE CENTER c.1800
Very rare and just like the early ones traded to No. America. Strung on grass. Aver. size 9 mm W and L. 28" loop. Est. 100-175
WIRE-WOUND OVAL ROSE WITH HEARTS
Another early bead style dating back to 1800. This style was very popular in the early Indian trade and is often seen on medicine stones, pouches, and necklaces. Wire-wound. Aver. size. 8 x 12 mm L. 27" loop strung on grass. TRADING POST PRICE **$175(06)**
MOLDED TRANS. RED MELON BEADS c.1800
EXTREMELY RARE. A few still have the gold leaf paint in the depressions. Irregular sizes. Aver. size 10 mm W and L. 29" loop strung on grass. Est. 75-125
CORNALINE D'ALEPPO TRADE BEADS
Brick red with large green glass centers. This is the earliest style dating back to the 1700s. Smaller beads like this were common on early Indian sites, often times mixed with "Quartz" beads from the same period at West Coast sites. (See page 97 for old ones.) Irregular sizes. Aver. size 12 mm W x 14 L. 32" loop. TRADING POST PRICE **$45(06)**

BLACK BEADS WITH WHITE STRIPE c.1800.
If there ever was a "skunk bead,"* this must be it. Aver. size 9mm W x 6 mm L. This black lobed bead is characterized by a prominent central white stripe of varying widths. They were traded as early as 1800 throughout No. America and were esp. popular in the Northwest. TRADING POST PRICE 7 x 9mm **$4(06)** ea; 24" string **$75(06)**
See Fenstermaker, *Vol. VI-Northwest Coast Bead Chart,* 1978.
*Nowadays, this term has been erroneously applied to every color of eye bead, esp. black with white eyes. The origin of the term "skunk" bead seems to be from the Blackfeet and refers to a very early "large blue bead with meandering lines and white and red flowers," as recalled by elderly informants to John Ewers in *Blackfeet Crafts,* Haskell Inst. 1945: 33.

Beginning in the 16th century or earlier, this style of bead was first made with a trans. dk. green center (looks black until seen through light) and an opaque brick red outer layer. They appear to have been made using the drawn glass method and often are found at No. American archaeological sites along with the white "quartz" beads. Also, yellow center rose-red beads were found in large numbers after 1800 in the No. American Indian trade. There is no clear evidence as to when they were first made, but most collectors believe they pre-date the white center versions.

Modern French reproduction Crow, pony, and seed-beads were made with white centers in several shades of red (sometimes brick but not the old rose-red), pink, orange, green, yellow, and bright blue. (These factories are now closed.)

See Picard, Vol. IV, *White Hearts, Feather and Eye Beads,* 1988.

Woodward, Arthur. *Indian Trade Goods.* Portland. Oregon Historical Society 1967: 19-20, 35.

Ewers, John. *Blackfeet Crafts.* p.32.

OLD ROSE-RED WHITE LINED BEADS
c.1800-1840.
Includes many variations of Cornaline d'Aleppo trade beads. Some have yellow centers, which pre-date the white center ones. Most are plain but a few have white twisted stripes. Largest aver. 15mm. diam. and smallest is 5mm. diam 40.5" loop. Est. 85-195 **SOLD $150(05)**

BLACK EYE BEADS
White glass droplets are melted to the surface of each bead to form dots or eyes. Some will say that the term eye beads originated as an honor to the beautiful eyes of 18th century singer Kitty Fisher and still others say these beads were worn as protection from the feared evil eye. It is doubtful if most American Indians ever heard of either, but they certainly did like this bead. Indians used them on clothing and necklaces, and attached them to medicine stones, pipes, and bundles. Apx. 10 x 10mm
    van der Sleen, p. 48
    Woodward 1965, p. 13-14
Black with red and/or blue (over white) or white eyes. TRADING POST PRICES **$5 ea(06)**
RED EYE BEADS (*Same history as black eye beads*) These are wire-wound with white center. The surface is covered with white dots or "eyes." 10 to 12mm
RED or ROSE $5 ea(06) Mixed strings, apx. 56 beads. TRADING POST PRICES **$95-$200(06)**

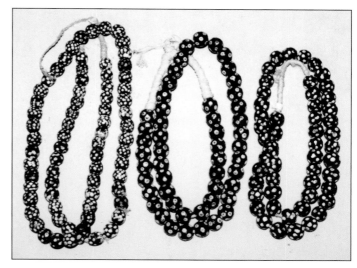

(Left to right) **BLACK EYE BEADS** 19th C.
Each bead has many (the best) white eyes with pink and blue dots within each "eye." Avg, 11mm. diam. and 34" loop. Nice collection with great patina. Est. 145-375 **SOLD $225(05)**
BLACK PROSSER EYE BEADS c.1890?
Prosser invented a method for molding glass shoe buttons in 1840. Soon after, molded beads were made using this method. These have large white eyes with red spots. 13mm. diam. x 29"L. Est. 50-150 **SOLD $50(05)**
LARGE BLACK EYE BEADS 19th C.
White eyes with red dots. These are a rare extra large size. Avg. 12mm. diam. on 29" loop. Exc. cond. Est. 85-175

WHITE CENTER ROSE WITH TRAILED FOLIATE DESIGNS
Stylized trailed floral patterns like this have been made in Venice since the late 18th century, possibly earlier. (Jargstorf 1995, p. 150) Average size 10 x 10 mm. TRADING POST PRICE **$12 ea(06)**

(Left) **WHITE CENTER ROSE WITH FANCY FOLIATE DESIGNS**
c.1850 or earlier.
This is a select string of a very early style bead. They are lamp wound beads probably made in Murano, Italy before 1850. They were made singly, so no two are alike. 62 beads strung on buckskin. Avg. 10 x 10mm. 29.5" loop. Est. 295-400
(Right) **STRING OF WHITE LINED ROSE EYE BEADS** c.19th C.
These have white eyes (dots) and average 11mm. diam., 27.5" loop. Nice old patina. Est. 75-180 **SOLD $85(05)**

(Left to right) **FANCY TRADE BEAD NECKLACE** 39 black eye beads having pink or blue dots over white eyes, 6 black with white and red eyes, 6 black with white eyes, 5 white lined red with white eyes, 4 milky with blue and red dots over white eyes, 2 white with dot marks, 2 small with blue and red eyes. Strung on buckskin. Apx. 29"L. Total of 64 beads. Est. 190-275 **SAME.** Six black spiral striped beads, 8 very old eyes, 27 black with white eyes, 8 yellow varied beads, 2 green faceted Vaseline beads, 1 large brick red with yellow blue and white stripes. Strung on buckskin. Apx. 29"L. Total of 52 beads. Est. 95-165 **SAME.** 34 black floral patterns, 8 white lined rose with floral designs, 2 black "six" beads, etc. Total of 63 beads. Strung on buckskin. Apx. 29"L. Est. 300-450 **SOLD $275(02)**

Millefioris

MOSAIC and MILLEFIORI BEADS are made from a wound glass core (usually black) with thin slices (called murrine) of multi-layered drawn canes melted onto the surface. Many interesting and beautiful patterns have been made. Millfiori means "1000 flowers" in Italian. As far as we know, this bead was not used by American Indians prior to 1900. They are Venetian and probably not made much before 1890. They gained popularity in the 1920s, with most being traded to Africa. Each one is unique.

TRADING POST PRICES **(06)**: SMALL under 25mm, **$4 ea**; 25-30 mm, **$6 ea**

See Picard, *Vol. 7-Millefiori Beads.*
Harris, Elizabeth. *Late Beads in the African Trade* . Lancaster, PA, Fenstermaker. 1984.

(Top to bottom) **MILLEFIORI CURVED AFRICAN CHIEF'S BEAD** c.1900 Black core with murrine (millefiori slice) in brick red, white, black, and yellow. Small chips on both ends. (apx. 2"L) 50 x 12 mm. TRADING POST PRICE **$12(06)** Murrine are yellow background with tiny red dots outlined with white and black. 20 x 10 mm. (apx. 3/4"L) TRADING POST PRICE **$8(06)** Murrine are placed in rows over green glass. Blue, yellow, and brick red. 26 x 12mm. TRADING POST PRICE **$6(06)** Murrine are six layer chevron patterns in blue, brick red, white over yellow. 34 x 13 mm. TRADING POST PRICE **$8(06)**

Murrine are six layers of blue, white, brick red and yellow all-over pattern. 38 x 14 mm. TRADING POST PRICE **$10(06)**

Old Pony (Pound) Beads

In the old trading post invoices, these beads are listed as pound beads—the price based on weight. In recent times, they are called pony beads, even though most of them were shipped up the Missouri River on steamboats!

See Woodward 1965, pp. 11-12.

STRIPED PONY BEADS
These beads show up on some old Indian items (see Crow medicine stone, following photo). Mostly yellow, white, or brick red background with various colored stripes. Each string is different—basic color of blue, red, or yellow. Apx. 4 x 6mm. TRADING POST PRICE **$10(06)** /Apx. 190 beads per string.

ROSE W. HEART PONY BEADS c.1860
3 mm W. 24" loop TRADING POST PRICES **$15(06)**; RED W. HEART (not shown) **$10(06)**
WIRE-WOUND RED W. HEARTS
Collected in Burma. Exc. cond. with varying shades of tran. red and rose. Aver. 3 x 6 mm. 26" loop on heavy string. TRADING POST PRICE **$15(06)**
GREEN CENTER BRICK PONY BEADS
Earliest style of lined bead in No. America. Aver. size 3 mm L and W. Strung on grass. 25" loop. TRADING POST PRICE **$18(06)**

(Left to right) **ROSE-RED W. HEART PONY BEADS** These are made at the same Italian glass factories as those made for the Indian trade in the 1800s. Apx. 24" loops. Sizes vary from 2 to 5 mm. TRADING POST PRICE **$15(06)** **WHITE PONY BEADS** on string. c.1860. 3 mm W and L. 25" loop. TRADING POST PRICES **$8(06)**; Black (not shown) **$8(06)**

ORIGINAL CROW MEDICINE STONE Pre-1860
Preston Miller Collection. Acquired c.1960 from Robert Riggs in Philadelphia, PA. A fossilized ammonite covered with buckskin and seed beaded lanes in pumpkin, robin's egg blue, and greasy blue; striped pony beads (pink/blue on white) cover the seed beads in horizontal lanes. Buckskin thongs are strung with primarily med. blue (some lt. and dk.), wire-wound beads in many varying shapes and sizes. There are four round rose white hearts, five "fancies," two hawk bells, various Bohemian "Russian" facets, smooth dentalium, 2"L. abalone pendant and clam disc shell beads. Hangs 7"L.

Solid Color Beads
PROSSER BEADS

Richard and Tom Prosser invented a machine to mold glass shoe buttons in England, c.1840. This method was quickly adapted to making beads. Prossers are easily recognized by the middle raised ridge of glass and their uniformity. They became immediately popular in the Indian trade and show up extensively after 1850 on cradle boards, dresses, medicine stones, and necklaces, to name a few. TRADING POST PRICES (06):

COBALT BLUE: 7 x 8 mm, apx. 78 bead string, **$15**; 5 x 7mm, apx. 97 bead string, **$12**

BODMER BLUE (sky blue) or LT. BLUE: 6 to 8mm, apx. 75-94 beads, **$20**; 5 x 6mm, apx. 104 beads, **$15**; 3 x 4mm, apx. 174 beads, 24" loop. **$12**
CHEYENNE PINK: 5 x 5 mm, apx. 158 bead string, **$15**
MILKY WHITE: 5 x 6mm, 109 bead string **$12**; 8 x 10mm, 68 bead string, **$18**

PADRE BEADS

The term "padre" bead has been applied to a turquoise blue wound bead that is said to have been given to Indians by Spanish missionaries in the Southwest.* Though the story can't be easily proven, the application of the name has certainly helped sell thousands of these beads. The truth is that beads of this color blue were popular with most all North American tribes. In the early 1800s, explorers Lewis and Clark presented variations of this bead to many of the tribes they visited. TRADING POST PRICES (06):

LT. BLUE: 7 x 10mm, 83 bead string, **$22**
WHITE: 6 x 9mm (24" loop), 93 beads, **$18**

*Sorensen, Cloyd. "The Enduring Intrigue of the Glass Trade Bead." *Arizona Highways.* Phoenix. July, 1971: 10-34.

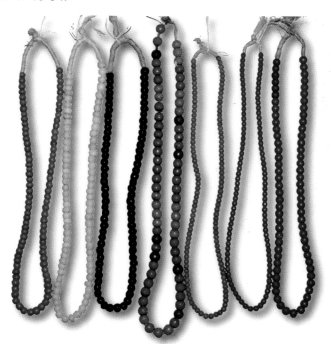

(Left to right) TRADING POST PRICES
ROBIN'S EGG BLUE PADRES, c.1820 6 x 13 mm. 20" loop. **$20(06)**
MILKY WHITE PADRES 6 x 10 mm. 22" loop. **$20(06)**
BLACK PADRE TRADE BEADS 80 beads. Avg. size, 10 x 6 mm. 20" loop. Not available '06.
LARGE SKY BLUE and PINK PROSSER TRADE BEADS c.1840 Avg. size-10 mm. 26" loop **$20(96)**
SMALL CHEYENNE PINK PROSSER TRADE BEADS Avg. size, 6mm. 23" loop **$15(06)**
SMALL SKY BLUE PROSSER TRADE BEADS c.1840 100 beads. Avg. size, 6mm. 23" loop. **$15(06)**
LARGE SKY BLUE PROSSER BEADS 6 mm. 22" loop. **$20(06)**

COBALT DONUT BEADS 19th C.
Popular wound ring (annular) bead used for earrings and spacers. Quite variable in size and shape (less commonly found in amber, clear and green). **T**RADING POST PRICE **(06):** 3 x 12mm **$2 ea $75.00**/string (apx. 132 beads)
See Francis, p. 72.

The next six lots of lace bobbins were purchased in a little village in the Cotswolds region of England. They are of interest because of the wonderful patina and the use of old beads for counter weights. A great variety of molded, fancy, and faceted beads were used on these bobbins; some are the same type as those traded to the natives of North America. Other beads used were unique and made specifically for this purpose, i.e.; called "square cuts." According to Richard Green, a long time member of the Bead Society of Great Britain: "They are not 'cut' (this is merely a colloquial term). They were wound glass beads usually with impressed file marks on four sides... made for English lacemakers by English 'lapidaries' (some of whom were also from bobbin-making families) from the late 18th and throughout the 19th century. Much later in the 19th century, almost when the English handmade lace industry was in decline, square beads which resemble the older English ones (but in general are much larger in size) were made in the Bohemian /German bead industry." (personal communication, 5/06)
(Top to bottom) **BONE LACE BOBBIN WITH TRADE BEADS** c.1800s.
This beautiful example has 1 Bodmer blue Crow bead, 2 clear glass, and 2 trans. rose molded Bohemian beads and 2 small cobalt blue Russian trade beads. The beads are attached with wire. The bobbin is carved from bone and has 6 metal bands as part of the decoration. This is an exceptionally nice bobbin. It is 4"L. Exc. cond. Est. 75-150 **SOLD $75(04)**
WOOD LACE BOBBIN WITH TRADE BEADS c.1800s.
Fancy central bead is trans. milky white with pink lines; 2 cobalt blue Russians, 1 trans. light blue, and 1 amber Russian and 2 molded Bohemian beads which are similar to the early file-impressed ones mentioned above. The dark rosewood bobbin has brass wire wrappings as part of the decoration. Bobbin is 3.5"L. Exc. cond. Est. 25-55 **SOLD $50(04)**
SAME
6 milky blue pound beads with one large trans. yellow Russian trade bead. Bobbin is 3.75"L. Exc. cond. Est. 25-55 **SOLD $25(04)**

"Buckingham Pillow Lace" displayed at Pitt Rivers Museum, Oxford Univ., England. Note the variety of wooden and bone bobbins and the use of beads "to keep the bobbin steadier against the pillow." The ring of beads attached to the bobbins by wire is usually called the "spangle" or "jingle," depending on the vicinity in the Midlands. The bobbins of the East Midlands Region of England are unique and highly decorated to suit each individual lacemaker, who sometimes added personal charms or mementos, i.e.; buttons, shells, or coins, as seen in this display. Frequently a large central bead is used, such as an "eye" bead or other Venetian "fancy" lamp worked bead. (Hopewell, Jeff. *Pillow Lace and Bobbins*. Buckinghamshire, England: Shire Publ. Ltd., 1999: 15-22.)

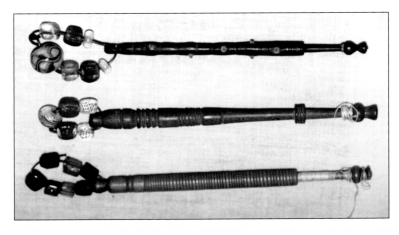

Author's collection. (Top to bottom) 1) Central fancy lamp worked bead, 2 clear and 2 rose with 2 opalescent smaller beads. 2) Central fancy lamp worked bead; 4 molded Bohemian beads (2 rose and 2 clear), which are similar to the early file-impressed ones mentioned above 3) Central clear red "square cut" (or molded Bohemian) bead with 4 cobalt and 2 blue Russian faceted beads.

Genuine North American Trade Beads

QUARTZ BEAD. An early opaque glass white bead, usually unevenly shaped as a result of the manufacturing process. Extensively found in Northwest and California sites (see photo examples following).
See Woodward 1965, p. 34 & 36

(Top to bottom) **TRADE BEAD NECKLACE**
Beads Found in Amadu Co., Calif. c.1800. Nice mixture of old beads includes white quartz beads (4mm. diam.), cobalt blue Russians (6mm. diam.), unusual large milky glass Russians (9mm. diam.), also a couple rare brick red Russians and green center Cornaline d'Aleppos. 26.5" loop. Exc. found cond. Est. 60-150 **SOLD $60(05)**
TRADE BEAD NECKLACE c.1800-1850.
Brick red with green center Cornaline d'Aleppo beads and glass "quartz beads." *Both of these beads originated in the 1700s. Green center beads like this pre-dated yellow and white hearts.* Both of these beads are common on early Indian sites on the West Coast found from Calif. to Alaska. At the bottom are three old and large brass uniform buttons. Beads are about 5 or 6 mm. diam. Exc. cond. 29.5" loop. Est. 75-150
TRADE BEAD NECKLACE
Beautiful necklace of beads dating from about 1800 to 1850. There are oval white l. rose (11mm. L.), cobalt blue Russians (5mm. diam.), milky cream colored Prossers (6mm. diam.), and 10 old blue chevrons. Strung on buckskin and ready to wear. 27.5"L. Est. 95-200 **SOLD $100(05)**

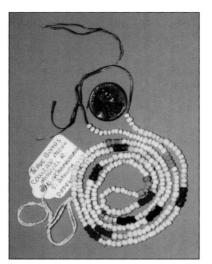

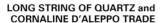

STRING OF POUND (PONY) BEADS c.19th C.
These were found along the Missouri R. north of Chamberlain, S. Dakota. Most of them are white with white lined rose, Bodmer blue, greasy yellow and cobalt blue. Excavated patina. 26"L. string. Est. 65-110 **SOLD $80(04)**

(Left to right)
PONY BEADS FOUND IN WESTERN CANADA c.1820.
We were told these were washed out by the rain. Incl. white, red, green, blue, etc. 37"L. Est. 40-85 **SOLD $60(00)**
MAIDU INDIAN GLASS TRADE BEADS c.1800.
Found in an open flat field near Placerville, Ca. at the foot of the Sierra Nevada Mtns. by Mary Temple about 1961. Quartz and Cornaline d' Aleppo beads. Graduated sizes. 45"L. Est. 75-150 **SOLD $75(00)**
SAME. 38"L. Est. 75-150 **SOLD $85(00)**
SAME. 27"L. Est. 55-110 **SOLD $55(00)**
CALIF. TRADE BEADS c.1800
From Amadu Co., Calif. Quartz and green center brick red Cornaline d'Aleppo beads. Excavated patina. 28"L. Est. 45-95 **SOLD $45(00)**

SAME c.1800.
This string includes 8 small dark blue and 7 larger milky white Russian trade beads along with "quartz" and Cornaline d'Aleppo. Est. 80-200 **SOLD $95(00)**

LONG STRING OF QUARTZ and CORNALINE D'ALEPPO TRADE BEADS c.1800 or earlier.
Harold and Irene Hanneman Collection from Browning, Mt. on the Blackfeet Reservation. The quartz bead is a very early type bead found all the way from northern Calif. up to Alaska and other areas of the northwest. The Cornalines have trans. green glass centers. Avg. 6 to 8mm diam. on 62" loop of 291 beads. Great patina. Est. 150-250

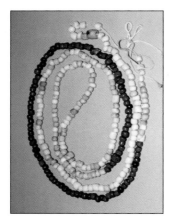

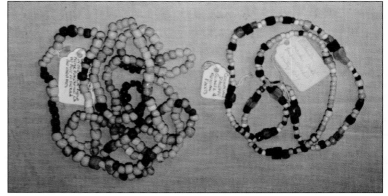

(Left to right) **LONG 50" STRING OF MAIDU TRADE BEADS** c.1700s.
These were found about 1961 by Mary Temple in an open flat field near Placerville, Calif. at the foot of the Sierra Nevada Mtns. on an old Maidu Indian village site. There are white quartz beads and green center brick reds (Cornaline d'Aleppo, the green centers are the earliest version). Est. 100-175 **SOLD $180(02)**
26" STRING Same provenance as above.
These are "pony bead" size quartz and green center brick reds interspersed with cobalt blue and milky white "Russian" facets. Est. 85-150 **SOLD $180(02)**

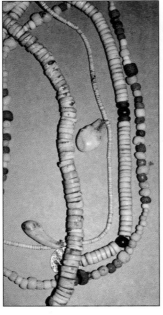

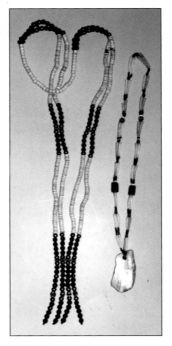

(Left to right) **GRADUATED CLAM SHELL DISC BEAD NECKLACE**
No. Calif. Pre-historic with excavated patina. Smallest are 3/8"
diam. Largest are 1/2" diam. Total 31"L. Est. 175-300 **SOLD $175(00)**
NEZ PERCE SHELL WAMPUM BEAD and ELK TEETH NECKLACE
Bull tooth in center is gold capped and other six are female. Wampum is
extra fine—1/8" dia. Total L. 49". Est. 125-275 **SOLD $150(00)**
OLD NEZ PERCE SHELL WAMPUM NECKLACE c.1890 (see full view of
necklace in photo at right).
*These were the most popular beads used by the Nez Perce and other
Plateau tribes. The women of these tribes value these beads highly and
wear them with their traditional and every day dress. They are made
from white clam shells.* This necklace is original, with two abalone shell
pendants, rare white lined rose disc beads, and brass and faceted glass
beads. Wampum is 5/16" diam. 47"L. Est. 400-650 **SOLD $425(01)**
QUARTZ and GREEN CENTER CORNALINE D'ALEPPO TRADE BEADS
c.1800.
These were found in Amadu Co., Calif. Excavated patina. 26"L. Est. 50-95
SOLD $40(00)

(Left to right) **PLATEAU
WAMPUM SHELL NECKLACE**
c.1900?
From Warm Springs Res., Ore.
White clam disc (7mm diam) with 8mm black iris facets and round brass
beads in a double strand with leather spacers. White glass tile beads at
top; 4 fancy black eye beads at bottom. Hangs 27"L. Hard to find traditional old-style piece. Exc. cond. Est. 250-500 **SOLD $250(03)**
HUPA (CALIFORNIA) TRADITIONAL DENTALIUM NECKLACE with abalone pendant. c.1890
Interspersed with yellow red heart "barrels," rose w. heart, t. blue Peking
Crow beads; black, white, pony trader blue and early green heart brick
ponies. Smooth dentalium is graduated from 7/8" to 1.25"L. Beautiful
varying shades of white/ivory (one is broken) 17". Est. 150-300

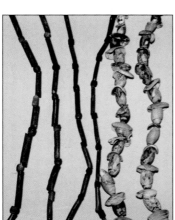

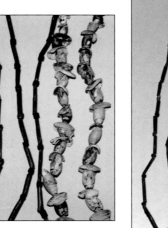

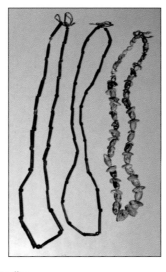

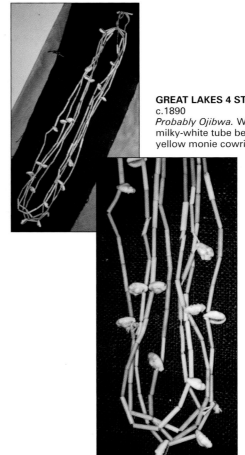

GREAT LAKES 4 STRAND NECKLACE
c.1890
Probably Ojibwa. Wonderful patina on
milky-white tube beads strung with old
yellow monie cowries on buckskin. Hangs
apx. 22"L. Est. 250-
350 **SOLD $200(02)**

(Left to right) **INDIAN-MADE
ROLLED COPPER BEADS and
WHITE LINED ROSE BEADS** c.1800 or earlier.
*Found by Leroy Gienger and his father on Wapmer Island on the Co-
lumbia River above the Dalles, Ore.* Beads average 1- 2"L. Strung on old
sinew 31"L. loop. Est. 65-135 **SOLD $77(02)**
SIMILAR.
Same provenance. The only difference is that this string is spaced with
old cobalt blue faceted Russian trade beads. Est. 75-150 **SOLD $100(02)**
KLAMATH INDIAN OLIVELLA SHELL BEADS c. pre-1800.
Ex. Gienger Collection. Found at Klamath Lake near Chiloquin, Oregon.
30" loop necklace strung on old sinew with exc. patina. Est. 65-125
SOLD $50(02)

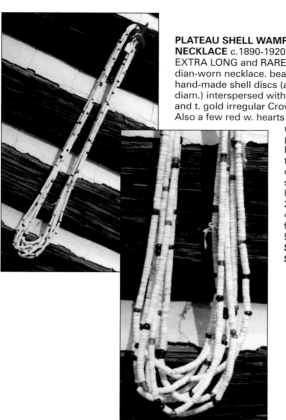

PLATEAU SHELL WAMPUM NECKLACE c.1890-1920
EXTRA LONG and RARE. Old Indian-worn necklace. beautiful white hand-made shell discs (apx. 1/4" diam.) interspersed with t. cobalt and t. gold irregular Crow beads. Also a few red w. hearts and four mother-of-pearl thin buttons tied. Eight continuous strands hang apx. 29"L. or 464"L (38.88 feet). Est. 500-875 **SOLD $500(03)**

SHELL DISC BEADS FROM CALIFORNIA 18th C.
Nice collection of graduated white shell beads and two large disc beads. 15"L. Est. 100-175 **SOLD $85(00)**

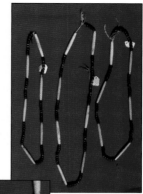

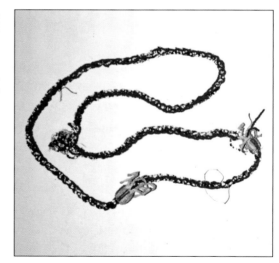

OLD BONE HAIRPIPE NECKLACES c.1870
Michael Johnson Coll., England. These are genuine old 2.75"L hairpipes with exc. age patina. They are interspersed with royal blue Crow beads and round brass beads. Strung on twisted cloth, which was often used for old Sioux and Cheyenne necklaces. (Left to right) A) Est. 175-300 **SOLD $175(98)** B) Est. 195-350 **SOLD $195(98)** C) Est. 175-300 **SOLD $200(98)**

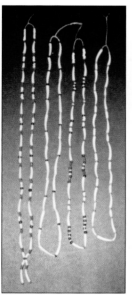

(Left to right) **SMOOTH WHITE DENTALIUM SHELL NECKLACE** strung with old glass trade beads including white pony, green center brick red, and Bodmer blue beads. *These are the old time dentalium shells that have a smooth surface.* 16 shells, 43" loop strung on imitation sinew. Exc. cond. Est. 50-125 **SOLD $35(99)**
SAME. 28 shells interspersed with white, pink, and cobalt pony beads. 37" loop. Est. 40-100 **SOLD $55(99)**
SAME. 16 shells with green center brick red, white, trans. blue and 4 old faceted Russian trade beads. 36" loop. Est. 50-100 **SOLD $30(99)**
SAME. 17 shells interspersed with white seed beads and blue pony beads. 34" loop. Est. 50-100 **SOLD $40(99)**

PLAINS SEED BEADED NECKLACE c.1870.
This is probably an old medicine necklace from a Plains tribe, perhaps Sioux or Cheyenne or possibly Ute. This is a very interesting necklace of braided beads strung on sinew. There are two fringed buckskin bead-covered balls (colors are brick and amber). The necklace colors are cobalt blue and old "salt and pepper" colors. Apx. 37"L Est. 150-250 **SOLD $175(02)**

TURTLE MOUNTAIN SIOUX BRAIDED SEED BEAD NECKLACE
Collected by Maurice Oliver between 1895-1920 (see full provenance on p. 23). This necklace is braided with thread using a "salt and pepper" assortment of beads (there are many old time colors). There is an interesting medallion at the bottom with a section of round Peyote-style stitching. It is 26"L. Perfect cond. Est. 75-200 **SOLD $100(03)**

FACETED RUSSIAN TRADE BEADS. Collectors and museums have for many years attributed this style of bead to early Russian traders. The truth is they were most likely made in Bohemia (where they were called *Sprengperlen** according to Jargstorf) and traded by most early traders. They were made in many sizes and were already a popular trade bead by 1820, especially on the Northwest Coast.

The term *Sprengperlen* is also a general term (derived from the word *Absprengen*) applied in Germany to drawn beads that are broken off from a raw cane or tube, which has been expanded to include cut or chopped drawn beads as well. (Neuwirth, Waltraud. *Beads from Gablonz.* Vienna, Austria: 1994: 201.)

See van der Sleen, p.12

Picard, *Russian Blues, Faceted and Fancy Beads,* 1989.

Jargstorf 1998, p. 55* and 81.

DRAWN GLASS CANE WITH GROUND FACETS
Contemporary.
This hexagonal cane has a dark blue center and clear outer layer (see end of cane detail photo). It has a 10mm diameter. Beads were broken, chopped, or cut off to form individual faceted beads. As in old "Russian" facets or *Sprengperlen* (see definition above), there will be a burr left by this process that can be seen upon close examination.

These are cobalt blue with sharp facets. TRADING POST PRICES **(06):**

Small 4 to 6 mm **$5 ea**
Medium 7 to 10mm **$6 ea**
Large 11 to 16 mm **$10 ea** (see following photo)

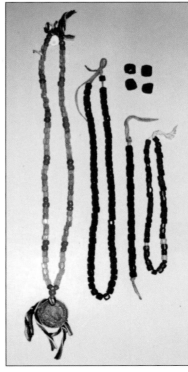

(Detail photo, left to right)
RARE LARGE DARK COBALT RUSSIAN BEADS c.1800
Collected from an Indian family on the Warm Springs Res. in Oregon. Apx. 12-13 mm. sq. Est. 10-15 each **SOLD $10 ea(00)**
RARE NECKLACE OF OPALESCENT TRANSPARENT FACETED RUSSIAN TRADE BEADS mid-19th C.
72 Russians, 8mm. diam. 29 rose white hearts (same size). Pendant is an 1828 Mexican silver dollar. 29"L. Est. 190-350 **SOLD $265(00)**
Same as next photo (center)
Same as next photo (far right)
RARE RUSSIAN FACETED TRADE BEADS c.1800.
Many colors including amber, green, blue, and opalescent white. 8-12 mm. diam. 15"L. Est. 110-185 **SOLD $110(00)**

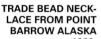

NOTE: The next three lots of Russian trade beads are the very dark cobalt blue type that was traded to North American Indians. These have a shiny polished surface and not the matte surface that is found on beads coming through the African trade. These are very scarce and difficult to find.

(Left to right) **STRING OF 51 LARGE DARK COBALT BLUE RUSSIAN FACETED TRADE BEADS** c.1800. *These were collected from an Indian family on the Warm Springs Reservation in Oregon.* They are all about the same size, 13 mm diam. The string is 28"L. Strung on buckskin. Exc. cond. Very rare. Est. 495-800 **SOLD $600(05)**
STRING OF 21 DARK COBALT BLUE RUSSIAN FACETED TRADE BEADS c.1800. *Collected on the Nez Perce Reservation, Columbia River, Washington.* Avg. about 9mm. diam. 7.5"L. string. Strung on buckskin. Exc. cond. Est. 150-250
STRING OF 75 DARK COBALT BLUE RUSSIAN FACETED TRADE BEADS c.1800. Avg. 9mm. diam. 25" loop. Strung on buckskin. Exc. cond. Est. 275-500

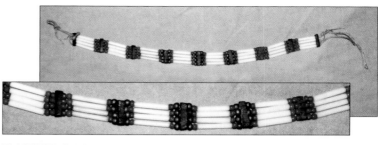

BLACKFEET GLASS CHOKER NECKLACE c.1890.
This style necklace was used by most Montana tribes including the Crow, Flathead, and Blackfeet. This one was made by a Blackfeet Indian. The long white beads are milky white glass and the beads on either side of the harness leather spacers are brass and white lined rose. The brass beads that are next to the spacers have developed a nice green verdigris. 13.5"L. Unusual to find a real one of these in good condition. Great patina. Est. 200-400 **SOLD $200(02)**

WIRE-WOUND CROW BEADS
Kilo package stamped *"Made in Western Germany."* These are from the well-known Plume Indian Trading Co. stock found in their NYC warehouse when they went out of business. Strung on twisted paper strings. These date to pre-1940, however, they are identical to those made for the Indian trade in the mid-1800s. Est. 10-25 string.

TRADE BEAD NECK-LACE FROM POINT BARROW ALASKA
c.1860.
Collected by A. Eddes around 1955. Bodmer (deep greasy) blue oval and round beads plus white l. rose beads strung on braided sinew. Worn as a choker-style necklace. 18" loop. Est. 100-175 **SOLD $75(05)**

Reference books for further reading:

Ewers, John. *Hair Pipes in Plains Indian Adornment.* Smithsonian Institution, B.E.A. Bulletin #164, Anthropological Papers, #50, 1957.
Pakes, Fraser J. "Dentalium and Plains Indian Aesthetics." *The People of the Buffalo, Vol. 2* editors Colin Taylor and Hugh Dempsey. Germany: Tatanka Press, 2005.
Stearns, Robert E. C. *Wampum and Dentalium.* 1887 Smithsonian Inst. reprint 1999. Hummelstown, PA: Tucquan Publishing.
Woodward, Arthur. *Indian Trade Goods.* Portland, Oregon Historical Society, 1965.

3. Trade Blankets

All blankets in this section are made of wool.

References and suggested reading for this section

Hanson Jr., Chas. "The Point Blanket." *The Museum of the Fur Trade Quarterly,* Vol. 12, #1. Chadron, Nebr. Spring 1976, pp. 5-11.

——. "Some Additional Notes on Trade Blankets." *The Museum of the Fur Trade Quarterly,* Vol. 24, #4, Chadron, Nebr. Winter, 1988, pp. 5-10.

Hanson, James. "Point Blankets." *The Museum of the Fur Trade Quarterly,* Vol. 33, #3, Chadron, Nebr. Fall 1997, pp. 6-13.

Swagerty, W. R. "Going Back to the Blanket: Origin and Production of the Indian Trade Blanket." *The People of the Buffalo, Vol. 2.* Taylor, Colin & Hugh Dempsey, eds. Wyk, Germany: Tatanka Press, 2005.

Tichenor, Harold. *The Blanket—An Illustrated History of the Hudson's Bay Point Blanket.* Toronto, Canada: Madison Press Books, 2002.

——. *The Collector's Guide to Point Blankets of the Hudson's Bay Company and Other Companies Trading in North America.* Bowen Island, Canada Cinetel Film Productions Ltd., 2002.

Hudson's Bay "Point" Blankets ad on back cover of *The Beaver* (official HBC magazine), Sept. 1927. The sizes are listed as 3 point, 3-1/2 point, and 4 point; colors are red, green, empire blue, gray, khaki, and white. Note label shown has "Made in England" line.

HUDSON'S BAY BLANKETS

The best known items traded by the HBC were the popular "Point Blankets." These blankets were never made by the Company itself but were instead contracted out to English woolen manufacturers. Among the most famous was the firm of Thomas Early in Witney, England, who was apprenticed as a blanket weaver in 1669. The HBC began marketing "Point Blankets" about 1780 and they have retained their popularity up to the present. Dark lines or "points" about 4-1/2" long were woven near one corner and each stripe was symbolic of one "Made Beaver." (*See Hudson's Bay section, p. 54, for photos of the company's "beaver tokens" which were coined in 1/8, 1/4, 1/2, and 1 "Made Beaver" denominations.*) Thus, four stripes meant the blanket was worth four beaver skins. Blankets came in sizes ranging from 1, 1-1/2, 2, 2-1/2, 3, 3-1/2 and 4 "Made Beaver." In modern times, even 6 and 8 point blankets have been available. The number of points indicated the blanket's size and weight. Presently, the number of points indicates the size of the blanket, with a four point being 72" x 90". The earliest color was the white with a black stripe as seen in this photo. Notice the small embroidered HBC tag (c. mid 1920s*), which was replaced with a larger tag about 1940. Tags that have *"Made in England"* on them indicate the blanket was made after 1890. Earlier blankets generally have a fluffier nap, which can be seen on the four points on this blanket. HBC blankets never have the ends whip stitched at the time of manufacture. This is a good way to identify blankets that were made for the Hudson's Bay Company. Some later colors were scarlet, green, and blue with a black stripe at each end. Starting about 1880, a white multi-color version with black, yellow, red, and green stripes became the most popular. Many people identify these multi-striped colors as "Hudson's Bay" or "Chief's Blankets." Used blankets in excellent condition are collectible and usually sell got between $75 and $150.

See Hanson, 1988: pp. 2 - 10,
*See Tichenor, *Collector's Guide* p. 59.

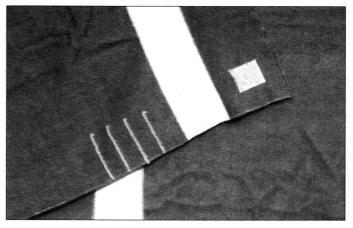

DOUBLE HUDSON'S BAY CO. QUEEN ELIZABETH II CORONATION BLANKET c.1953.
These are now rare blankets made by HBC to celebrate the Queen's coronation in 1953.* They are a beautiful "royal" purple with white stripes and Beaver Points. This is an uncut double blanket. It has two labels and is in mint condition. Both blankets total 14' 6"L x 6' W. Est. 500-2000 **SOLD $550(03).**
eBay Sale Feb. 2003. This blanket was sold in halves, each bringing $360 totaling $720 for both (not shown).
    *See Tichenor, *The Blanket,* p. 57.

Opposite page:
(Left to right) **3-1/2 POINT HUDSON'S BAY BLANKET**
Small tag indicates made in the mid-1920s.* *This white with black striped blanket is the earliest point blanket. Indians used this size for wearing blankets as well as capotes. It provided winter camouflage for a hunting or raiding party. Stacks of these same size and color blankets can be seen in pre-1900 Northwest coast potlatch photos.* White and fluffy thick nap. 63" x 78". Exc. clean cond. Frayed ends. Est. 175-275 **SOLD $175(00)**
4 POINT HUDSON'S BAY BLANKET
Small tag indicates made in the early 1930s.* VG nap worn as in light use. Slightly off-white from age with black stripes and points. Frayed ends. 71" x 82". Est. 125-225 **SOLD $135(00)**
3-1/2 POINT HUDSON'S BAY BLANKET
Small tag indicates made in the mid-1920s.* Beige color with dk. brown stripes and points. Has remnants of real silk binding on ends. Exc. cond. Medium nap. 61" x 77.5". Est. 125-250 **SOLD $140(00)**
    *See Tichnor, *Collector's Guide,* pp.59-63.

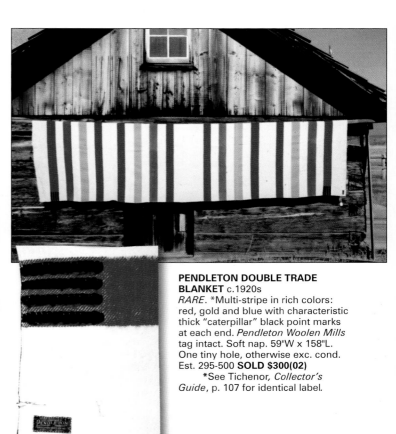

PENDLETON DOUBLE TRADE BLANKET c.1920s
RARE. *Multi-stripe in rich colors: red, gold and blue with characteristic thick "caterpillar" black point marks at each end. *Pendleton Woolen Mills* tag intact. Soft nap. 59"W x 158"L. One tiny hole, otherwise exc. cond. Est. 295-500 **SOLD $300(02)**
    *See Tichenor, *Collector's Guide*, p. 107 for identical label.

EARLY DOUBLE TRADE BLANKET Pre-1900
Very RARE. Beautiful tight nap fine wool is natural varying grey with narrow indigo and red strips each end. 5' x 12-1/2'. One finger size hole otherwise exc. cond. Est. 200-350 **SOLD $250(04)**

4 POINT TRADE BLANKET
Old Oregon City Woolen Mills, has label which is raveled. Original white wool felt binding on ends. Rich unfaded colors: cobalt, gold, green, and yellow with cobalt point marks. 61.5" x 78" Exc. cond. No holes. Est. 200-400

(Left) **3 POINT BLACK and WHITE HUDSON'S BAY CO. BLANKET** c.1890-1900
Examples this size and in this good of condition are very hard to find. *It was one of the most popular styles in the Indian trade.* This one is heavy and has only one small moth hole. 55"W x 67"L. Tag is missing but it had the small size HBC tag.* Est. 95-250 **SOLD $105(05)**
*See Tichenor, *Collector's Guide,* p. 57 for identical label.
(Right) **RED SQUARE WEAVE BLANKET WITH 2 BLACK STRIPES** c.1935?
Nice heavy blanket in exc. cond. 77"W x 81"L. Est. 125-200 **SOLD $135(05)**

(Left) **RED WOOL WITH BLACK STRIPED TRADE BLANKET** c.1870-1910.
This style blanket was very popular in the Indian trade. The black binding on either end is somewhat worn but the rest of the blanket is in exc. cond. Some small moth holes scattered here and there. 70" x 78". Diagonal weave with good wear and patina. Est. 65-150 **SOLD $78(05)**
(Right) **GRAY INDIAN WARS PERIOD BLANKET WITH BLACK STRIPES** c.1870s or 80s.
Hard to find example. Solid tight weave in very exc. cond. Black stripe is 2.5"W. Blanket is 60"W x 76"L. Est. 125-300 **SOLD $100(05)**

(Left) **WITNEY BI-CENTENNIAL BLANKET**
*Made in England for 1976 America's Bicentennial Celebration. This is the famous mill that once had the contract for making HBC blankets as early as the 17th century. Specialty blanket made again **only for this year** as historic replica from an older original.* 72" x 90" double bed size. Exc. cond. White with wide blue and narrow red stripe each end. Est. 250-400
(Right) **"TRAPPER POINT" TRADE WOOL BLANKET** c.1920s
Made in England by T. Eaton Co. * Beautiful lt. brown with wide black stripe. Hard to find 3-1/2 point blanket. 63" x 79". Est. 200-300
　　*See Tichenor, *Collector's Guide,* p. 89 for identical label.

4 POINT "TRAPPER POINT" TRADE BLANKET c.1920s*
Same provenance as previous blanket. Deep blue with black stripe and points. Excellent tag with Indian head. 66" x 78". No holes or mothing. Frayed on one edge. Est. 125-200 **SOLD $100(02)**

PENDLETON GLACIER PARK TRADE BLANKET c.1930
Multi-stripe colors: red, yellow, black, and green with thick black point marks. Nice mountain goat label intact*. Dense nap. Some mothing at one end, otherwise exc. cond. 53" x 73". Est. 75-150 **SOLD $85(02)**
*See Tichenor, *Collector's Guide,* p. 108 for identical label.

(Left) 3-1/2 POINT HUDSON'S BAY MULTI-STRIPED BLANKET c.1940
Unusual tiny tag reads "All wool-Made in England." No HBC label. *This size was the most popular Indian wearing blanket.* Black, yellow, red, and green stripes. Frayed ends. Very light mothing. Three small pin holes. Clean medium nap. 64" x 75". Est. 95-150 **SOLD $95(00)**
(Right) MULTI-STRIPED BLANKET
Probably J.C. Penney's. Royal blue, yellow, and red. No tag. Machine whip-stitched ends. No point marks. Exc. cond. Medium nap. 74" x 83". Est. 60-125 **SOLD $50(00)**

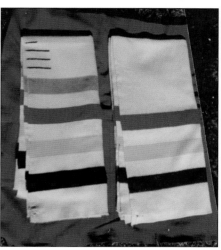

ROYAL CANADIAN MOUNTED POLICE BLANKET c. 20th C.
Grey blanket with black stripes and stenciled *"R. C. M. P."* in center. *Ottawa Valley Woolen Mills* label. Only two tiny holes. 59" x 74". Exc. cond. Est. 100-250

(Left) GLACIER PARK BLANKET, PENDLETON WOOLEN MILLS, OREGON c.1930.*
5 point white blanket with green, red, yellow, and black stripes. Exc. cond. with complete label. 66" x 82". 100% wool. Est. 95-200 **SOLD $100(03)**
*See Tichenor, *Collector's Guide,* p. 108 for identical label.
(Right) YELLOWSTONE PARK BLANKET, PENDLETON WOOLEN MILLS, OREGON c.1930s*
Beautiful white blanket with narrow black, green, and red stripes and perfect label. 100% wool with a few small brown stains in center of one side. 62" x 84" Exc. cond. Est. 95-200 **SOLD $100(03)**

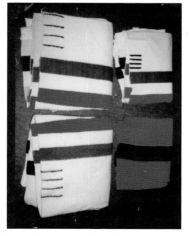

(Left to right, top to bottom)
HUDSON'S BAY CO. BLANKET
White blanket with multi-color stripes (black, yellow, red, and green) and 4 black "Beaver Point" stripes to indicate size. Many years ago someone sewed silk ribbon binding on each end; it is now disintegrating. Exc. used clean cond. 5' 7" x 7' 2" Est. 100-200 **SOLD $105(99)**
PENDLETON "GLACIER PARK" BLANKET c.1950
White blanket with multi-color stripes (black, yellow, red, and green) and 4 black beaver points (unusually thick and short stripes). Tag is disintegrated. Exc. used clean cond. 4' 5" x 6' 2" Est. 100-175 **SOLD $95(99)**
HUDSON'S BAY CO. BLANKET
Small 1.5" x 1-5/8" *"Seal of Quality"* tag dates this blanket to the mid-1920s. White blanket with multi-color stripes (black, yellow, red, and green) and 4 black "Beaver Point" stripes to indicate size. This is the old style blanket with the heavy napped wool. Exc. clean cond. 5' 1" x 7' 4" Est. 125-300 **SOLD $100(99)**
RED with 2 BLACK STRIPES BLANKET.
No identifying tag but the edges are whip-stitched so it is not an HBC. Exc. clean cond. 4' 2" x 6'. Est. 75-150 **SOLD $85(99)**

4. Photo Essay – History and Use of Trade Cloth in North America

by Carolyn Corey

Daniel Defoe wrote in 1724:
*"Be their country hot or cold, torrid or frigid, 'tis the same thing, near the Equinox or near the Pole, **the English woolen manufacturers clothe them all.**"* (In Corey 2001: 2)

Note: terms shown in uppercase are defined within this article.

English Origins

Early trade cloth that was distributed to North America was the product of the European BROAD-CLOTH industry, with England being primarily, but not exclusively, the supplier. Contemporary BROADCLOTH is a fine-napped and pressed WOOLEN fabric. However, in the Middle Ages it was characterized as very coarse with a plain (square) weave. It was used for all types of under and outer garments. As England's most ancient WOOLEN cloth, it was produced in many grades and was woven on a wide loom, from 54 inches (apx. 1.4 m) to 63 inches (approx. 1.6 m) or wider. There was a great demand for coarse BROADCLOTH, it being widely used by most of the population. The gentry, however, were more discriminating in purchasing mainly the finer quality cloth (*Ibid* 2001: 33, 38).

WOOLEN yarn was spun from the short fibers of the fleece and is processed after weaving to become dense and heavy, "with BROADCLOTHS the stoutest and best" of various WOOLEN cloths that were made in this manner (Goodrich 1850: 237). In England, as early as 1197, BROADCLOTH was regulated by statutes to control the length, the width "within the LISTS" and quality, so that taxes could be collected on behalf of the King. (Heaton, 1920: 126). By an Act of Richard the 3rd in 1483: BROAD-CLOTH was to be 2 yards within the LISTS.

A LIST is an obsolete term for the bordering strip on the edge of the cloth, which was frequently made of a different fiber than that of the cloth; for example, mohair or a coarser fiber.

A SELVEDGE literally means **self-edge**: the border or edge of cloth finished so as to prevent raveling.

A PIECE is a length of cloth, such as 40 yards.

PIECE DYED cloth is dyed after being woven.

"DYED-IN -THE -WOOL" cloth is woven from dyed yarn or dyed raw wool made into yarn.

SAVED LIST is a dye resist edge list on piece-dyed WOOLEN cloth that blocks the dye from penetration, resulting in an undyed LIST, which is usually white. (Corey 2001: 2-4 and 33-38)

FANCY LIST is a woven edge on "dyed-in-the-wool" cloth. Midgley defines "fancy" as fabric "having a pattern which is developed by weaving" rather than from dyeing, i.e., "piece dyeing" or any other process (Midgley 1932: 248).

GREY LIST is a woven edge on white (or piece dyed cloth), which has black warp threads and white weft threads.

STROUD CLOTH .The early 18th century cloth was called "stroudwaters," later shortened to "strouds" and was named for the town of Stroud in Gloucestershire. Stroud was located on the Stroudwater River and became famous for its fine quality military broadcloth called "Stroudwater Reds." At this time, the cloth had a single or triple-striped black LIST or a SAVED LIST that was white or with black stripes. By the mid-18th century, a change in quality occurred when the manufacturing center shifted to the north and the West Riding area of Yorkshire, a region of coarse indigenous wool. After 1828, both good quality and coarse wool were used in the making of STROUD CLOTH for the American Fur Co., and later the Hudson's Bay Co. "STROUD CLOTH" was now characterized as having a triple-striped black LIST, some dyed in the PIECE with a SAVED LIST. (For more information on the complex and enigmatic history of STROUD CLOTH, See Corey 2001: 27-32; 37 and Corey 2005: map p. 132; 138-139.)

In 1552, a clothing statute was passed in England establishing the standards of wool-making and requiring the use of LISTS to distinguish between various grades of BROADCLOTH. By 1606, SELVEDGES were categorized into "broad, narrow, plain and stop-listed." This early BROADCLOTH was graded by degrees of fineness: superfine, second, and inferior (Corey 2001: 13). It was possible to look at the LIST and identify the type and quality of the cloth. By the late 1700s, there were more than three hundred laws covering all aspects of wool manufacture. However, all of these cloth laws were repealed by Parliament in 1821 due to the difficulty in enforcing the statutes. (Heaton 1920: 417-18). Nevertheless, a market to the North American Indians had already been developed, which depended on the sale of BROADCLOTH with decorative borders.

Early American Trade

At about the same time that the 1552 decree was enacted in England, the first BROADCLOTH was introduced to Natives on the East Coast of America by English and French traders. As early as 1609, it was readily available. (Lyford 1945: 20). At first, the Indians took whatever came their way, but soon they were making demands for their preferences.

The earliest reference that I have found to what is probably "SAVED LIST" is in 1704, when Thomas Bannister of Boston wrote to London inquiring about bays, "after a sort fit for the Indian trade without any nap with white stripe thru the SELVEDGE. They must be all blews...next to the blews the red sells best and next...purple." Later Bannister says that by bays he means "lo prized blew broad cloath. And if you please, leave out the purple. Those nobody chuses to buy." (Montgomery 1984: 159) Significant here is the early discrimination for principally blue and red cloth, even though other colors were available, which is also documented in early fur trade records. (See "STROUD CLOTH, the Sacred Cloth," pp. 110-111)

Early Use of Trade Cloth by Plains Indians

The early pictorial records of the Plains Indians suggest that there was considerable status to be gained by the wearing of brightly colored cloth. Examples can be found in several of the paintings by the Swiss artist Karl Bodmer, who traveled to the Plains tribes in the 1830s. Equally significant is the implied meaning of spiritual qualities attributed to red cloth, as seen by close examination of the ceremonial and warrior regalia portrayed by him. An important Blood chief is pictured wearing a red "SAVED LIST" shirt along with a large peace medal (**Photo 1**). When Bodmer created a portrait of a Blackfoot chief at Fort McKenzie in his war dress in August 1833, he carefully delineated the use of a fine fur "medicine necklace"[1] which was embellished with a red striped "SAVED LIST" showing at the bottom edge (**Photo 2**). Furthermore, the highly revered hero of the Mandans, *Mato-Tope*, was painted in his "grandest dress." He wears a large horned ermine headdress, which Maxmilian describes as worn only by distinguished warriors who have performed many exploits. What is barely evident is the long red "SAVED LIST" trailer, described by Maxmilian as "hanging down behind as far as his calves." Also, there is a triangular bib on the front of his war shirt that is made of half-red and half-blue cloth. (Maximilian 1839: 76-77). (NOT SHOWN)

PHOTO 2. Ikas-Kinne (the low horn), a Siksika Blackfoot chief. Karl Bodmer painted this image at Fort McKenzie in August 1833. Maximilian describes him, at this time, as "a tall, well-looking man with a very marked countenance. He wore a otter's skin over his shoulders which was ornamented all over with pieces of shell." (Thomas-Ronnefeldt 1984: 115 and 141) This elaborately decorated otter skin "necklace"[1] was mounted on scarlet striped "saved list" stroud cloth. This style of trade cloth, from Stroud, Gloucestershire, England, was traded as early as 1714 to Indians in colonial America. Later, after 1800, this striped selvedge "stroud cloth" was mainly manufactured in the northern county of Yorkshire, England, for the American Fur Company and distributed to their Upper Missouri River fur posts. Although the mother-of-pearl clam shells on this garment were probably taken from the nearby Missouri River, the sea shells (abalone), the brass, and other metal buttons, as well as the gorgets pictured here, were popular trade items listed in the Fort McKenzie inventory. (Chronister 2001:9-10) Numerous examples of shells and buttons were found at the site of Fort McKenzie during an archaeological excavation in 1952. (Shumate 1973:30-32)

Bodmer depicted a leader of the Mandan buffalo bull society at Fort Clark in 1834 holding a massive black shield heavily laden with large pieces of red cloth (some with "SAVED LIST") along with medicine objects, i.e., blue thunderbird cut-outs (**Photo 3**). This same figure and his shield are central in a dynamic painting of bison dancers in front of their medicine lodge (Thomas and Ronnefeldt 1982: 172). Bodmer also pictured a Minnetaree chief at Fort Clark wearing a red with white "SAVED LIST" dog dancer society sash (**Photo 4**). A similar Hidatsa or Mandan sash collected in 1846 is now in the Berlin Museum (**Photos 4A and 4B**).

PHOTO 1. Stomik-Sosak (the Bull's Back Fat), a Blood chief. He was painted by Karl Bodmer at Fort McKenzie in 1833. Maximilian described him as "a very good old man" and "great friend to the Whites, and resolved, with his small band, to remain faithful to the fort." (Thomas-Ronnefeldt 1984: 119 and 136) Note the large silver Presidential peace medal necklace strung with trade beads which he proudly wears as evidence of his high esteem and friendship with the "Whites." Significant here is the scarlet "saved list" trade cloth that forms the main body of his shirt. The white border of the cloth is deliberately placed to form decorative stripes at the shoulder seams. Also, there is a double selvedge created by an extra layer of cloth at the neck, possibly a bib, which emphasizes the wealth and status of the wearer who could afford such a luxury. "Scarlet saved list" was among the trade cloth inventoried from Fort McKenzie when it was closed in 1844. Stomik-Sosak's face is colored with red vermilion, a popular trade item at Fort McKenzie. (Chronister 2001: 9-10).

PHOTO 3. Leader of the Mandan Buffalo Bull Society. Karl Bodmer painted this image at Fort Clark in 1834. The large, black, lavishly ornamented shield is a very dominant and dramatic item. Its unusual size is about half the size of the dancer who holds it (approx. 30-36" in diameter). Scarlet cloth is the predominant feature, some of which has white "saved" lists. The red gunstock club motif and blue painted rawhide thunderbirds are medicine symbols which, in conjunction with the colors of red, black and/or blue, were very likely associated with power and conquest through warfare. (Thomas-Ronnefeldt 1984: 217) (Also see "STROUD CLOTH, the Sacred Cloth," pp. 110-111.)

Bodmer also painted a bison dance being performed at Fort Clark with this same figure as the central image. Maximilian wrote that "nine men of the band of the buffalo bulls came to the fort to perform their dance, discharging their guns immediately on entering. *Only one wore the entire buffalo head*; the others had pieces of the skin of the forehead, a couple of fillets of red cloth, their shields decorated with the same material." (*Ibid*: 172, 202, 217). Close examination of the latter painting reveals that the shields of the other dancers are comparatively smaller (probably 24" diameter) and less ornate.

This is fabricated of both blue and red trade cloth ornamented with dyed porcupine quillwork; the "SAVED LIST" is given prominence as a decorative feature of the sash itself. The contrasting colors of black (or navy blue) and red, used in this context, were most likely significant of power and conquest through warfare. This belief and use was documented amongst the Plains-Ojibwa ca. 1850, a tribe whose domain was in close proximity to Fort Union (Howard 1965: Map 10) (See "STROUD CLOTH, the Sacred Cloth.") Examination of this particular artifact reveals that it is made of a very coarse fabric (Miller: 93).

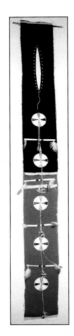

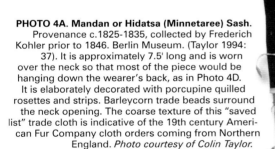

PHOTO 4. Minnetaree Dog Dancer, Pehriska-Ruhpa (the two ravens). He is pictured here at Fort Clark by Karl Bodmer in 1834. His dress fits the description of the Mandan dog dancers, as one of the chiefs of the dog band. According to Maximilian (March 7, 1834): "The four principal dogs wore round their neck a long slip of red cloth, which hung down over the shoulders, and, reaching the calf of the leg, was tied in a knot in the middle of the back." (*Ibid*: 198, 201, 223)

PHOTOS 4C & 4D. Contemporary replica of the Dog Society Sash. Made to the exact specifications of the original out of coarse old square weave blanket dyed by the author. The custom-made Czech quillwork is sinew-sewn.

PHOTO 4E. Michael Terry, well-known speaker, craftsman, and re-enactor, models the replica sash at the 2002 Material Culture of the Plains, Plateau & Prairie Conference in Great Falls Montana. He is a master horseman and re-enacts a buffalo hunt in the dynamic old Indian way—on horseback with a bow and arrow.

PHOTO 4A. Mandan or Hidatsa (Minnetaree) Sash. Provenance c.1825-1835, collected by Frederich Kohler prior to 1846. Berlin Museum. (Taylor 1994: 37). It is approximately 7.5' long and is worn over the neck so that most of the piece would be hanging down the wearer's back, as in Photo 4D. It is elaborately decorated with porcupine quilled rosettes and strips. Barleycorn trade beads surround the neck opening. The coarse texture of this "saved list" trade cloth is indicative of the 19th century American Fur Company cloth orders coming from Northern England. *Photo courtesy of Colin Taylor.*

PHOTO 4B. Close-up of the original sash on display at the Berlin Museum. Photo is partially over-exposed, obscuring the white "saved list" but is included here to show quillwork detail and the coarse texture of the cloth. *Photo courtesy of Mark Miller.*

Coincidentally, in 1832 an American Fur Company (AFC) Fort Union record states that the "scarlet cloth this year is the most inferior ever brought to the Upper Missouri." In spite of this problem, examination of the AFC fur trade records indicate a lively cloth trade on the Upper Missouri at this time. Their headquarters were built at Fort Union in 1828. Thereafter, the majority of AFC cloth orders were sent to this location; between 1827 and 1840, shipments included "GREY LIST" and "saved grey list," as well as "FANCY LISTS" in 1834 and 1836. In 1838, a large annual order included "indigo blue fancy list 1 in cloth." (Corey 2001: 23-24).

"FANCY" was a cloth almost certainly of multi-colored striped lists. This striped woven fancy list cloth, which was DYED-IN-THE-WOOL, was very likely a more expensive WOOLEN cloth. PIECE dyeing was a more economical process that produced the bright solid colors, primarily of red and blue, which the Indians coveted for both sacred and secular use. These are the factors that determined what the traders ordered to satisfy demands. However, it is clear that the Northern Plains tribes persisted in their demands for a contrasting white list on trade cloth. For example, a letter, dated 1811, by United States government officials who were attempting to compete with the fur trade companies for the Indian trade, states that, "The Indians never change their fashion, and are very particular…for instance, a cloth without a white stripe on the edge will not be worn by an Indian." (Peake 1954: 270-71)

Farther east, in present day Minnesota, the Chippewa tribe had access to a coarse cloth with a GREY LIST. This was also probably supplied by the AFC, which had permanent posts in the area as early as 1825. It is documented as being one of four kinds of BROADCLOTH traded by tribes in the region for furs, the most common being "the cheapest quality…dark blue coarse BROADCLOTH with a white border." This trade cloth was further described as "white list cloth with white edge that was coarser than the gray [list or edge]." (Densmore 1929: 32, 140-141).

From the mid to late 19th century, the Oglala Sioux developed a special preference for dark blue cloth for men's wearing blankets, which had a prominent white stripe created by the overlapping "SAVED LIST" seams down the center of the wearer's back. They also made use of both red and blue "SAVED LIST" for large "dress blankets" (courting blankets). These were fabricated from one red and one blue blanket which had overlapping white list seams that became an integral part of the decorative motif. (Powers 1980: 40-47 and Corey 2001: 25) (**Photo 5**). Among the Crow, a bright green cloth was highly prized for women's dresses. This was introduced on the Upper Missouri River as early as 1828 by the AFC: "grass green cloth, SAVED LIST, list to be clear white as possible." (Corey 2001: 12)

reveals a three-band striped SELVEDGE called "rainbow." This is a rare documented photo of the use of this style of fabric c. 1900 by a Northern Plains tribe. Most likely, it resembles the earlier "FANCY LIST" sent to Fort Union as early as 1834 (one year after Bodmer's visit there in 1833), but it was not distributed in the Southern Plains until after the 1860s.

PHOTO 6. Sioux mother and child, photo by Jesse Hastings Bradley, taken between 1896 and 1900 at Pine Ridge, South Dakota (Denver Museum of Natural History, Colo. #245). The mother is wearing a typical dress of indigo blue "saved list" trade cloth. Her daughter's dress hem reveals a three-band "rainbow list" cloth.

PHOTO 5. "Gambling Game Practised by the American Indians" W.H. Martin. 1909. Note blanket worn over head of the Sioux man (front left), which is actually two blankets with overlapping white selvedge seams forming a center stripe on the "Skunk" blanket. *Postcard from the Preston Miller Collection.*

The Lakota favored the use of indigo-dyed white SELVEDGE trade cloth in women's dresses, as seen in this photograph of a Sioux mother and daughter taken in the late 19th century (**Photo 6**). The daughter's dress hem

Extensive use of indigo blue, white edge "SAVED LIST" cloth (usually called simply "list cloth" by the traders) was recorded amongst the Plains, Woodland, Prairie, and Plateau tribes throughout the 19th century. It was the ubiquitous cloth for garments, i.e., men's war shirts, breechclouts, and leggings. (See **Photo 7**, Crow men wearing trade cloth breechclouts.) According to anthropologist James Howard, the Plains-Ojibwa made use of both red and blue "STROUD CLOTH" for men's breechclouts, called azians as "an indispensable item of male apparel." The older male warriors and chiefs wore exceptionally long breechclouts, which touched the ground in both front and back, as "a mark of masculinity." "Leggings, like the breechclouts, were often made of red or blue STROUD CLOTH." (Howard 1965: 60-61)

PHOTO 7. *"Crow Indian Dancers,"* c.1890? Color tinted postcard. All four men wear "saved list" breechclouts. Note the breechclout with fancy beadwork and "pinked" cut selvedge. *Four Winds Auction, 2001.*

STROUD CLOTH, the Sacred Cloth

In 1972, Douglas Light, Curator of the Ethnology Department of the Glenbow Museum in Calgary, wrote a monograph entitled *Tattooing Practices of the Cree Indians.* His Cree informant for the account of the tattooing bundle's creation was Solomon Bluehorn, an elderly man "well versed in all aspects of Cree and Saulteaux religion." Anthropologist David Mandelbaum had employed Bluehorn as an interpreter during the 1930s. Here is what Bluehorn had to say about the bundle:

> Not everyone had the right to perform the tattooing ritual for the power had to be given in a dream. Such a shaman would become the owner of the tattooing bundle, containing the articles needed for the ceremony...Long ago, in the buffalo days, a man had a dream. A buffalo spirit came to him and said "My Grandson, I am the most powerful spirit of the Plains Cree. If you follow my instructions I will give you a great gift; it is a tattooing bundle." This spirit was called "Buffalo that Walks like a Man" and...taught the first owner the proper tattooing procedures, songs and prayers...the man was considered to be one of the most influential medicine men of the Cree.

Like other bundles, it was wrapped in STROUD CLOTH, which the Cree referred to as *munto-ee-gun* (sacred cloth), the two popular colors being *mee-kway-ah-gun* (red cloth) and *kus-kee-tay-wee-gun* (black cloth) or navy blue. Whenever the bundle was opened, a cloth offering was added to the outer wrappings. Over a number of years, when some of the wrappings became tattered, they were "put away" in the bush with tobacco, as an offering to the spirit giver (Light 1972, 13).

The religious tattoo designs given to men included buffalo heads, the spirit "Buffalo Who Walks like a Man," thunderbirds, etc. One of these bundles, with ownership dating back to the mid-19th century, is called the Four Sky Thunder Bundle, and was ceremonially transferred to Light. He then describes in detail the red stroud wrappings and contents of this bundle in his possession (*Ibid*: 7-18).

Earlier, anthropologist James H. Howard described the contents of two war bundles, which were owned by individuals (rather than communally). Howard obtained both bundles directly from Plains-Ojibwa shaman John Daniels, "an aged medicine man" of Long Plain Reserve, in 1958. Daniels referred to the red and black ribbons on the badger war bundle as war colors of his tribe. This bundle may date back as early as 1850 (Howard 1965: 88).

Many other Plains tribes used trade cloth as medicine wrappings, i.e., the Blackfoot favored the triple striped SAVED LIST (STROUD CLOTH) for ceremonial pipe wrappings and medicine bundles. The Crow used red "SAVED LIST" cloth to wrap rock medicines (used in healing the sick) and for trim on war shields. Rawhide rattles used in ceremonies throughout the Plains were frequently wrapped in blue or red "SAVED LIST" cloth. Trade cloth pipe bags, usually red, are known to have been in use on the Northern Plains at an early period.

Ojibwa Religious Objects

The use of red and blue trade cloth as an integral part of medicine objects and/or ceremonies appears to have had a widespread use in the Northern Plains tribes. This use is frequently in conjunction with important universal religious symbols such as the thunderbird or manitou.

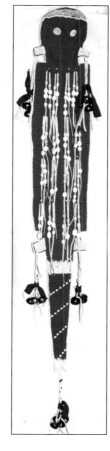

Contemporary Otter Medicine Bag, which closely resembles one formerly on display at the Glenbow Museum in Canada. Most Ojibwa bags are made of real otter skins, but this one is made of cloth. It follows closely the shape of an otter and is used in a Mediwiwin religious ceremony. A Mediwiwin ceremonial drum on display at the Milwaukee Public Museum has sides covered in half red and half blue trade cloth. *Made by Allen Chronister; cloth dyed by the author.*

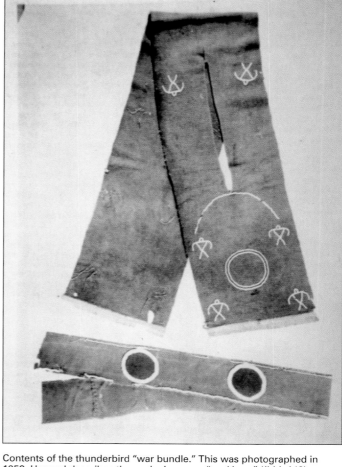

Contents of the thunderbird "war bundle." This was photographed in 1958. Howard describes the neck piece as a "necklace." (*Ibid*: 143)

John Daniels, a Plains-Ojibwa shaman on the Long Plain Reserve, Manitoba, in 1958. States Howard, "He is wearing the 'thunderbird' war bundle regalia." This includes a red "saved list" neck ornament. "...although of cloth, [it] is clearly patterned after the animal skin type described by Skinner. It could be inferred that the original owner claimed the thunderbird as his spirit helper or guardian in battle." The piece is beaded with fourteen thunderbird symbols plus circle and rainbow motifs. The cloth belt has appliqué blue "stroud" circles surrounded with white beads. Howard describes this ceremonial paraphernalia in exacting detail[2] (Howard 1965: 71, 86-88).

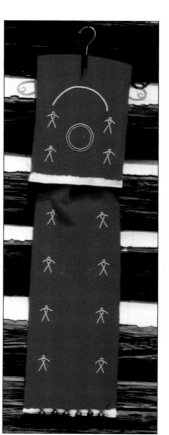

Contemporary reconstruction of the original "necklace." Note addition of hawk bell ornaments that Howard described as missing on the original artifact. *The exact specifications were used in the new piece, which was made by Allen Chronister. Cloth dyed by the author.*

Endnotes

[1]Although white men named these article "sashes" or "tippets," the Indians called them "necklaces." (Razcka 2003). Also see the medicine "necklace" later documented by Howard's Plains-Ojibwa informant John Daniels., p. 111.

[2]A "Bungi" (Plains-Ojibwa) Sun Dance priest, Talking Horse, is shown in the 1930s wearing a similar war bundle beaded sash and belt, also made of cloth (colors not known). He and another man in the photo also carry rawhide rattles "of a Sun Dance Priest and Sun Dance offering banners." (Howard:82)

Bibliography

Chronister, Allen. "The Fall of Fort McKenzie," in *The Museum of the Fur Trade Quarterly*, Vol. 37, No.3. Chadron, Nebraska. 2001.

Corey, Carolyn. *The Tradecloth Handbook.* St. Ignatius, Montana: Four Winds Indian Trading Post, 2001.

——. "Coveted Stripes," in *People of the Buffalo, Vol. 2.* Taylor, Colin & Hugh Dempsey, eds. pp. 131-146. Wyk, Germany: Tatanka Press, 2005.

Densmore, Frances. *Chippewa Customs.* Reprint 1979: Minnesota Historical Society Press, 1929.

Goodrich, Chas. A. *The Family Encyclopedia*. Hartford, Connecticut: Belknap and Hamersley, 1850.

Heaton, Herbert. *The Yorkshire Woolen & Worsted Industries from the Earliest Times Up to the Industrial Revolution.* Oxford, UK: Clarendon Press, 1920.

Howard, James H. *The Plains-Ojibwa or Bungi.* Vermillion, South Dakota: University of South Dakota Museum, 1965.

Light, Douglas W. *Tattooing Practices of the Cree Indians, Occasional Paper #6.* Calgary, Alberta: Glenbow-Alberta Institute, 1972.

Lyford, Carrie A. *Iroquois Crafts*, reprint 1982. Wisconsin: Schneider Publications, 1945.

Maxmilian, Prince of Wied. *Travels in the Interior of North America During the Years 1832-1834*, reprint 2000. London: Taschen, 1839.

Midgeley, Eber. *Textile Terms in the Textile Trade: Vol. II, General Terms.* Manchester, UK: Emmot & Co. Ltd., 1932.

Miller, Mark. Personal communication. Kalispell, Montana, 1990.

Montgomery, Florence M. *Textiles in America 1650-1870.* New York: W.W. Norton & Co., 1984.

Peake, Ora Brooks. *A History of the United States Factory System 1795-1822.* Greeley, Colorado: Colorado State College, 1954.

Powers, William K. "The Art of Courtship Among the Oglala," in *American Indian Art Magazine,* Vol. 5, No.2, pp. 40-47. Scottsdale, Arizona, 1980.

Raczka, Paul. "Ohkinikski: War Medicines of the Northwest Plains," in *The People of the Buffalo, Vol. 1.* Taylor, Colin & Hugh Dempsey, eds. pp. 130-138. Wyk, Germany: Tatanka Press, 2003.

Shumate, Maynard. "Fort McKenzie (1832-1843): Historic Site Salvage Archaeology," in *Archaeology in Montana,* Vol. 14, No.2. Cascade, Montana, 1973.

Taylor, Colin F. *The Plains Indians.* London: Salamander Books, 1994.

Thomas, David, and Karin Ronnefeldt. *People of the First Man*. New York: Prometory Press, 1982.

III. Replicas – Reproductions Of Traditional Indian Art

1. Clothing and Accessories

War Shirts, Leggings, & Vests

EARLY CROW-STYLE WAR SHIRT *Copy of an original worn by Lakota warrior Slow Bull during the 1868 treaty signing at Fort Laramie, WY. Color copy of the original included. This is an excellent replica of the original sold by Sotheby's for $200,500 in 1996.* Beautiful appliqué-stitch bead colors on 2.5"W. strips: pred. lt. turq. blue with Crow pink, t. cobalt, and gr. yellow blocks. Narrowly bordered with Crow pale blue and t. dk. cobalt. Bib is painted red ochre with white lane-stitched beaded stripes. "Scalp locks" are 80% real human hair—the rest is horse hair and ermine strips, each wrapped with red thread "firecracker-style." Shoulders-imitation bear claw and imitation hawk feather. Top half of shirt dramatically painted dk. brown. Beautiful bighorn sheep brain-tan hides; old-style tanned with all appendages and dew claws intact with hair-on edges—an expert job. 28"L. Side appendages are 51"L. 54" underarms. Made in the Netherlands. Est. 3000-4500 **SOLD $2700(04)**

References on this specific shirt: Colin Taylor article in *Studies in American Indian Art.* p. 48 shows Slow Bull wearing this shirt; also on p. 28 in Taylor's book *Iho'lena;* also Sotheby's *Catalog #163*, 1996.

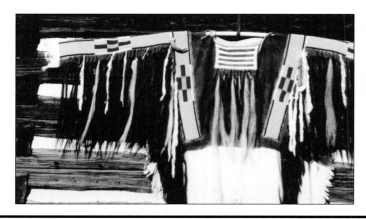

CROW-STYLE WAR SHIRT *Reservation period style. Strips were beaded by Cecile Lumpry, Coeur d'Alene-Flathead.* Blue-green painted hides with brown stripes and dots very effectively done in powder paints mixed with hide glue. Sleeve and shoulder strips are beaded in geometric patterns: mustard, t. dk. cobalt, lt. blue, Crow pale blue rose w. heart and white. Red wool trim at neck laced with leather thongs. Ermine drops at sleeve are bound with red "saved list." Est. 4000-5000 **SOLD $4500(04)**

Opposite page:
The authors (with their Australian shepherds) displaying some of the replicas in their personal collection. Carolyn is wearing a Salteaux-style strap dress that she beaded and made from her "saved list" trade wool. Preston wears a bandolier that he made and a shirt and bonnet made by Allen Chronister, who made two of the bandoliers, quiver, skunk anklets, pony-beaded blanket strip, back rest panel, and Cree blanket pictured, as well as most of the pipe bags. Other artisans are Mark Miller, Bob Brewer, Ric Carter, Dave Powell and Cecile Lumpry (who did the beadwork for the large bandolier, blanket strips, pad saddle, and rifle case). The shield over Preston's head is the one made by Bill and Kathy Brewer featured on p. 155. *Photograph by Craig Tice.*

UPPER MISSOURI RIVER-STYLE WAR SHIRT *Bodmer Period Style*.
Body is made from red "saved list" trade cloth (white selvedge at shoulder seams). 24"W. Rough texture buckskin sleeves. Pony beaded front has 5" diam. rosette. 1.5"W strips and sleeve trim in t. "Montana" blue (similar to old "pony trader blue") and white old-time block designs. Armholes have nine ermine tubes, red wool wrapped, and three black horse-hair "scalp locks," white quill-wrapped. 36"L. Open on sides old-style. Est. 625-750 **SOLD $575(02)**

CROW-STYLE WAR SHIRT c.1860-style*
Smoked brain-tanned buckskin. Muted brown and red-ochre painted stripes. Red wool wrapped horsehair locks. Bibs have red/black wool inlay with white pony-beaded borders; quill (yellow) and yarn (red and navy) wrapped buckskin fringes with pony trader blue and white spacer beads. Pred. gr. blue, with dk. cobalt, Crow pink, gr. yellow, red w. hearts and white strips; apx. 29" x 3"W. Sleeve strips: 18.5" x 3". Arm to arm: 64"W x 43"L. Average man's size. Est. 3000-4000
*See original in Penney, pp. 158-9.

CROW-STYLE "HORSE STEALING" SHIRT
Brown painted buckskin with red ochre stripes on sleeves. Red ochred sleeve fringes, bottom fringes, tabs, and bibs. Red wool inlaid bibs are white and black pony beaded triangle design (both sides). Shoulders and bottom are beaded in typical Crow colors: lt. blue, C. pink, muted red w. heart, gr. yellow, white, Sioux green, and cobalt. Beaded medicine bags each side of front: 1) pony trader blue and white pony bead edging and wrapped seed beads; 2) white pony bead wrapped with black and white pony bead edging. Lt. blue morning star motifs on sleeves have red wool centers with scalp lock dangles. Thong tied sides. 42" chest. 23"L. Est. 625-950 **SOLD $675(00)**
See *Four Winds Guide to Indian Artifacts* p. 194 for trade cloth variation.

Jerry (Pinto) McClure, Salish-Pend O'Reille from the Flathead Indian Reservation, is shown here wearing the following garments. Jerry is Chief Charlo's great grandson. He is posed next to a Metis cart parked in front of the original 1862 Jocko Agency building that was re-located to Four Winds. (Breastplate and bandolier are pictured separately on pp. 118-119)

HIDATSA EARLY STYLE WAR SHIRT c.1840-style
Heavy brain-tan hide painted natural brown with red ochre buckskin fringes (apx. 3"L) on sleeves and bottom. Painting reflects individual war exploits including specific weapons, etc. (see detail). Bib (both sides) is smoked buckskin with half red and half navy triangle (prob. symbolizing buffalo pound) bordered with white and pony trader blue pony alt. pattern. Shoulder beadwork is same bead design and colors; each shoulder has diff. attachment: one has otter strips with carved antler ornament, the other has red-ochred ermine strips with flat brass button. 22"L including fringe, 41" chest. Expertly-made. Est. 500-750 **SOLD $425(99)**

EARLY NO. PLAINS STYLE PAINTED WARSHIRT c.1950s
Lt. weight, somewhat stiff brain-tan hides. Dk. grey vertical body stripes and sleeve horiz. Red wool at neck opening. A few red wool wrapped hair-locks at armholes. Appendages left old-style. Somewhat crude but effective. 50" chest-apx. 40"L. Est. 250-400 **SOLD $150(99)**

EARLY NO. PLAINS STYLE PAINTED LEGGINGS c.1950s
Lt. smoked med. weight brain-tan painted charcoal black (faded) horiz. lines and tadpole designs. Red-ochred bottom tabs are fringed. Human hair lock fringes are alt. black and red wool wrapped. 34" inseam. Est. 250-400 **SOLD $150(99)**

BLACKFEET-STYLE PERFORATED SHIRT
This type of garment is known as a Lord's Shirt...the earliest ones were made of buckskin with holes representing bullet holes. "There were... three reasons for the existence of such shirts. As transferred articles, used mainly for power in battle;"... for regalia worn by society members; and as expressions of visions...which directed the making...of such garments." (Adolf Hungry Wolf, p. 21) Red-ochred shirt with perforated stripe and Christian cross motifs. Gr. blue, white, and black pony beaded at shoulder and on bib. Red and navy cloth inlaid bib; red crenolated wool neck opening. Est. 1200-2000 **SOLD $1200(98)**

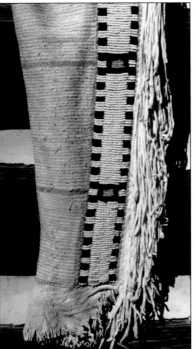

PONY BEADED BUCKSKIN LEGGINGS 1840-style
Lightly red-ochred over narrow grey horizontal stripes. 2"W strips are white and black ponies with yellow seed beads. Long white side fringes apx. 10"L. Top fringed tabs hang apx. 24"L. Soft thick hide is very nice comm. one—looks and feels like brain-tan. Strips 25"L. 33" inner leg measurement. Very subtle and correct for the period. Est. 600-950 **SOLD $500(00)**

SIOUX STYLE BEADED BUCKSKIN LEGGINGS
Traditional lane-stitched strips are a beautiful peri-winkle bkgrd. with step-triangles and crosses: bottle green, red w. hearts, and gr. yellow. White vertical beaded lane has bottle green and red w. heart box motif. Lt. ochred and smudged hide looks old. 30"L includ. top tabs. 23"L inside leg measurement. Strips are 3"W x 23"L. Side fringes 6-9"L. Heavy hide. Est. 600-900 **SOLD $480(00)**

METIS-STYLE QUILLED BUCKSKIN VEST
Beautiful lt. smoked brain-tan hide with tailored finish; red Fox braid bound lapel and false pocket flaps have floral sewn quilled motifs. Flowers are brick and lavender single band technique; stems and tendrils are single line in gold and olive. Brass stamped domed button front. Back has tailored tie closure. Mattress ticking lined. Man's large size 42-44. 25.5"L. Exc. cond. Est. 500-800 **SOLD $450(00)**

Head Gear (Bonnets, Hair Ornaments, etc.)

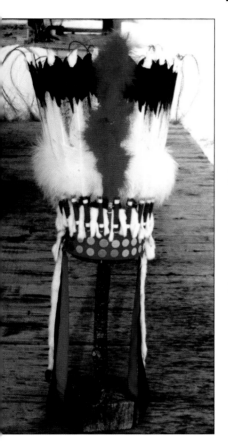

BLACKFOOT-STYLE STAND UP BONNET
23 hand-painted "legal eagle" feathers have red wool covered wooden dowel base with white fluffs; ermine fur top attachments have red horsehair. Red fluffs cover central plume. Band is 4.5"H red wool with old-time flat brass buttons and ermine strips; old checked gingham backed. Silk ribbon (three red and one black) and full ermine side drops. 18"H. Apx. 9" diam. with buckskin ties. Est. 650-800 **SOLD $700(03)**

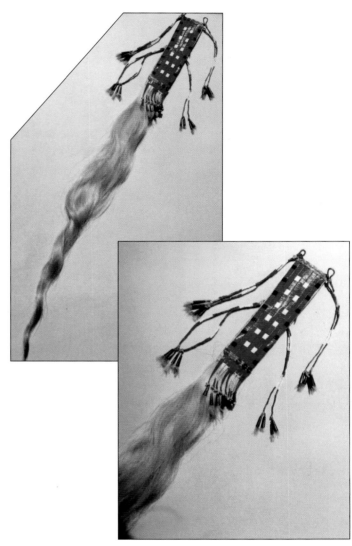

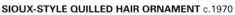

SIOUX-STYLE QUILLED HAIR ORNAMENT c.1970
Red quill-wrapped slats with white and black. Brass sequin trimmed. Tin-cone bottom fringes with purple fluffs. 4 prs. of alt. red/white quill-wrapped extensions with hand-made tin cones with purple fluffs. Yellow-dyed horse tail. Panel 2" x 9"L, rawhide backed. 28" total L. Exc. cond. Est. 200-350 **SOLD $200(04)**

SPLIT HORN REPRO BONNET
Fringed ermine strips cover buckskin base. Brow band is red wool with beadwork design in dk. cobalt blue, turquoise, old rose w. hearts, red, and navy blue ribbon. Crow bead suspensions: alt. red white-hearts and periwinkle blue plus hawk bell and red horsehair drops. Red and cobalt Prosser beads and hawk bells strung between split buffalo horn tips. Large imitation eagle feather (11" x 3"W) suspensions on back have quill-wrapped slats in red, black, and white and trimmed with white feather fluffs and red hackle drops attached with white ermine. Double layer of long ermine tubes, red wool wrapped with cobalt bead separators and black horsehair tips. Red, yellow, green, and navy ribbons each side. Dark red hackle feathers at base of horns on either side. Hangs 40"L. Est. 800-1200 **SOLD $625(98)**

Miscellaneous Ornaments

PRE-1850 STYLE GRIZZLY CLAW NECKLACE
Imitation prairie grizzly claws (apx. 3"L) mounted on otter fur with cobalt Prosser bead spacers. Red trade cloth backed. Triangular otter back piece bound with muslin. Well constructed. Hangs apx. 17.5" in front and apx. 21" in back Est. 450-650 **SOLD $350(98)**

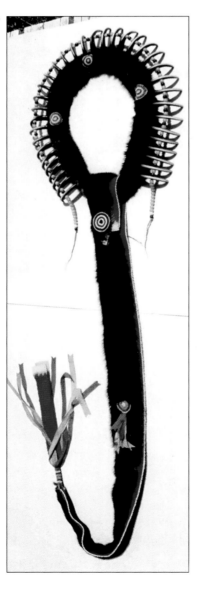

PRAIRIE-STYLE GRIZZLY CLAW NECKLACE
c.1830-style
Imitation prairie grizzly claws are stained horn (4"L) interspersed with red trade wool that is white pony edge beaded. Gr. blue Crow bead spacers. Very well-made. Est. 350-500 **SOLD $275(99)**

PRAIRIE STYLE GRIZZLY CLAW OTTER DROP NECKLACE
36 large imitation claws interspersed with cobalt and gr. yellow prosser trade beads. Red "saved list" backed otter drop is 42"L + 12"; real silk ribbon/cloth drops, bead wrapped. Five medallions are Chey. pink, gr. blue, t. cobalt, and t. forest green. Superb workmanship and attention to detail. Est. 1500-2000

HAIRPIPE BREAST PLATE c.1950s
Aged 4.5" celluloid hair pipes, probably from the old Plume Trading Co. (This a rare item due to the unavailability of these hair pipes today.) Heavy harness leather separators with C. pink and t. blue pony bead central panel. T. red and topaz Crow beads at sides with buckskin thongs forming fringes (red ochred). Hand cut large brass cross hangs from top. 10.5"W x 17.5"L. Est. 350-500 **SOLD $175(99)**
See p. 115 for a photo of this bandolier and breast plate being worn together.

DEW CLAW BANDOLIER

c.1950s
Multiple carved shapes all hand-made; buckskin tied to leather strap (1/2"W) with cobalt Crow beads. Tiny cloth med. bag at top. Very convincing work—looks Indian made. Hangs 26"L. Est. 150-350 **SOLD $85(99)**

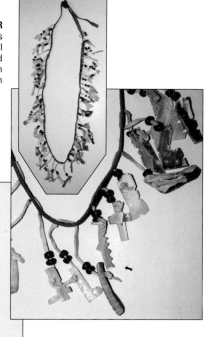

OLD-TIME FINGER and BEAD WOVEN SASH and MATCHING GARTERS

c.1980
Made by renowned late weaver Dick Carney. Includes his business card, "Powhatan Originals, Doyline, LA" etc. A legend in his lifetime—a man who loved his craft and had a reputation for his fine authentic work. Very rarely do these come up for sale. Beautiful soft wool yarn in muted tones of indigo, and shades of red and yellow ochre. Authentically woven with interspersed white pony beads. Very few people know how to do this! A wide 7" x 62" sash plus 18" long braided fringes interspersed with same beads! Garters: Soft shades of yellow and red ochre interspersed with white ponies. 1.5"W x 27"L plus 8"L. braided and beaded fringes. Exc. cond. Est. 500-1000 for the set. **SOLD $500(05)**

NO. PLAINS DEW CLAW BANDOLIER c.1960

Apx.45 (2"L) deer dew claws strung on brain-tan thongs with dk. cobalt and white tile beads. 3/4"W x 64" loop on heavy harness leather. Exc. cond. Est. 80-200

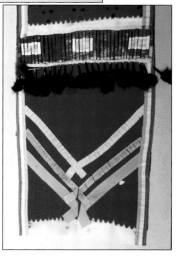

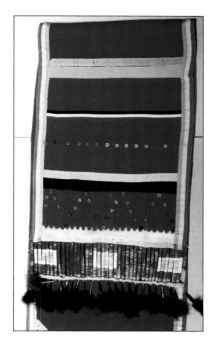

STAMPED GERMAN SILVER LARGE ORNAMENTS

Worn by prominent tribal members 19th C. and earlier. These are nicely patinaed to look old. *Made in Germany.*
(Left) **CROSS** with crescent at bottom. Scallop stamped on borders with lightning and cross patterns. 10"L. Buckskin thong. Est. 125-250 **SOLD $125(00)**
(Right) **PECTORAL** has hanging circles at bottom. Stamped fancy star/cross motif. Buckskin top thong. Hangs 6"L x 7.5"W. Est. 125-250 **SOLD $125(00)**

SIOUX-STYLE "SAVED LIST" WOOL BREECHCLOUT WITH QUILLED PANEL c.1950

Clear red dyed heavy plain (square) weave wool has hobbyist "clamp" white selvedge*. Nicely faded red/white/blue grosgrain binding. Chevron-configured ribbons are pale yellow, grey, and yellow. Tarnished brass sequin decorations in 1/4" and 3/8" sizes. Front has navy silk-satin ribbon plus same grosgrain as back decor. Buffalo-rawhide slats wrapped with red, yellow, and white old-time box motifs. Hand-made tin cone drops have burgundy fluffs. Excellent cond. 12" x 52" cloth + 3" quilled panel Est. 150-350 **SOLD $150(04)**
*See Corey *The Tradecloth Handbook,* p. 10 for explanation of this hobbyist method.

2. Ornamented Blankets and Hides

CROW-STYLE MAN'S FULLY BEADED MOCCASINS
Appliqué stitched on comm. tanned thick elk. Looks like brain-tan! Chey. pink background with lt. periwinkle, muted red w. heart, old-stock gun-metal facets. Border colors: White, Crow pale blue, Arapaho green, gr. blue, and gr. yellow. Yellow-ochred. Very thick hard sole. 11.75"L. Ankle-wrap. Exc. cond. Est. 450-650 **SOLD $380(99)**

CROW-STYLE TRIANGULAR BELT POUCH
Background bead colors incl. Chey. pink, chalk blue, white, and hortensia. Design bead colors: dk. navy, cranberrry, gr. yellow, Sioux green, t. lt. am-ethyst, pink w. hearts, and traces of gun metal tri-cuts. Appliqué stitched. Bound with maroon cotton; inside flap is same color with polka dot lining. Commercially tanned leather bag is sinew sewn. White pony bead edg-ing. Patina. 10"L x 4.5"W. Est. 250-350 **SOLD $270(99)**

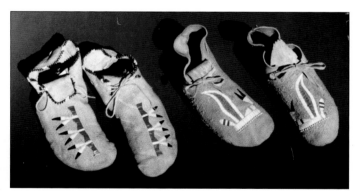

QUILLED BUCKSKIN MOCCASINS 1830-style
Each is early style side fold one-piece construction, which preceded the hard-sole two-piece style. *Made in Europe.*
(Left) Lightly red-ochred buckskin with simple band technique feather motif in red ochre, white, and black. Sinew-sewn. Cuff and tongue are edge-beaded in Pony trader blue and white ponies. 10.75"L. Sole shows wear. Exc. cond. Est. 200-400
(Right) Brain-tan buffalo hide with beautiful simple band technique quill-work in white, red ochre, dk. brown, and lt. purple. Red ochred buckskin in design center. White pony bead borders on design front. Shows light wear. Sinew-sewn. 10.75"L. Est. 200-400

SIOUX-STYLE PAINTED BRAIN-TANNED BUFFALO HIDE
RARE Complete old-time configuration with head and ears. Early-style box and border design in red ochre, deep green, yellow ochre, black with white lines, all natural pigments. Rich color smoked hide. Still has outside loops from tanning process (used to have a beaded strip). Apx. 85"L x 38"W. Est. 1500-2500 **SOLD $950(01)**

PAINTED ELK HIDE
Signed "Frank Shortey '91" Traditional pictographic style depicts Confederate soldiers and Indians as well as Winter Count. Black and white stylized feather motif has small laced hoop with bead-wrapped horsehair drop—to symbol-ize catching the enemy. Hair on back. Exc. cond. 76"L x 63.5"W. Est. 375-500 **SOLD $350(98)**

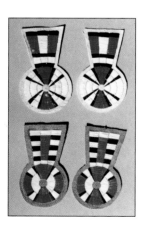

(Top to bottom) **"KEYHOLE" DESIGN QUILLED MOCCASIN TOP SETS** Early-style. *Made in Czech Republic.* Red, black, and white sewn, fully-quilled. Simple band stitched on leather. Expertly done. Quillwork is 4"L x 2.25"W. Est. 200-300 set **SOLD $200(99) Similar.** Orange, black, and white quills. Est. 175-250 set

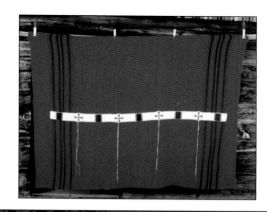

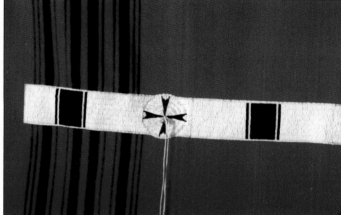

**PAINTED MULE
DEER HIDE**
*Signed "M. Locke
'94"* Central tipi motif
and feathers with four
Indian warriors on
war-painted ponies.
Yellow-orange, red,
yellow, cobalt, and
blue brightly painted.
Exc. cond. 46"W x
51.5"L. Est. 250-450

SIOUX-STYLE FULLY-BEADED STRIP ON RED STRIPED BLANKET
Early Classic pattern: seven rows lane-stitched pred. white with simple
blocks in t. dk. cobalt and gr. yellow. Rosette (3.5" diam) motifs are t.
cranberry and t. dk. cobalt. Long buckskin thongs with 1/2" hawk bells
suspended from each rosette center. Strip is 3"W x 68"L. Red wool blanket
is early Canadian with multi-black stripes on each end. 78"L x 62"W in rare
pristine cond. Est. 1250-2500 **SOLD $1200(04)**

3. Pouches and Bags

Shoulder Bags, Bandoliers

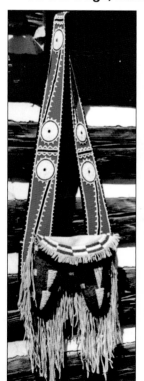

SO. PLAINS-STYLE FULLY-BEADED SHOOTING POUCH c.1830
Probably Kiowa. *This piece is in the Rijksmuseum voor Volkenkunde, Leiden, Holland;
purchase included a color Xerox of the original
unpublished photo of the original.* * Unique
combination of styles. Bag is smoked moose
hide ALL SINEW-SEWN and fully-pony-beaded
in w. center cranberry with white simple block
and triangle motifs. Tied apx. 8"L. buckskin
fringes all around. Pouch is 9"L x 9.5"W, exc.
fringe. Choctaw style-beaded strap is an early
Southeastern-style expertly pony-beaded in
classic pre-historic scroll motif; white with
black on red "saved list" trade wool. Bound
with navy "saved list" wool. Appliqué stitched.
Backed with aged mattress ticking. Light patina.
Strap is 3.5"W x 56"L. Est. 800-1200
SOLD $900(01)
    See Chronister, Allen, "Southern Plains
Decorative Arts in the Early 19th Century:
Berlandier's Comanche Bag Revisited," in *The
People of the Buffalo, Vol. 2.* Taylor, Colin &
Hugh Dempsey, eds, pp. 206-217. Wyk, Germany: Tatanka Press, 2005. *Photo of this original
bag is on page 212 and the correct description
is on page 212 labeled "Fig. 5."
    See *Four Winds Guide To Trade Goods
and Replicas,* p. 127, for more photos of this
specific style of bag.

NO. PLAINS-STYLE BANDOLIER

Pouch is a woven piece of wool assomption sash, pred. red. Striking black and white loomed pony-beaded strap is backed with red wool; long warp braided fringes are red and green. Upper pouch is red wool bound with black Fox braid and bordered with white appliqué seed beads. Old checkered gingham lining. Two brass buttons trim. Hangs 30"L. Pouch is 7.25" x 11.5"H. Strap is apx. 2"W. Est. 250-450

EARLY-STYLE CANADIAN BANDOLIER

Appliqué floral abstract beaded on red wool in beautiful old-time colors of Sioux green, cranberry red, Chey. pink, cobalt, gr. yellow, pumpkin, lt. blue, white, and gr. blue. Dk. green Fox braid binding. Silk ribbon tabs on top of strap are red and black. Backed with mattress ticking. Bag is 12"L. x 9.5"W. Strap is 23.25"L x 4"W. Est. 600-900 **SOLD $500(99)**

BLACKFOOT-STYLE FULLY-BEAD-ED BAG

Worn by Stoney, Sarcee and Blackfoot warriors to carry war medicine. Flathead Indian appliqué-stitched in gorgeous design and colors. White central panel and flap with gr. yellow and C. pink diamonds and triangles outlined in dk. cobalt; wide border is gr. blue with gr. yellow and rose w. heart step pattern; roll beaded sides are dk. cobalt. Lined with old muslin flour sack. Shoulder strap (3/4"W) is brain-tan elk with double row of gr. blue Prosser beads laced with thongs. Elk bottom fringes, 11"L. Buckskin backed. Pouch 11"L x 8"W. Strap hangs 24" + fringes. Nicely aged. Came with copy photo of Western Canadian Indians wearing similar bag. Est. 850-1500

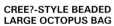

CREE?-STYLE BEADED LARGE OCTOPUS BAG

Pastel symmetrical floral beadwork on black velvet (beaded same both sides). Large central stylized flower is t. rose, lt. blue, white, and Crow pink, Other colors include mustard, Sioux green, t. turq., and red. All edge-beaded in white seed beads; also bordered in same white beads. Double carrying straps are all white bead wrapped. Est. 800-1500 **SOLD $800(04)**

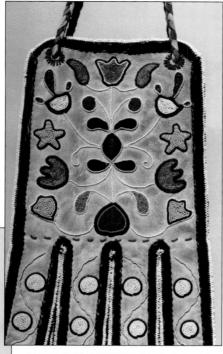

METIS-STYLE BEADED OCTOPUS BAG
Buckskin panels have "High Plains Metis"* abstract floral patterns in mustard, gr. blue, t. red, pale blue, t. bottle green, transl. pink, and t. dk. cobalt outlined with white. Diff. patterns and colors each side. Dk. blue silk borders and white seed-bead edged all around (including tabs). Madder red yarn bottom tassels. Carrying strap is braided silk ribbon; pale yellow, lt. red, and lt. olive green. Lined with bright chintz pattern. Superb piece with attention to every detail. 18"L x 7" top opening. Hangs apx. 40"L. Est. 750-1200

*See *Metis Legacy* by Barwell, Dorion and Prefontaine, 2001, p. 228 for similar example.

Also see *Expressing Our Heritage,* Gabriel Dumont Inst., 2002, pp. 85-89 for discussion of this interesting group of people.

(Left) CHEYENNE-STYLE LARGE PIPE BAG
Classic stripe bead design: dk. cobalt, white; inner stripe is red w. heart, gr. blue, and pumpkin. Roll beaded top and sides same colors. Typical edge-beaded top tabs have tin cone and red horsehair drops. Quill-wrapped rawhide slats are red, yellow, and pale blue. 14"L. yellow ochred bottom fringe. 36"L total x 5.5"W. Yellow-ochred comm. hide. Est. 600-850 **SOLD $550(99)**

(Right) CHEYENNE-STYLE PIPE BAG
Classic stripe design in white, old-stock t. bottle green; inner stripes are Crow pale blue and gr. yellow, highlighted w/dk. cobalt. Top is roll bead edge and sides beaded same colors in nice 3 lane motif. Bottom fringes are yellow quill-wrapped. Hand-made tin cones on fringes and tabs. Char. top tabs are edge-beaded in white and bottle green w/tin cone drops. Made on beautiful Indian tanned hide. Hangs 27"L x 5.5"W. Est. 600-800 **SOLD $650(99)**

CHEYENNE STYLE PIPE BAG
Elaborate Classic beadwork designs: stripes are t. red and white with t. forest green, Chey. pink, gr. yellow, and turq. Middle of bag (under the cones) has triple overlapping star design. Made on heavy stiff commercial hide, which is nicely yellow ochred. Top roll beaded with four beaded tabs with hand-made tin cones and red-dyed horsehair. Bottom quill-wrapped panel is pred. red with early box design in white, purple, and golden yellow. Fringed buckskin bottom. Excellent craftsmanship and beadwork. 6"W x 19.5"L. Est. 700-850 **SOLD $600(98)**

OLD-STYLE BEADED BLADDER BAG
Buckskin beaded band in t. forest green, t. red and white; tin cones over red ochred leather fringes. Red beaded medicine wheel on bottom with red quill-wrapped buckskin thong drop with tin cone and red feather fluffs. Light yellow ochre patina overall. 12" x 12" circumf. Est. 195-275 **SOLD $220(98)**

(Left) SIOUX-STYLE PIPE BAG
Lane-stitched on soft smoked brain tanned hide. White bkgrd. with red w. hearts, pumpkin, with pony trader blue outline. Diff. design each side. Roll beaded top. Quilled rawhide slats are red and yellow (5.25"L) Buckskin bottom fringe 10"L. 32"total L x 5.5"W. Exc. cond. Est. 650-850 **SOLD $750(99)**
(Right) Similar to previous bag. Lane-stitched on lt. smoked brain-tan. Gr. blue bkgrd. with gr. yellow, red w. hearts, and dk. cobalt design elements. Diff. design each side; other side also has gr. green and white. Roll beaded top and sides. Quilled bottom slats (5"L) are red with purple and yellow designs. 30" total L x 6"W. Buckskin bottom fringe 9"L. Exc. cond. Est. 650-850 **SOLD $750(99)**

CHIPPEWA-CREE STYLE BEADED PIPE BAG
Beautifully contoured abstract beadwork is diff. on each side. Gr. green, t. dk. cobalt, t. gold, transl. pink, t. amethyst with white contoured bkgrd. Roll beaded panel edges. Red yarn wrapped bottom fringes. Buckskin top edge beaded with gr. blue pony beads. White bkgrd. Looks old and completely authentic! Nice patina. Hangs 29"L. 5-3/8"W. Est. 500-750 **SOLD $500(05)**

(Left) LARGE EARLY UPPER MISSOURI-STYLE QUILLED PIPE BAG
Mandan-Hidatsa style unique diamond patterns. Multi-quill plaited panels are white with pale pumpkin and lt. turq. on one side, white and turq. with red on other side. Incredible perfect, flat quillwork ALL SINEW-SEWN. 6"H. quill-wrapped rawhide slats; white with red and turq. concentric box double motif. T. dk. cobalt beaded bands with pale gr. yellow and dk. red w. hearts. Roll beaded top same colors. 14"L. buckskin fringes. 5"W x 36"L. *Made in Czech Republic.* Est. 950-2000 **SOLD $1000(01)**
(Right) CROW-STYLE BEADED PIPE BAG
Beaded both sides same block design, diff. subtle old-time colors each side: lt. blue, t. cobalt, t. forest green, gr. yellow, Crow pink, Sioux green, gr. blue, lavender, red w. lined, and white. Lightly red ochred with faint red ochre dots wrapped; red wool overlay top and bottom borders. White top edge-beaded. Alt. red/navy bottom fringes with white pony bead spacers. Attention to every detail in this beautifully made piece. Hangs 30" incl. fringe. 4.5"W x 13.5"L. bag. Light patina. Est. 600-800 **SOLD $600(01)**

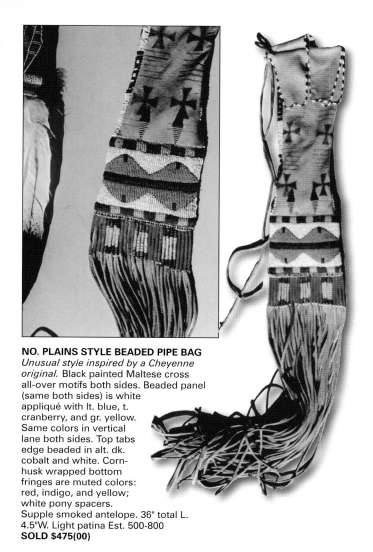

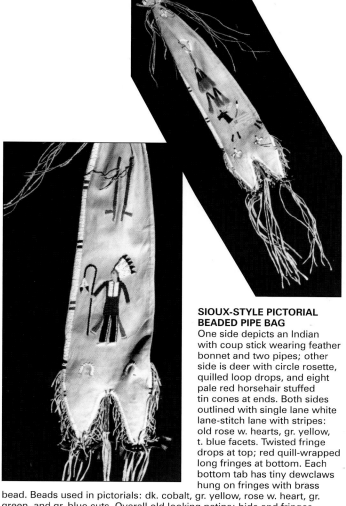

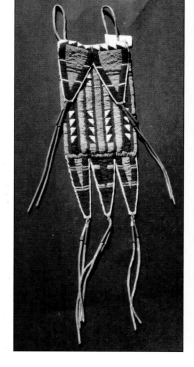

NO. PLAINS STYLE BEADED PIPE BAG
Unusual style inspired by a Cheyenne original. Black painted Maltese cross all-over motifs both sides. Beaded panel (same both sides) is white appliqué with lt. blue, t. cranberry, and gr. yellow. Same colors in vertical lane both sides. Top tabs edge beaded in alt. dk. cobalt and white. Cornhusk wrapped bottom fringes are muted colors: red, indigo, and yellow; white pony spacers. Supple smoked antelope. 36" total L. 4.5"W. Light patina Est. 500-800 **SOLD $475(00)**

SIOUX-STYLE PICTORIAL BEADED PIPE BAG
One side depicts an Indian with coup stick wearing feather bonnet and two pipes; other side is deer with circle rosette, quilled loop drops, and eight pale red horsehair stuffed tin cones at ends. Both sides outlined with single lane white lane-stitch lane with stripes: old rose w. hearts, gr. yellow, t. blue facets. Twisted fringe drops at top; red quill-wrapped long fringes at bottom. Each bottom tab has tiny dewclaws hung on fringes with brass bead. Beads used in pictorials: dk. cobalt, gr. yellow, rose w. heart, gr. green, and gr. blue cuts. Overall old looking patina; hide and fringes are grey smoke color, looks old. All sinew-sewn. Bag 6"W x 28"L. +12" fringes. Est. 500-900 **SOLD $550(00)**

(Left) EARLY-STYLE POSSIBLES BAG
Author's collection. Lightly red-ochred. Pony trader blue and white pony bead stripes with attachments of tiny strips of red wool; edge-beaded flap and lane-sewn sides same bead colors. Long bottom thongs. Smoked moose hide carrying strap. 8"W x 6"H. Est. 200-300 **(Right) NO. PLAINS EARLY-STYLE PIPE BAG**
c.1830 style *Unique bag inspired by one in a private collection.* Red plain weave (square) wool has white and med. blue pony beaded panels (both sides). Long buckskin triangular tab has black and white pony bead borders; roll beaded top same colors. 10"L tab +buckskin fringes 10"L. Bottom buckskin fringes (11"L) each have 1.5" tin cone with red wool drops. Bag is 13.5"L x 4.5"W. Est. 300-450 **SOLD $325(02)**

INTERMONTANE-STYLE FULLY BEADED BELT BAG
Double triangle flaps, triple triangle drops, and front panel all in luscious pastel lane and appliqué beadwork. Colors: lt. blue, t. pony trader blue, gr. yellow, dk. red w. heart, gr. green, Chey. pink, and white. Flaps and tabs white bead-edged. Panel has roll beaded edge. Tin cones and brain-tan thong trim. Dark patina looks old! 4.5"W x 17.5"L. Unique piece. Est. 350-500 **SOLD $450(05)**

Small Bags

EARLY-STYLE NO. PLAINS MIRROR BAG *1830 bag.* Appliqué stitched in white, pony-trader blue, and red w. hearts. Different design on either side. Sides are roll beaded and top is bead-edged. Red wool trade cloth at bottom and on strap. Sinew sewn on heavy smoked moose. Soft fringe bottom. Med. patina. 7"L x 5.5"W. Est. 450-650 **SOLD $350(00)**

(Left to right) **BLACKFOOT-STYLE QUILLED BAG**
Sewn simple band rosette (4.5" diam.), band with stylized leaf patterns; top bordered with complex unusual checkerboard pattern (one side only). Colors: white, pumpkin, gold, and chestnut brown. Lightly smoked buckskin, 6" bottom and side fringes. Flat brass central button. 9"L, 6"W bottom, 5"W top. Est. 400-650
EASTERN WOODLANDS-STYLE QUILLED KNIFE SHEATH
Four diff. styles of sewn quillwork on this piece!! Red sawtooth quilled edging on all sides and top; simple band horiz. border; three vertical bands of two quill diamond stripe motifs in gold, red, and blue-grey; tiny lanes and designs of single line quillwork in red, white, and grey. Smoked buckskin covered rawhide sheath. Dk. red horsehair filled tin cone suspensions at top and bottom. Case is 9.75"L + cones 3.25"W. Buckskin strap at top. Est. 450-600 **SOLD $500(01)**
MANDAN-HIDATSA-STYLE QUILLED POUCH
Multi-quill diamond technique is white with brick and black. Top flap has two quill diamond technique in stripes. Navy wool side binding. White pony beads along bottom. 5" bottom buckskin fringes. Hangs 13.5"L. Pouch 6"L x 5.5"W. Crow beads on hanging strap. Est. 300-450

UPPER MISSOURI RIVER-STYLE MIRROR BAG
Unusual style. Made on smoked brain tan. Hourglass design; beaded on one side only in appliqué stitch. Chey. pink bkgrd. with gr. yellow, red w. hearts, apple green, gr. blue w. hearts, and dk. cobalt. Strap also has fully-beaded tabs, same colors. White bead-edged handle and top; thimbles, hawk bells, brass cones, and bone beads, ermine skin drop embellishments. Lined with grey wool also forms scalloped bottom tab and handle top. Patinated. Bag 6"L x 4"W. Strap 17"L x 1.75"W. Fringe 6.5"L. Est. 450-650 **SOLD $450(99)**

(Left) **NO. PLAINS-STYLE QUILLED STRIKE-A-LITE BAG**
Made in Czech Republic. Unusual piece has half indigo-half corn yellow simple band sewn quillwork; horned spirit figure on half yellow ochred half red ochred bag. Zig-zag sewn quilled flap and bottom border is white with indigo and red. Bottom tin cone fringes. Top corners have thongs with dew claw suspensions. Bottom corners have thongs with brass beads dew claws with red cut feathers. Sides are seed bead edged in pony trader blue. 3.5"W x 5.5"H. Buckskin braided carrying strap. Exc. cond. Est. 140-300 **SOLD $135(04)**
(Right) **ASSINIBOINE-STYLE FULLY-BEADED AMULET**
Made in Czech Republic. Charming little diamond-shaped piece has four horse tracks inside divided triangles. Colors are gr. yellow, white, t. cranberry, gr. green bordered with med. blue. Each corner has four buckskin thongs with t. green Crow beads, brass beads, and tin cones. 6"L x 3"W. Exc. cond. Est. 125-250

SIOUX-STYLE PICTORIAL QUILLED BAG
Central buffalo and two birds in flight with red line bkgrd. bordered with gilded brass sequins. Simple band sewn quillwork in red and white. Smoked brain-tanned buckskin with 8"L side fringes. Braided buckskin handle. Beautifully done. Bag 13.25" x 16.5" incl. fringe. Est. 250-475 **SOLD $200(00)**
See original in Walters: 46.

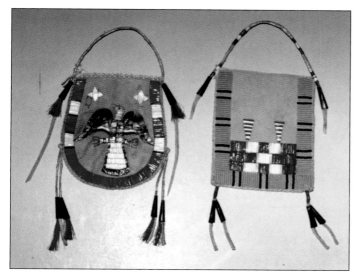

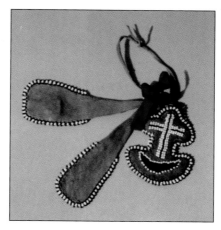

APACHE-STYLE MEDI-CINE CHARM
Sinew sewn. Dk. cobalt and white beaded design. Edged in same. Navy silk ribbon tied to top. Smoked buckskin with expertly "artifaked" patina. 3.25"L x 2.75"W. Tabs are apx. 6.25"L. Est. 50-85

See original in Alan Ferg, *Western Apache Material Culture*, Univ. of AZ Press, 1987: plate #28.

(Left) NO. PLAINS-STYLE U-SHAPED QUILLED POUCH
Made in Czech Republic. Varying blues, orange, rust, white central eagle motif with border primarily red, white, and dk. brown (one side only). Yellow quill-wrapped handle and side drops embellished with red horsehair tin cones. White edge-beaded opening. 3.75" x 4.5"L. pouch. Est. 200-300 **SOLD $200(03)**

(Right) NO. PLAINS-STYLE SMALL BEADED/QUILLED POUCH
Made in Czech Republic. Central geometric sewn-quillwork primarily red with white and yellow. Handle quill-wrapped in same colors. Borders are "lane" stitched lt. periwinkle with pale gr. yellow and pony trader blue (one side only). Red quill-wrapped bottom drops with tin cones. 3.75" x 4.5"L. pouch. Exc. cond. Est. 85-175 **SOLD $125(03)**

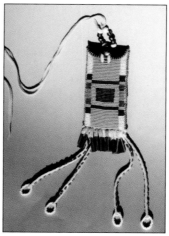

QUILLED DEER HOOF BAGS
Made in Czech Republic. Hair-on fronts with panel of simple band sewn quillwork. (Left to right) Quillwork blocks of red and white with dk. brown. Pony edge-beaded flap. Quillwork blocks are orange, white with dk. brown. Quilled flap is white and black. Pony trader blue lower border. Buckskin fringes and braided handle. Hang 17" total L. Bags 5"W x 8" + 6"L buckskin fringe. Est. 130-200 each **SOLD $100(02)each**

CROW-STYLE WHETSTONE CASES
(Left to right) Fully-beaded buckskin front in classic Crow geometrics. Tin cone bottom fringes with long buckskin beaded loop drops. Back and flap are harness leather. Edge-beaded sides and flap. Crow bead top loop. 2.25"W x 4.25"L. Pale blue with white, t. emerald, t. cobalt, Crow pink, lt. blue, gr. yellow, and w. lined red in med. blue. Est. 200-350 **SOLD $150(01)**
Crow pink, white, t. cobalt, t. emerald green, red w. heart, and lt. blue. Edge-beaded in opal white. Brass cone bottom fringes. Est. 200-350

CROW-STYLE LOOM BEADED WATCH FOB
Unusual. White bkgrd. with two tabs ornamented with four brass cones and red horsehair. Blue Russian facets and green thread wrapping. Multiple subtle old-time bead colors. Brass cone and Crow bead top. Hangs 8"L x 1"W. Est. 85-125

(Left) EASTERN SIOUX-STYLE QUILLED STRIKE-A-LITE POUCH
Made in Czech Republic 1830-style. Beautifully "zig-zag" quilled, all sinew sewn with authentic colors: "dog" is black with red geometric motifs and orange borders. Flap is also quilled in black and white. 6"L lower buckskin fringes quill-wrapped in white and connected with gr. blue ponies. Four partially quilled loop drops. Eight hand-made tin cones with red horsehair. Braided buckskin strap. Hangs 14" total L. Bag is 5.25"L x 3.25"W. Est. 400-550 **SOLD $400(03)**

(Right) NO. PLAINS-STYLE TRIANGULAR FLAP POUCH
Yellow ochred buckskin sinew-sewn sides. Flap is white, t. red, and t. gold lane-stitched. Partially red quill-wrapped loop drops; two red horse hair tin cone drops. Braided handle. Flap 12"L x 4"W pouch. Est. 95-200 **SOLD $125(02)**

CROW-STYLE WOMAN'S FULLY-BEADED AWLCASES

Rawhide insert with beaded buckskin covers. Two entirely different styles here, both beautifully made. (Left) Buckskin beaded top has tin cone ornaments and white bead edging. Case is bead-wrapped in lt. blue, Crow pink, gr. yellow with red w. heart and t. cobalt stripes. Tin cone bottom beaded thong drops 8"L. 7"L case. Est. 300-400 **SOLD $225(01)** (Right) 4"L fully-beaded flap edge-beaded in t. red. Case is bead wrapped in pale blue, t. rose, gr. yellow with white and dk. cobalt stripes. 4.5" buckskin bottom drops are edge-beaded in alt. t. red and white beads. Brass and Crow beads at top loop. Case 6.5"L + drops. Est. 200-300

4. Weaponry

Large Weapon Cases/Weapons

CROW-STYLE LANCE CASE

Crow woman carry these upright on horseback even today in Crow parades. Painted rawhide (parfleche) case bound with red trade wool and buckskin laced. Fully-beaded top panel is Crow pink with wonderful blend of traditional colors: t. forest green, lt. blue, Sioux green, outlined in white with pony trader blue stripes. Touches of red w. heart, gr. yellow, and gr. blue. Two drops in same colors with t. blue morning star motifs on red wool with navy wool inlay. All panels white edge-beaded. Heavy lt. smoked fringes top wrapped with alt. navy and red thread and spaced with white pony beads. Two brass hawk bells at top. 4' 5"L. Long fringes apx. 20"L. Est. 875-1500 **SOLD $800(00)**

Also see Czech-made lance case on p. 176.

WOOD GUN STOCK WAR CLUB

Hefty stock is embellished with brass tacks, and N.W. brass dragon from a trade fusil. 6" steel dag blade. Ermine strip drops with four old-time hawk bells; top has buckskin strap; wrapped red Fox braid. 1.25" thick x 30"L wooden club. Est. 150-300 **SOLD $100(01)**

ARAPAHO-STYLE STONE HEAD WAR CLUB

Fancy club with lane-stitch beadwork on handle and club in pred. white, with t. red, pumpkin, and cobalt. Natural oval-shaped stone head held in place by beaded and fringed buckskin. Rawhide wrapped handle. 26"L. Est. 400-500 **SOLD $275(99)**

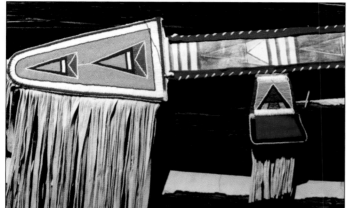

SIOUX-STYLE RIFLE CASE
Traditional lane-stitched beadwork: periwinkle bkgrd. with typical box and diamond patterns in cobalt with gr. yellow, Sioux green, C. pink, and red w. heart (same both sides). Heavy elk case with lightly red-ochred and twisted long fringes at both ends (26"L front, 18"L butt end). 51"L. 7"W opening, tapers to 3"W. Exc. cond. Est. 800-1200 **SOLD $500(99)**

CROW-STYLE PARFLECHE LANCE CASE and SWORD
Skillfully made with beautiful beadwork colors: pale blue, rose w. heart, gr. yellow, gr. green, cobalt bordered in white, bottom tabs also have Crow pink. Painted parfleche is cobalt with red and yellow ochre and pale green. Bound with red saved list; bottom red wool tabs bordered with navy saved list. 43"L. Old sword is 40"L. Brass guard, unmarked blade, brass-wire wrapped handle. All in exc. cond. Est. 935-1250 **SOLD $935(02)**

CROW-STYLE RIFLE CASE
Smoked deer hide with moose hide panels each end in Crow pink, white, Crow pale blue, t. dk. cobalt with red w. hearts. Red wool inlay. Very long buckskin fringes apx. 36"L. Case apx. 40"L. Est. 1000-1500

OKLA.-STYLE LOOM BEADED RIFLE CASE
Panels are lt. blue bkgrd. with multi-color feather and geometric motif. Fringed buckskin case is supple comm. tan—looks like unsmoked braintan. Hawkbell trim. Narrow fringe-laced case is well-made. 45"L. 7" butt-end x 3.5" barrel end. Est. 175-295 **SOLD $175(00)**

SIOUX EARLY-STYLE BEADED QUIVER and BOWCASE
Lt. smoked comm. tan—looks like brain-tan. Lane-stitched beadwork at each end is white with classic concentric box motif in muted red w. hearts, gr. blue, and gr. yellow. Case openings laced navy trade wool; quiver support laced red wool covered dowel. Buckskin strap is both yellow and red ochred with lanes white beads and long fringes. Case ends have long fringes apx. 12"L. Bowcase is 41"L. Quiver 25"L. Exc. construction, lt. patina; could pass for old. Est. 450-750

CROW-STYLE OTTER BOW and ARROW QUIVER
Ornate beadwork drops are white, lt. blue, t. rose, rose w. hearts, t. emerald green, gr. blue, gr. yellow, t. dk. cobalt, and Crow pink inlaid with red wool. Quiver panels have additional lime green. All beadwork bound with navy Fox braid and white bead edging. Roll beaded quiver openings same colors. Otter fur quivers and lavish use of otter fur on carrying strap plus otter fur backed drops and decorative strips. Red wool carrying strap backed and bound with white muslin; beadwork and silk ribbon trim. Hardwood bow (45"L) with sinew-string and sinew-wrapped grip. Metal tipped feather fleched arrow. 33"L bow quiver. 23"L arrow quiver. Straps 9"W. Hangs apx. 48"L. Est. 1500-2500 **SOLD $1800(05)**

BOW and ARROW QUIVER
Comm. hide dark patina quiver with long fringes red ochred. Beaver fur trim has pink eye bead trim; horse-hair locks. 22"L. Bowcase apx. 43"L. Red painted triangles on "locust" wood bow; red and black seed bead wrapped grip with beaver fur; horse-hair at end. Sinew-strung. 45"L. Three arrows: "birch shafts" have wavy incised lines and green or red painted stripes near end. 26-27"L.; obsidian and chert knapped points; turkey feather fletching. Hand-written tag has full-description. Est. 425-650

CROW-STYLE RAWHIDE BEADED KNIFE CASE
Preston Miller Collection. Pastel geometric beadwork with typical white outlines; brass tack trim. Red-ochred and painted with green lines, red wool welted seam with white pony-bead edging. Bottom drop is bead-wrapped fringed red wool and twisted ochred buckskin thongs with alt. white and gr. blue bead trim. All sinew-sewn. Case 12"L + 12"L extensions. Est. 450-650

NO. PLAINS-STYLE BEADED KNIFE SHEATH and CAMP KNIFE
Preston Miller Collection. Stylized bear paw motif on top panel and striped side strip in lt. blue, t. cobalt, Crow pink, and gr. green. Heavy rawhide sinew-sewn case. Nice patina. 11.5"L x 4"W. Expertly made heavy duty camp knife has *J KITCHIN SHEFFIELD* stamp (see close-up photo). Wood handle has three brass rivets. 12.5"L. Blade 7.5"L. Est. 800-1200 Set

INTERMONTANE-STYLE LARGE BEADED/QUILLED KNIFE SHEATH

Made in Germany. Top and side panels are white, old rose w. heart, t. pony trader blue, Sioux green, corn yellow, and Crow pink. Sinew sewn. Red-ochred buckskin over rawhide. 3/8" brass tack borders. Thick buckskin side fringes apx. 14"L alt. wrapped with pale yellow quills and red yarn. Pony bead spacers. Sheath 12.5"L x 4.75"W. Est. 600-850

SIOUX-STYLE FULLY BEADED KNIFE SHEATH and KNIFE

Made in Czech Republic Pred. gr. blue with pale gr. yellow step triangles with t. cranberry, black and white. Lane-stitched and sinew-sewn. Aged tin cone fringe with dk. red dyed horsehair; same tin cone/horsehair on top corners and bottom on white wrapped quilled thong. Buckskin covered heavy rawhide. Expertly made. Includes 7" blade Green River old-style butcher knife. Twisted buckskin hanger. 10"L sheath x 3.5"W. Est. 250-400 **SOLD $250(04)**

SIOUX-STYLE FULLY-BEADED KNIFE SHEATHS

Each is lane-stitched in traditional designs. Unsmoked buckskin. ALL SINEW-SEWN. Top buckskin straps. (Left) White bkgrd. with gr. blue, red w. heart, black, and gr. yellow. Black bead-wrapped bottom buckskin drops. Case only 10"L x 3" top W. Est. 175-250 **SOLD $175(01)**
(Right) Colorful motifs in lt. blue, gr. yellow, red w. hearts, dk. cobalt, gr. yellow, and white. Rawhide insert. 9"L + buckskin drops 6"L. Est. 175-250 **SOLD $175(01)**

CHEYENNE-STYLE FULLY-BEADED KNIFE SHEATH

Top half is lane-stitched, using dk. cobalt, t. red, and mustard stacked triangle motif. Bottom half is appliqué stitched; thunderbirds dk. cobalt and t. red. Rawhide liner. Top bound with red trade wool. 5" side fringe and trade cloth welted seam. Brain tan smoked hide. Beautiful craftsmanship. 3.5"W x 11"L. Est. 275-400 **SOLD $325(98)**

TAHLTAN-STYLE DAG CASE

Red wool trade cloth is partially appliqué-beaded in white, porcelain white, gr. blue, and dk. navy design elements. Both strap and case edges are bound in blue twill braid. Strap has an overlay of black trade cloth early "sausage" motifs. Strap lining is mattress ticking; moose-hide case. 14.5"L x 4.25"W. 26" strap. Very authentically-made by an expert craftsman. Est. 300-400 **SOLD $300(99)**
See Duncan:164-167. This knife case was inspired by typical design motifs on two pictured knife cases.

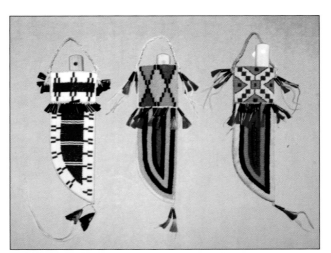

SIOUX-STYLE FULLY BEADED KNIFE SHEATHS WITH KNIVES.

Made in Czech Republic. Lane-stitched and sinew-sewn. Buckskin covered heavy rawhide. Each includes 7" Green River old-style butcher knife. Twisted buckskin hanger 11"L x 3.5"W.
(Left to right) White with red w. heart and pony trader blue. Tin cone fringes and side trim. Deer dew claws on bottom thong. Est. 250-400 **SOLD $250(04)**
Elegant colors are pred. Cheyenne pink with mustard and gr. blue step-triangles outlined in t. dk. cobalt. Aged tin cone fringe with varying shades of red-orange dyed horsehair; same tincone/horsehair on top corners and bottom. Est. 250-400 **SOLD $275(04)**
Sioux green, white, red w. hearts, and t. dk. cobalt; red horse hair tin cone fringes, side and bottom trim. Est. 250-400 **SOLD $250(04)**

PLATEAU-STYLE LARGE PARFLECHE KNIFE CASE
With old butcher knife (15"L). Very heavy rawhide with red, dk. red stripes, dk. green with heavy cobalt border and outline. Buckskin laced. Very convincing piece, looks old. 16"L x 5.75W. Est. 125-275 **SOLD $124(98)**

EARLY ASSINIBOINE OR EASTERN SIOUX-STYLE FULLY-BIRD QUILLED KNIFE CASE
Copy of original in Volkerkunde Berlin, Germany. Made in Germany. Beautiful soft earth tones of rust, gold, off-white, and dk. brown. Horiz. striped bands on bottom; vertical simple band on top. White sawtooth quilled top edging. Buckskin fringes (4"L) and top hanger are partially porky quill-wrapped in white and red. Hand-made tin cone decorated fringes. Nicely patinaed all-over. Rawhide insert also aged. 9"L. 2.5" top W. Est. 550-800 **SOLD $600 (01)**
For more info. see *American Indian Art magazine*, "Bird Quillwork" by Norm Feder, Summer '87, pp. 46-57.

IROQUOIS-STYLE QUILLED NECK POUCH WITH DAGGER.
This is a fabulous set: smoked buckskin case is sewn red quill-edged; central panel is *loom woven* in step-diamond pattern of red, white, purple, and yellow (1/2"W x 3.5"L); borders are 2-color (red and white) zig-zag; outline borders all done in white single-line; and there is one panel of simple band technique! Loom woven quillwork is the most time-consuming technique as well as the most sturdy. All sinew-sewn. Hand-made antler handle knife (6.25"L) with quill-wrapped drops; tin cone and red horsehair ends. Buckskin neck strap. 6.75"L case. Est. 500-750 **SOLD $500(00)**

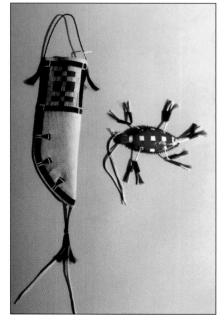

(Left) **NO. PLAINS-STYLE QUILLED KNIFE CASE**
Buckskin covered rawhide case has simple band sewn quilled panel in pale yellow, dk. red, and pale blue lane-stitch beaded border in "Montana" t. blue with white. Red quill-wrapped handle. and bottom drop with tin cones and dk. red horsehair. 10"L. 3"W. Pristine. Est. 350-500
(Right) **SIOUX-STYLE FULLY QUILLED LIZARD AMULET**
Simple band sewn red with white. Pony trader blue pony edge-beaded. "Legs and tail" are white quill-wrapped thongs with aged tin cones with red horsehair. Nice early style. Body 4.5"L. Est. 120-200 **SOLD $120(05)**

5. Toys, Dolls, and Miscellaneous Accessories

CROW-STYLE TOY HORSE WITH GEAR
Author's Collection. Fantastic beaded horse gear includes keyhole forehead ornament, bridle, martingale (neck collar), saddle blanket, high pommel riding saddle with stirrups, lance case, crupper, painted shield, saddle bags, cradle, and hoof covers! Incredible attention to detail. Coarse-weave wool covered toy horse (c.1925) on wooden platform with wheels. 22"H x 22"L. Est. 1800-2500

Allen Chronister made this to order. When he outfitted the horse with all of the paraphernalia, Preston said "BUT where are the beaded hoof covers?" They arrived in the mail the following week!

SIOUX-STYLE FULLY-BEAD-ED FEMALE DOLL
This doll was made by the late Domiani, who maintained a shop which produced large quantities of fully-beaded items similar to this doll. Spectacular pictorial dress has ledger drawing-style horses and Indians on horseback motifs on both sides. Solid red bkgrd. with white and mustard shoulder trim. Bottom hem border is narrow Sioux green and white with mustard stripes.

Horses are t. rose, mustard t. cobalt pink, and gr. blue. She sports a fully-beaded belt and knife case, moccasins, and leggings. Head and arms are smoked buckskin. Body is canvas. Black hair. Old-time beaded face. Tiny white bugle bead choker necklace with leather spacers and teeny brass beads looks like mini-hairpipes. 17.5"H. Est. 800-1250

SMALL 1830-STYLE DOLL and CRADLE
Buckskin cradle is pony-beaded in gr. blue, white, and black with red wool strip attachments. Doll is buckskin with red beaded wool dress, beaded leggings, and real hair. Cradle apx. 12"L. Est. 125-200 **SOLD $125(99)**

NEZ PERCE-STYLE DOLL CRADLE BOARD
Original in the Smithsonian Coll. from Nez Perce Res. c.1876.*. Red wool appliquéd top and hood with simple double star and stripes motif: white, gr. blue, pony trader blue, and forest green. Nice smoked buckskin. Old pink padre loop with abalone pendants across front. Muslin head "doll" with old calico wrap. Very close replica of the original, same size of 15"L. Exc. cond. Est. 450-700 **SOLD $400(00)**
   *See photo of original in *American Indian Art Magazine,* Autumn '99, p. 63.

NO. PLAINS-STYLE FULLY-QUILLED LIZARD AMULETS
Made in Czech Republic (Left) Sewn quilled top on buckskin; buckskin thong legs are quill-wrapped with red horsehair tin cones. Apx. 6"L. Red and white "picket fence" quillwork with red quill-wrapped legs and tail. Est. 125-195
(Right) Red, indigo, and white "zig-zag" quill-work with red and blue wrapped legs and tail. Est. 125-195
SOLD $125(02)

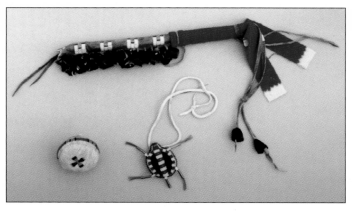

(Top to bottom) SNAKE MOTIF RATTLE
Face and body of snake is sewn quilled in simple band and single line technique: white, chestnut brown, and orange on red ochred buckskin. Handle of rattle is covered with red "saved list" wool. Dewclaw rattles hang from red-ochred thongs. Finely crafted. 14"L. 12" fringe at back. Est. 150-250 **SOLD $150(99)**

FULLY BEADED TURTLE AMULET
Lane-stitched, t. emerald green bkgrd. with red w. hearts, porcelain white, and pumpkin. Tin cones and red horsehair for legs, and tin cone tail. Bead edged. On buckskin neck strap. 2.75"L x 2"W. Est. 45-75 **SOLD $35(99)**

PARTIALLY BEADED BUCKSKIN BALL
Beaded on buckskin in gr. blue, gr. green, pumpkin, dk. cobalt, cranberry, and gr. yellow. Beaded strip around circumf.; cross on either side of ball. 3" diam. Est. 25-50

PAIR OF NO. PLAINS-STYLE WILLOW BACK RESTS
Bound with red saved list trade wool on top and sides. Canvas top loop. 17.5"W top, 29" bottom, 48"L. Nicely peeled willow, graduated small on top to larger on bottom. Est. 300-400 pair **SOLD $325(02)**

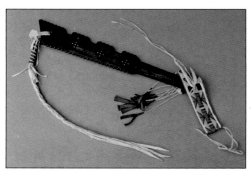

(Left) PRAIRIE-STYLE HORSE EFFIGY MIRROR BOARD
Made in Czech Republic. This style was carried by grass dancers. Dk. stained wood, carved and lead inlaid horse head (both sides) and weeping heart cut-out. Brass tack trim. Buckskin loop hanger. 3.25" sq. inlaid mirror. 10"H x 4.5"W. Similar to one described as "Iowa" in *American Indian Art* by Feder, p. 50. Est. 150-250 **SOLD $150(04)**.
(Right) NO. PLAINS-STYLE MIRROR BOARD
Made in Czech Republic. Dk. stained wood with horse head carved top, brass tack decorated. Inlaid round 5" diam. mirror. Buckskin thong hanger in drilled hole. 10.75"H. Est. 125-225

SIOUX-STYLE WOODEN QUIRT
with fully beaded wrist strap in lt. blue and gr. yellow, dk. cobalt and red w. heart. Lt. and dk. blue bead edged. Ends of strap have twisted fringe with tin cones and red cloth.
Hand-carved and stained wood embellished with brass tacks. Buckskin braid whip wrapped with red cloth. Expert workmanship. Wood 20"L x 2"H x 2.5"W. Strap 20"L x 2"W. Hangs apx. 48"L. Est. 350-500

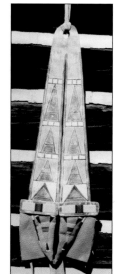

CROW-STYLE CRUPPER
Preston Miller Collection. Hand-made rawhide is painted in yellow and red ochre, olive green outlined in dk. cobalt. Smoked moose hide embellished with beadwork in typical pastel Crow colors. Beaded rectangular panels bordered with pale green silk; white edge bead trim. 35"L. Est. 500-750

BUFFALO HORN SPOON WITH QUILLWORK
This could be easily mistaken for an old piece! Carved handle portion wrapped with yellow and blue-grey plaited quillwork. Hole at end has same color quill-wrapped drops (6") with tin cones and blue-grey horsehair at ends. Thong handle. 8.75"L. Est. 200-350 **SOLD $275(00)**

CROW EARLY-STYLE PR. of CRUPPER ORNAMENTS
Preston Miller Collection. Rawhide with red and navy trade wool overlay bordered with white pony beads. Blacksmith-made iron spoon dangles make wonderful musical tinkle from movement. 11" total L. Est. 250-400

6. Painted Rawhide
Items (Parfleches)

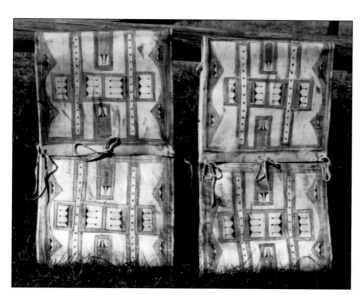

CROW-STYLE PARFLECHE BAG
Long buckskin side fringes (apx. 25"L). Flap and sides bordered with black wool. Bold yellow, red-orange, and green with heavy indigo outlines. Flap fringed with buckskin 2"L. Apx. 10" x 9". Est. 200-350 **SOLD $190(00)**

CHEYENNE-STYLE PAIR OF PARFLECHES
Expertly painted and patinaed. Heavy hand-scraped rawhide. Soft green and lt. red ochre with black outlines. Back is bordered with red ochre lines. Three sets of buckskin ties. 27"L x 15"W. Hard to tell from the real thing! Exc. cond. Est. 650-1500 pr. **SOLD $700(04)**

PLATEAU-STYLE FLAT PARFLECHE BAGS *Each is replicated from originals in Cheney-Cowles Museum, Spokane, WA.*

(Clockwise, left to right) Beautiful 30"L. white brain tan side fringes. Flap and front are apple green, pale yellow, and indigo with indigo outlines. Very subtle and nicely made of heavy rawhide. 9.5" x 10" bag. Est. 200-300 **SOLD $250(01)**
Unusual painted design of double-diamonds in faded indigo, soft green with red ochre vertical bands of stripes inside diamonds and along border. Red "saved list" wool bound on sides; buckskin laced. Med. weight rawhide. Interesting piece. 9" x 13.5". Est. 175-250
Elaborate geometric patterns in red ochre, pale yellow, faded indigo, and soft green outlined in faded indigo. Buckskin side lacing and flap ties. Flap is solid red ochre. Med. weight rawhide. 11" x 14". Est. 150-225

PLAINS/PLATEAU PARFLECHE SHOULDER BAG
Masterfully made to look old. Delicately painted in lt. red, green, yellow, and blue faded hues. Outlined in dk. brown. Long side and bottom fringes (12"L) fasten piece together. Wide buckskin strap hangs 20". Buckskin thong flap closure. Convincing patina. 13"W x 10"H x 5"D. Est. 400-750 **SOLD $400(04)**

(Left) **CROW-STYLE CYLINDRICAL PARFLECHE**
Beautiful clear colors: red with green and yellow; indigo outlines. Tops also painted with red inner circle and indigo sawtooth border. Brain-tan thong ties and laced fringes. Nice opaque rawhide. Great for a feather bonnet case. Apx. 20"L x 5" diam. Est. 175-275
(Right) **BLACKFEET-STYLE PARFLECHE CYLINDER**
Heavy rawhide with long thick brain-tanned fringes (23"L.). Design colors: green, red, and blue with fine black outlines. Design also on ends. Exc. craftsmanship. Est. 18"L x 6" diam. Est. 225-350
See Torrance, p. 188.

PAIR OF CROW-STYLE PAINTED PARFLECHE CASES
Red wool borders are laced with smoked buckskin fringes; 27"L on sides. Heavy rawhide painted in red ochre and dk. brown outlined with black ink. Brown patination. Bottom case is 13" square; top one is 10.5" x 6"H. Est. 250-400 **SOLD $225(02)**

SIOUX-STYLE PARFLECHE BOX
Heavy rawhide with muted painted designs in red ochre, yellow ochre, and indigo, outlined in black. Red wool bound laced corners. 20" x 9" x 10"W. Est. 250-400 **SOLD $250(99)**

More horse gear, made by Czech craftworkers, see pp. 175-176.

Pipes and stems made by Czech craftworkers, see p. 169.

Bibliography For Reproductions (Including Czech Repros)

AKICITA Early Plains & Woodlands Indian art from the collection of Alexander Acevedo. Exhibition Catalog. Los Angeles: Southwest Museum, 1983.

Conn, Richard. *Circles of the World.* Denver Art Museum, 1982.

Duncan, Kate. *Northern Athapascan Art.* Seattle: Univ. of Wash. Press, 1989.

Feest, Christian, editor. *Studies in American Indian Art.* Seattle: Univ. of Wash. Press, 2001.

Hanson, James. *Spirits in the Art.* Kansas City: Lowell Press, 1994.

Hungry Wolf, Adolf. *Blackfoot Craftworker's Book.* Skookumchuck, BC, Canada, 1983.

Orchard, Wm. C. *The Technique of Porcupine Quill Decoration among the Indians of North America.* New York: Museum of the American Indian, 1971.

Penney, David W. *Art of the American Frontier-The Chandler-Pohrt Collection.* Seattle: Univ. of Wash. Press, 1992.

Taylor, Colin. *The Plains Indians.* London: Salamander, 1994.

———. *Iho'lena.* Wyk auf Foehr, Germany: Tatanka Press, 1998.

Torrance, Gaylord. *The American Indian Parfleche.* Seattle: Univ. of Wash. Press, 1994.

Walters, Anna Lee. *Spirit of Native America.* San Francisco: Chronicle Books, 1989.

CROW-STYLE INCISED PARFLECHE
c.1850-style.
Tag reads *"Natural brown Buffalo rawhide. Hand incised."* Green wool welting. Intricate cross-hatched patterns on front, flap, and rawhide hanger. Apx. 8" x 10". Considerable patina. Est. 125-275 **SOLD $150(99)**

SIOUX-STYLE PARFLECHE
Masterfully made to look old! Beautiful design on flap and front is yellow ochre, red ochre, Sioux green, cobalt, and black outlined in black fine lines. Very heavy rawhide. Buckskin laced aged red "saved list" side binding. Thick buckskin ties. Expertly patinated. 12"W x 13"L. Est. 450-700 **SOLD $495(05)**

(Left) SIOUX-STYLE PARFLECHE BOX
Yellow ochre, red ochre, faded indigo, Sioux green outlined in black fine lines. Triangular cut out flap. Side lacing and flap ties are heavy smoked brain-tan. 14" x 8" x 5"D. Est. 225-325
(Right) SIOUX-STYLE PARFLECHE BOX
Same colors and configuration as previous box. Est. 225-325 **SOLD $200(01)**

IV. Photo Essay – The Story of "Indian Hobbyists" Around the World

Introduction:
What is an "Indian Hobbyist"?

According to William Powers, the term "hobbyist" first developed in the United States to describe non-Indians who "have a wide range of interest in American Indian subjects, …mainly arts and crafts, Indian dancing and singing. Although…regarded as a movement, hobbyism has no national organization but rather comprises independent groups organized at the local state and regional levels." Their main activity is giving powwows and dressing in Indian outfits, which are representative of the various North American tribes. (Powers 1988: 557) Colin Taylor adds that in Europe, "…the interest of a committed hobbyist generally begins at an early age…[and] as the interest develops, individuals often choose one or more activities such as craftwork, collecting, camping (generally in tepees), joining political support groups in aid of American Indians, lecturing, researching and writing." (Taylor: 1988, 562) Note that Taylor makes no mention of dancing, because the hobbyist movement in England didn't really get its start until the 1970s with the first appearance of Powwows there. Michael G. Johnson says that in the U.K. many independent researchers don't consider themselves "hobbyists" because the term "appeared to stem from U.S. Scout and summer camp organizations geared mainly to Indian dancing, singing and craftwork in the 1950s." (Johnson: pers. comm., June 2006) British Boys Scouts never developed Indian lore as they did in America, nor was there anything comparable to the Order of the Arrow. The Boy Scouts of America had a significant impact on the early development of hobbyism, which later spread to youth in other countries.

American Hobbyist Movement

How Did This Movement Begin and What Were the Influences?

Although hobbyism has prospered since the end of World War I, its origins can be found in various youth organizations[1] that were established around the turn of the 20th century in the United States.

Boy Scouts of America, est. 1910, was the largest of many youth organizations having genuine (or what were perceived to be real) American Indian themes. For the Boy Scouts, this Indian convergence was brought about by several of its co-founders, Daniel C. Beard, outdoorsman and author of children's books, and Canadian Ernest T. Seton, naturalist, illustrator, and author. (See further discussion of these men under "Books" below.)

The Boy Scouts learned Indian dancing, sign language, and how to make Indian outfits and other crafts, resulting in an Indian Lore Merit Badge in 1911. By 1915, the Order of the Arrow was founded, with initiation ceremonies based on Indian themes and Indian names for the local chapters. (Powers: 1988, 557) Some Boy Scout groups, such as the Koshare Boy Scout Troop 232 of La Junta, Colorado, founded in 1933, made Indian lore "the very foundation of their programs." The previous military-style terms were gradually replaced with Indian ones, i.e.; brave, chief, etc. "They dedicated themselves to the public performances of…vanishing Indian cultures." This group even started its own museum, featuring genuine Indian artifacts along with their own replicas. (Deloria 1998: 135-136). The Koshare Indian Dancers gained world-wide fame; a book, *Koshares,* was written about this organization by Jack Kelly in 1975. During the 1930s and 40s, scouting encouraged groups such the Koshares to concentrate more on scouting themes. Most groups compromised but others became independent and "became the nucleus of hobbyist groups." (Powers: 1988, 558) Today, however, the Koshares are still active within the Boy Scout "Order of the Arrow" program.

Also see Indian Dance Teams, pp. 141-142.

Books Influential To the Scouting Indian Lore Programs

ERNEST T. SETON *The Birch Bar Roll of Woodcraft* (1902), *Two Little Savages* (1903), *Book of Woodcraft and Indian Lore* (1912). Seton was a Canadian. In 1901, he started a youth organization called "Woodcraft Indians." He later introduced summer camps based on outdoor Indian lore. He and Beard, co-founders of the Boy Scouts, had a philosophical difference of opinion on basic issues and became rivals. By 1915, Seton had left the Boy Scouts, claiming that he was opposed to the "militaristic policies" of that organization.

DANIEL BEARD *The Boy Pioneers: Sons of Daniel Boone* (1909). Beard advocated pioneer ideals as a basis for youth reform rather than the model of the Indian chosen by Seton. He founded the "Sons of Daniel Boone" and wrote handicraft and wood lore articles for *Boy's Life.*

LESTER GRISWOLD wrote *Handicrafts* in 1925 and was a Boy Scout leader and instructor in handicraft. He was influential in the development of the Koshare Indian Dancers. He also was a consultant for national youth organizations, YMCA and YWCA, Campfire Girls, Boy Scouts, Girl Scouts, and 4-H Clubs.

ARTHUR C. PARKER *The Indian How Book* (1927).

RALPH HUBBARD *Handicraft* (1927) and *American Indian Crafts* (1935). Hubbard was a Montana rancher, school teacher, Boy Scout leader, Indian dancer, writer, and "hobbyist icon [who] personified the hobby's diverse origins." (Deloria: 1998, 138-139) He traveled throughout the United States and Europe producing Indian pageants that featured his special repertory of so-called "Indian" dances, i.e.; "Sioux Buffalo dance," "Great Plains War Dance," etc. (Powers: 1988, p. 558).

JULIAN H. SALOMAN *The Book of Indian Crafts and Indian Lore* (1928).

JULIA M. (BUTTREE) SETON *The Rhythm of the Red Man in Song, Dance and Decoration* (1930)

BERNARD S. MASON, Ph.D. *Woodcraft* (1939), *Dances and Stories of the American Indian* (1942), *The Book of Indian Crafts and Costumes* (1946). Mason was an authority on Indian crafts and lore, Indian dances, woodcraft, and camping. He left his job as a college professor to write and lecture on those subjects. During World War II, he wrote a survival manual for the U.S. Air Force (Mason: 1946).

W. BEN HUNT *Indian and Camp Handicraft* (1939), *Indiancraft* (1942), *The Golden Book of Indian Crafts and Lore* (1954), *The Golden Book of Indian Crafts and Hobbies* (1957). The national Scout magazine, *Boy's Life* featured articles by Ben Hunt (who was also known as "Lone Eagle"), making him widely popular with many boys who made their first Indian craft object through his detailed drawings. "Boy Scouts and youth groups from all over the world know of Ben Hunt." The major inspirations to Ben's life, which fostered his lifelong interest in Indians, were the tales his grandmother told him of the Indians of his native Wisconsin. Other strong influences were "Uncle" Dan Beard's craft articles in early *Boy's Life* and his interactions with Sioux Indians who came to Milwaukee with the Buffalo Bill Wild West Show.

Preston Miller's scrapbook from the 1950s, showing Ben Hunt articles on costume making. Left: 1955; Right: 1953.

The story goes that twelve-year-old Ben hung out in their tipi camp but was largely ignored until he suggested to the Indians that they all hunt rabbits in the park to eat for dinner! This strategy worked, so that not only did he share the hunt, the skinning, and the meal but he was honored as their special guest that night in the "Big Show." This resulted in a lifelong friendship and correspondence with "Standing Bear of the Wanblee Sioux." (Hunt: 1954, editors p. 4-5) When he died in 1970, a tribute appeared in *Powwow Trails* describing him as the "Father of the Indian Lore Hobby…he alone is probably responsible for influencing more people than anyone else in pursuing the study of the American Indian." (Vol. 7, April 1970, #1)

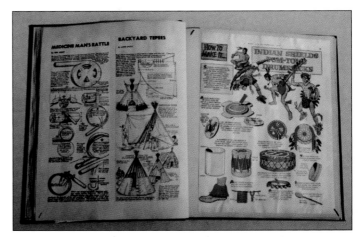

More Ben Hunt articles from Preston Miller's 1950s scrapbook. Left: Rattle and "tepee" construction. Right: Shields and "tom-toms" in 1957.

W. BEN HUNT and J. F. "BUCK" BURSHEARS *American Indian Beadwork* (1951). Jack F. "Buck" Burshears became a scout at age twelve in 1921, received his Eagle Badge in 1924 (the first one ever awarded in southeast Colorado), and was a Scoutmaster by 1930. According to Norm Feder, "he really got the 'bug' in 1930 when he was in college and worked with Lester Griswold and his Scouts." In 1933, he founded the now world famous Koshare dance group, who met in his basement for many years. "His whole life and energies have been devoted to the scouting program." (*American Indian Hobbyist*, Vol. II, #2, Sept. 1955) He fostered "…over 2000 boys who grew into young men as Koshares, and ensured a legacy that continues to this day, that has produced over 579 Eagle Scouts." He was the Scoutmaster of the Koshare Indian Dancers until his death in 1987. Buck was awarded the highest honors given to an adult Scouter—the Silver Beaver, the Silver Antelope, the Silver Buffalo, and the Distinguished Eagle Scout award, and was also awarded the President's Volunteers in Action Award by President Ronald Reagan. He was adopted by the Chippewa tribe and both he and his wife were also adopted into the Blackfeet tribe by tribal chairman, Earl Old Person.

The Koshares and Buck built the "Koshare Kiva" from the ground up; it opened in 1949 and is the home of the Koshares. It also houses Buck's extensive Indian artifact and craftwork collection. It includes an Indian art museum, theatre, recital hall, curio and handicraft shop, and dance practice area. The Koshare team became world famous and entertained all over the U.S.A., even at professional football game half-times! Their research center has thousands of books and slides, movies, records and tapes. (More about the Koshares on p. 157)

Hobbyist Magazines

When Norman Feder started *American Indian Hobbyist* in September 1954, it was a milestone in the development of the hobbyist movement. Feder was a former Boy Scout and wanted to see an alliance between independent groups and Boy Scouts. He became the catalyst that drew together all of the non-Indians who had similar interests in the ways and crafts of the American Indian. He spent his summers traveling around to Indian powwows, museums, and Indian study groups and eagerly reported all about these annual trips in the magazine. Feder wrote in an editorial in his newsletter, Jan. 1955: "Have you ever stopped to ask yourself, 'Why am I studying Indian Lore?'" Feder encouraged boys, whom he affectionately called Indian "bugs," to find a deeper meaning in learning about Indian religion, politics, and customs and not just crafts and dancing... "as an end to themselves...The American Indian has been chosen as an ideal to many youth movements; Ernest T. Seton's 'Woodcraft Indians,' the YMCA Indian Guide program, the Boy Scout Honor organization 'The Order of the Arrow,' etc. There is a good reason why these groups chose the Indian...[he] represents everything that our civilization considers to be good and wholesome." (Feder, 1955: Vol. I, #5, p. 1).

HOBBYIST MAGAZINE TIME-LINE:
American Indian Hobbyist (AIH) – founder/editor Norman Feder, Sept. 1954-Dec. 1959 (Los Angeles, CA)
American Indian Hobbyist – new editor Richard R. McAllister, Jan. 1960-Jan. 1961 (Alton, Ill.)
American Indian Tradition – (new name) Rich McAllister, 1961-63 quit publication (Alton, Ill.)
Powwow Trails – Wm. K. and Marla Powers, April 1964-1970. (New Jersey)
The Singing Wire – founder/editor Ty Stewart (CIHA newsletter), Jan. 1967-Jun 1969 (Panorama City, CA)
American Indian Crafts & Culture – (new name) editor/publisher Ty Stewart, Sep 1969-1974 (Panorama City, CA) He moved the magazine to Tulsa, OK in May 1970.
Moccasin Tracks – editor Jerry Smith (CIHA publication), Sep 1975-March 1986 (Corona, CA). New editor Kaysee Tsuji, April 1986 (Lakewood, CA) quit publication after Jan./Feb. 1987 issue.
Whispering Wind – (LIHA publication up to 1980) founder/editor Jack B. Heriard, Oct. 1967-present (Folsom, LA)

Indian Dance Teams

Numerous dance teams sprung up around the country; most were initially under the auspices of the Boy Scouts Order of the Arrow program. As they gained expertise and expanded their performances outside of scouting activities, many dance groups broke away to

gain more independence. (Also see Koshare Indian dancers, pp. 139-140).

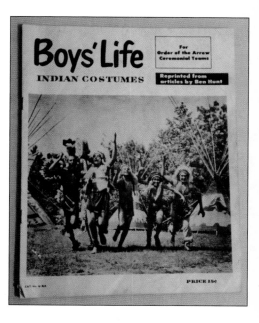

Special *Boy's Life* issue for the "Order of the Arrow" ceremonial dance teams, featuring illustrated articles by Ben Hunt. Undated issue, c.1950.

Each month, starting with its first issue in 1954, *American Indian Hobbyist* magazine featured an Indian dance group. In that same year, Norm Feder and Win Fairchild started the National American Indian Dance Association.

In Dec. 1954, *American Indian Hobbyist* featured the Baltimore Red Shield Boy's Club, formed in 1936 by the Salvation Army as a member of Boy's Clubs of America. "The Indian group sets its aims beyond making costumes and learning dances, as it strives to build leaders with the club, the camp and the community." Their summer home was Camp Puh'tok, where the Indian Dancers, who were also counselors, performed at special Indian Council fires. "This small group was destined to grow to surprising proportions," and by 1940 they were asked to perform at the New York World's Fair. In 1950, they performed at the Boy Scout Jamboree at Valley Forge, Pennsylvania. In the 1950s, they did over one hundred shows a year. (*American Indian Hobbyist*, Vol. I #4)

Another one of the groups featured in *American Indian Hobbyist* was the "Shupeda Indian Society of Interpretive Dancers" from Toledo Ohio, which was formed in 1948 at Camp Miakonda (Scout Camp.) (Vol. I, #8, April 1955) This group was originally associated with the Boy Scouts, but became independent soon after Benson Lanford joined them c. 1952. Thom Meyers, who now owns "Buffalo Chips" Trading Post in Billings Montana, was also a member of this group. Benson says, "We did performances in the area including dancing at the weekly council fires at the Boy Scout Camp Miaconda during the summer. We also attended some of the larger Ben Hunt-type Indian lore gatherings, one at Janesville, Wisconsin, and a couple at Jackson, Michigan. We were quite active for a number of years." Later Benson joined the Wakinyan Dancers in Detroit (means "Thunder and

Lightning" in Lakota). Another such group at the time was the "Ogle Wanagi Dancers" (Ghost Shirt Dancers) from Cleveland, Ohio. These groups also attended a large powwow sponsored by Dick Berry from Springfield Ohio. (Benson Lanford, pers. comm., 2006)

Shupeda Indian Dancers, c.1955. The meaning of "Shupeda" was understood to be Omaha for "White Buffalo." Benson Lanford is third from left, holding a feather staff. *Photo courtesy of Benson Lanford.*

In the early 1950s, Tyrone Stewart was active in Win Fairchild's Boy Scout "White Hawk Dancers" in southern California, but after his troop was regularly passed over for Order of the Arrow membership during a three year period, they formed their own independent dance team called the "War Chiefs." Later, his group was "tapped out" to become members of the Walika Lodge (a San Fernando Valley Council) and the "War Chiefs" became the majority of this very active Order of the Arrow dance team. (Ty Stewart, pers. comm. 2006)

Another dance team is described in a photo essay on "The Tuckahoe Indian Dancers" by Preston Miller in *Four Winds New Guide to Indian Artifacts*, pp. 189-192. Preston was a member of this Order of the Arrow Dance Team, which started in 1945 in York, County, Pennsylvania. "In 1954, our dance team traveled to the O. A. National Convention in Laramie, Wyoming where we won the National Champion Indian Dancing competition. We performed shows for schools, carnivals, T.V., etc. Eventually, we separated from the Boy Scouts because they frowned on our performances to groups outside the Boy Scouts. The new group became know as 'The Susquehannock Indian Dancers.'"

The Hunka Indian Dancers, part of Scout Troop 235, were formed in San Antonio, Texas in 1960. This was the only "Old Time" group in TIHA (Texas Indian Hobbyist Association) at the time. By 1962, they had split from the scouts and formed their own group sponsored by the local Optimist Club. (TIHA Powwow Program, 1965.) While in the OA in Texas, Jerry Farenthold met The Hunka Indian Dancers at an event and noticed how great their outfits looked, as opposed to the simple Boy Scout kits. The Hunkas really did their research. When he saw their old-style outfits he thought—"that's the way Indians really looked." "It was an epiphany that changed my life," noted Jerry. "The Hunkas had a sister group—The Red Shield Dancers in Baltimore, Maryland [see preceding page]—and one of our members, Jerry Garman, who was stationed in the service in San Antonio at the time,

was also a Red Shield. Fellow member Gene Marchesi also came to visit and taught us much more. Later Don Eberhardt, whose parents owned the Western Trading Post in Denver, was also stationed in San Antonio and he taught us much more and became an advisor to the group." They also learned singing, dancing, beadwork, quillwork, etc. Gordon and Janice Collins were their primary leaders, inspiration, and teachers; the group met at the Collin's tipi for craft sessions and dance practice twice weekly. (Jerry Farenthold, pers. comm., July 2006)

Hunka Indian Dancers, 1965. Back row (top left to right) are Jerry Garman, advisor; Harvey Skinner, director, the first bonnet wearer; Gordon Collins, advisor, second bonnet wearer. Jerry Farenthold is on Garman's right, back row. Janice Collins is in the second row, second woman from left, with braids and dress and stands in front of her husband, Gordon. Ron Rardin, advisor, is seen far right, third row in front of Collins, left. The elected Chief, Jim Skinner is at the far left, third row. *Photo courtesy of Jerry Farenthold.*

State Indian Hobbyist
Powwows and Organizations

A yearly gathering of California hobbyists, called the Witayapi (meaning "friendship" in Sioux), was started by Win Fairchild in 1954. There were about 350 participants the first year. Other similar annual Powwows sponsored by independent hobbyist groups started up in New York (Monroe Powwow), Cleveland (Oglewanagi Powwow), the "Detroit" Powwow, and Baltimore (Red Shield Powwow). (Powers, 560)

"White Indian Fairs and get-togethers seem to be starting up all over the country in an effort to keep pace with the growing interest in Indian lore," wrote John G.

Lotter in an article published in *American Indian Hobbyist Magazine* (Vol. II, #2, Sept. 1955). For example, Wa-Be-Ski-Wa (meaning "white" in Chippewa), the Indian Fair Association, was formed in the Midwest by a group of men interested in Indian dancing and Indian lore.

CIHA (California Indian Hobbyist Association) was organized by Ty Stewart and his wife Peggy in 1967. (Ty Stewart, pers. comm., April 2006) By this time, the Witayapi was held bi-annually and there were four such state groups in operation in Texas (TIHA), Florida (FIHA), and Louisiana (LIHA). (*Powwow Trails,* Vol. IV, #4, Sept. 1967, p. 6)

The origins of TIHA were in 1956 at an annual gathering of "interested persons in Indian Lore" at an Indian Exposition in Huntsville, later called an Indian Festival when relocated to Brenham. As it gained momentum, the name was changed to TIHA; the first powwow under that name was held in Austin in 1964. (TIHA Powwow program, Fort Worth, TX.: 1966) LIHA (Louisiana Indian Hobbyist Association) was formed on the model of CIHA and TIHA. Powers adds that others arose in the mid-60s in Pennsylvania, Greater New York, and New England based on the successful model of TIHA. (Powers, p. 561)

Suzie Bousquet at the 1980 "Wit" wearing beadwork she has made.

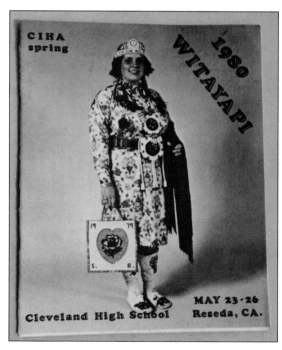

CIHA Spring 1980 Wityapi program cover featuring princess Suzie Bousquet. The entire Bousquet family was actively involved in CIHA; Suzie's father Chuck, mother Pat, and sister Terry were all on the early staff of Moccasin Tracks in the 1970s. Her sister Terry Bousquet was Witayapi princess in 1976. Brother Rick was an active dancer in CIHA; as a veteran he wore a dance outfit with American flag motifs that he beaded.

Putt and Jill (Redmond) Thompson at a Midwest Hobbyist Powwow in the early 1980s. The couple met through their activities in TIHA (Texas Indian Hobbyists Association). Jill Redmond and her sisters Peggy and Linda were members of the Latonka Indian Dancers of Houston, Texas in the mid-60s. Putt and Jill moved to Montana and established Custer Battlefield Trading Post on the Crow Reservation.

The Ikpoos, a non-affiliated informal group sharing interests in Northwest Coast as well as Plateau and Plains tribes, was started in the Seattle, Washington area in the early 1950s. Norm Feder wrote about the "Ickpoos" in 1956 as editor of the *American Indian Hobbyist*, Vol. III, #1, p. 8: "This group I feel is just about the best of any group I've seen from the standpoint of the interest of their members, the skill and beauty of their crafts and costumes, and their ability to reproduce dances. All this in spite of the fact that they have no formal organization and no group name." Bill Holm admits to starting the group along with Donn Charnley, who was a camp counselor on the San Juan Island in Washington State. Bill says that the "pre-Ikpoo" idea came about when Bill was a cub scout camp counselor in the 1940s. Later, the real Ikpoos developed a pledge, a silly dance, and initiation. This unconventional group didn't want to have the restrictions of rules. It may have been a silly name but the concept fostered creativity due to the group's relaxed atmosphere and lack of rules, hierarchies, restrictions, or a "grade" like in school. Bill says that the one rule they did have was that "ALL ARE CHIEFS." The group took their commitment to the study of Indian culture very seriously, through making "artifakes" and reproducing dances and songs. There was competition amongst them to do their best through different "Ikpoo Chieftanships." They continued meeting into the 1960s but Bill still considers himself to be an Ikpoo today, as many members still keep in touch. The small membership initially included Louis Jull, Michael Johnson, Larry Coffey, and later Richard Conn and Roger Ernesti. (Bill Holm, pers. comm., March 2006; also see "Introducing the Ikpoos" by Shari McEachern, *American Indian Hobbyist*, Vol. V, #5, Jan. 1959 pp. 51-52).

Although no national organization was "ever formed, national events were held, mainly due to the efforts of Tyrone H. Stewart." He organized the first National Indian Hobbyist Powwow in Denver, Colorado in 1969. The 2nd National Powwow in Sedalia, Missouri in 1972 had over 1000 participants (600 dancers) (Powers, 561). Others have been in Bedford, Indiana, and Danville, Illinois. They are held every four years—usually in the Midwest. (Farenthold, pers. comm., July 2006) Also see http://www.nationalpowwow.com.

They All Started as Hobbyists!

BILL HOLM is a prolific craftsman, painter, educator, author, and lecturer, and continues to be an inspiration and the "guru" for contemporary Indian studies. According to his wife Marty: "Bill became fascinated with the costumes and dances of the Indians of the Northern Plains…when he was a boy living in Roundup, Montana." His father taught him how to shoot and hunt. Three years later, his family moved to Seattle, where the Coast and Plateau exhibit at Washington State Museum "stimulated his interests in their dances, ceremonies and beliefs." (AIH 1958: Vol 4, #5-6, p. 48-49) Bill was an art teacher when he started writing articles in AIH—the now famous capote diagrams in Sept 1956, followed by "Plains Indian Cloth Dresses" in AIH Feb 1958. He was a founder of the "Ikpoos," a Seattle-based organization of people interested in Indians. (See above) He is the former curator of the Burke Museum and professor emeritus of art history at the University of Washington in Seattle. He has written numerous books about Northwest Coast Art.

Bill says that, "my first introduction to Ben Hunt was in 1937 in my Jr. High School library." There he found copies of the *Boys' Life* magazine where Ben Hunt's articles first appeared. Some of them were later incorporated into Hunt's first book, *Indian and Camp Handicrafts* (1939). "I think the first thing that I made was a roach," says Bill. "I still have the breastplate I made out of rolled paper!" However, he believes that Seton's *Two Little Savages* is the most universally read book that has influenced hobbyists around the world. He still has his first copy from the 1930s. (Holm, pers. comm., March 2006) On the last page of *Sun Dogs & Eagle Down,* a book commemorating Bill Holm's paintings, Lloyd Averill relates that in the summer of 1934, nine-year-old Bill discovered *Two Little Savages* on a bookshelf at his grandparents' farm in North Dakota. This is a story of two young Canadian white boys with an avid interest in outdoor life. Bill was mesmerized by the first paragraph and it would seem that "he never got over it." (Brown & Averill, pp. 186-187)

> "Yan [one of the characters in the book] was much like other 12 year old boys in having a keen interest in Indians and wildlife, but he differed in most in that he never got over it. Indeed, as he grew older, he found yet a keener pleasure in storing up the little bits of woodcraft and Indian lore that pleased him as a boy." (Seton, New York: Grosset & Dunlap, 1903, p. 15).

Bill says that "I wouldn't be where I am today if it had not been for my HOBBYIST background." Contrary to the opinion of many others in the academic world, Bill is comfortable with the term and proud to call himself a hobbyist. (Holm, pers. comm., April 2006) He believes that a profound learning experience results from the making of "artifakes," giving the craftsman unique insight and perception into that culture on many levels.

The following excerpts are from a paper Bill Holm gave at a conference in Los Angeles of the American Anthropological Association in 1978:

> My feelings on the usefulness of artifaking are very strong…I came into the academic world through this back door of making things—things that interested me. These things we called "artifakes," a term I first heard from Dick Conn about 30 years ago. I was not a "scholar," although my interest in Native American material culture was serious and intense. I was an "Indian Hobbyist" of the classic type. But something came out of this artifaking beyond the personal fun—the discovery that I was beginning to understand some things about certain aspects of Northwest Coast Indian art that had apparently escaped the attention and the understanding of others who had studied it, analyzed it and published on it before…
>
> Some kinds of artifaking have had a long history of usefulness in anthropological circles. Replicating stone tools makes a lot of sense to archaeologists who are trying to reconstruct whole cultures on the basis

of minimal evidence...But artifaking as an investigative technique in other areas of material culture has had less acceptance. Indian hobbyists, the principal practitioners, have been generally held in low regard by professionals, although there are more than a few ex-hobbyists among them. But because of their single-minded approach to artifaking, many of these hobbyists have acquired extremely detailed knowledge of the material they have chosen to work with. They often have clear and sometimes profound perception of the design principles and stylistic relationships involved. (Holm: 1978)

NOTE: It is important to keep in mind that Holm's original concept of "artifaking" is replication in its purest sense that is made for personal or educational purposes; not aged or antiqued nor used for commercial or fraudulent purposes, which can be the connotation in modern times. (See pp. 10-15 for further discussion on "artifake detection.") Also see a photo of Bill and one of his paintings in *Four Winds Guide to Indian Trade Goods and Replicas,* p.5.

NORMAN FEDER's interest in Indian culture began with his childhood in the multiethnic environs of Brooklyn and the Bronx in New York City, where he spent consider-able time in the local museums. His family moved to Los Angeles, where he started high school and later went to UCLA (Feest, p. 2-3). After leaving the army, Norman worked for Win Fairchild, owner of Fairchild Woodcraft, an Indian crafts store in Los Angeles. In 1954, not only did he start the *American Indian Hobbyist* magazine (see details above), but he and Win started the National American Indian Dance Association. His "...efforts with the *American Indian Hobbyist* magazine caught the attention of Dick Conn, [who was] the curator of Indian Art at the Chappelle House in Denver at the time." He went to Denver as Dick Conn's assistant, which led to the job as curator of American Indian Art at the Denver Art Museum. (Ty Stewart, pers. comm., April 2006) He also served as an assistant curator for the Museum of the American Indian, Heye Foundation, New York City, for one year in 1960. In 1961, he returned to the Denver Art Museum, where he served as curator until his retirement in 1973. Norm Feder's first major book, *American Indian Art* (1971), gave credence to the value of Indian artifacts viewed as works of art rather than solely for their ethnographic value. This publication coincided with the exhibit at New York's Whitney Museum where Feder was guest curator. Later, in 1977, he served as editorial consultant to *American Indian Art* magazine and was a prolific contributing writer to that publication until his death in 1995.

Bill Holm's studio in Seattle, Washington, 2001. His articulated mannequin, SuperKen, is wearing an original Nez Perce ermine bonnet that was featured in this book's companion volume, *Four Winds New Guide to American Indian Artifacts,* p. 21. On the back wall are some of the many replicas Bill has made, including a quill-wrapped moose hair blanket strip and war shirt.

REGINALD AND GLADYS LAUBIN devoted their lives to the preservation and interpretation of American Indian dances and culture. They wrote *The Indian Tipi* in 1957, a classic book that is still used by anyone who has ever put up a tipi. *Indian Dances of North America,* 1976, was followed in 1980 by *American Indian Archery*. The couple were popular performers of Indian dances and wrote articles for hobbyist magazines, etc.

JAMES HOWARD started dancing at age twelve and gradually went to tribal dances across the Plains and Woodlands. He published many scholarly articles while on the powwow circuit, and eventually became an anthropologist and professor at The University of No. Dakota. (Deloria 1998: p.140) He was a contributing writer and associate editor of *American Indian Hobbyist*. (See further references to Howard's work as an anthropologist on pp. 109-110 of this book.)

Grayhorse 1974. (Left to right) Ty Stewart, Wilbur Waters (Ponca, deceased), and anthropologist Dr. James Howard. "James Howard was a great supporter of hobbyist functions. We became friends after I moved to Oklahoma and enjoyed several events together. Jim was criticized by some anthropologists for associating with hobbyist dances." (Ty Stewart, pers. comm., July 2006) *Photo courtesy of Ty Stewart.*

WILLIAM K. POWERS made annual visits to the Pine Ridge reservation in So. Dakota in 1948 studying and performing Lakota music and dance. He wrote articles about this experience in *American Indian Tradition* between 1960-62 and was also an associate editor for the magazine. (Ibid: 139-140) He was Professor of Anthropology at Rutgers University and director of a graduate program in N. American Indian studies, which he founded in 1986. By 1990, he had written twelve books and over two hundred articles on American Indian culture, including *American Indian Art* magazine. (Powers, Wm. K., *War Dance,* Tucson: Univ of AZ Press, 1990)

RICHARD G. CONN, born and educated in Washington State, received an MA from the University of Washington in 1955. Later, he became the curator of the Denver Art Museum and published many fine material culture books. In 1959, he took a job as curator at the Eastern Washington State Historical Society. He returned to the Denver Art Museum in 1971 while Norm Feder took a sabbatical, and took over the curator's position again after Norm's retirement in 1973. When he was a member of the Ikpoos, Conn said that he was "...especially interested in craft techniques and making 'Artifakes.'" Bill Holm says that Conn "coined" the term "artifake," c. 1950. (See Bill's comments on page 144.) Conn took a position on the editorial board of *American Indian Hobbyist* in

1960 and was a frequent contributor (AIH 1960: Vol. 6, #7-8, p. 78 and 97). He was also on the editorial board of *Whispering Wind* and wrote articles for *American Indian Art* magazine.

TYRONE H. STEWART says that he first became "hooked" on Indian lore when he saw the 1938 movie *Last of the Mohicans,* starring Randolph Scott. Living in southern California, he was a "regular" at Fairchild Woodcraft (Indian craft store), which is where "Win [Fairchild] gave me a subscription form for *American Indian Hobbyist Magazine,* which had just published Vol. 1, #1." Later, "...at an Order of the Arrow gathering, I saw what a wonderful transformation had taken place in the O.A./Hobbyist world, strictly due to Norm Feder's efforts with A.I.H. Although I had a long time interest in Indians, this was really the beginning for me. I went to 'Witayapi' and fell in love with singing Ponca songs that were led by Jim Steiner, Mike Tucker, and Hans Duddenhaus...For years I had been a part of Win's dance group while in scouting." (See "Indian Dance Teams," page 142, for more of Ty's personal experience.) Ty and his wife Peggy organized the Californian Indian Hobbyist Association in 1967, "along with Pat Tearney, Richard Ely, Jerry Smith, et al. We planned workshops and dance sessions...and we grew by leaps and bounds. Mike Tucker, my former AICC partner, was in the Navy now, and headed for Vietnam. Jim Steiner organized a 'War Dance' for Mike (I did most of it) and sent for Lamont Brown and Sylvester Warrior to sing while they were in L.A. I recorded them for four hours, singing, translating, and explaining Ponca songs. The experience of War Dance or Hethuska was 'where it was at' for me, so I focused my passion. I got permission from Sylvester to form the Hethuska Drum or 'Fireplace' in California. That began in September, 1968." (Ty Stewart, pers. comm., April 2006)

Sylvester Warrior, Ponca. Nudahonga of Ponca Hethuska at Grayhorse Ilonska, 1972. At that time, the Ponca Hethuska was seated officially at Grayhorse. (Ty Stewart, pers. comm., July, 2006) *Photo courtesy of Ty Stewart.*

Ty started *The Singing Wire*, a CIHA magazine, as founder/editor in January 1967. The name was changed to *American Indian Crafts & Culture* in September 1969; he moved the magazine from Panorama City, California to Tulsa, Oklahoma in May 1970. Ty says that he was asked to chair the first National Pow Wow in Denver in July 1969, and later in Springfield, Missouri in 1972. (Pers. comm., April 2006) Wm. Powers credits Ty Stewart as being the principal motivator for starting this national event (Powers: 561).

Ty Stewart and son Marc at Ponca Hethuska, 1983. "Marc is ready to be seated in the society. Abe Conklin was the Nudahonga. Also in attendance were members from all of the non-Indian Hethuska groups: California Hethuska, Texas Lonestar Wardance Society, Whitebear Society, Chicago, Illinois, and the A.I.S. Wardance Society from New England." (Ty Stewart, pers. comm., July 2006) *Photo courtesy of Ty Stewart.*

DENNIS LESSARD's interest in Indian lore began in 1951; he was active on the Powwow scene on the East Coast and Detroit. In 1957, he started Del Trading Post. He received his Indian name "Hohu Ogle" (Bone Shirt) at Pine Ridge reservation in 1960. In 1961, he managed the Great Lakes Indian Museum in Cross Village, Michigan and in 1964 married Rosemary and spent time living with a Rosebud Sioux family. (*Powwow Trails* 1965: Vol. 2, #2) The family later moved to Mission, So. Dakota on the Rosebud reservation, where Dennis ran his trading post and amassed a large Indian collection. He was a frequent speaker at the Plains Indian Seminar at the Buffalo Bill Historical Center in Cody, Wyoming. He and his wife Rosemary also have written many material culture articles for hobbyist magazines and *American Indian Art* magazine.

BENSON LEE LANFORD is a collector, dealer, writer, speaker, lecturer, appraiser, consultant, and moderator. When Benson was in fifth grade he presented a little program to his class in imitation of Indians he had seen dancing at Wisconsin Dells. As a result of his performance, he was asked to join the Shupeda Indian Dancers. (See photo and description under "Indian Dance Teams, p. 142.) He did a good deal of craftwork and some beadwork at the time, including "the widest woven beadwork belt

of anyone in our dance group." During his high school years, after the Shupedas disbanded, Benson began attending powwows and Indian events throughout the Great Lakes area. In 1959, after graduating from high school, he met Milford Chandler and Dennis Lessard through the Wakinyan Indian Dancers based in Detroit. After graduating from college in 1965, Benson moved back to Detroit and became more actively involved with the Wakinyan Dancers. He solidified his friendship with Milford Chandler, who was a "mentor to a number of us, including Dennis Lessard and Ben (Bentley) Stone." Chandler moved to California in 1973 and Benson joined him later that year and was in daily association with him until Chandler's death in 1981. Since 1973, Benson has been moderator for five years as well as a presenter of twelve papers at the annual Plains Indian Seminar at the Buffalo Bill Historical Center in Cody, Wyoming. He is a frequent speaker at American Indian conferences. He has a total of 112 articles in print in various publications, including 11 on moccasin construction and identification. He is an editorial reviewer and has written articles for *American Indian Art Magazine.* He is currently a consultant for Christie's international auction house, American Indian Dept. (Pers. comm., May 2006)

"An image of Floyd Slocum (oldest dancer of our dance group in Toledo, Ohio) painting my face—front cover of the Sunday pictorial section of the TOLEDO BLADE, Oct. 10, 1954. I had just turned thirteen at the time. I beaded the white buffalo head (single outline) on the breechclout...and made the fiber hair roach, feather arm and wrist bustles, headband, and gun stock war club worn in this photograph." Benson says that in his childhood play he "NEVER was a 'cowboy'...ALWAYS an INDIAN!" *Photo courtesy of Benson Lanford.*

Benson Lanford, right, holding an old c.1900 Plateau vest at the MCPPP Conference in Rapid City, So. Dakota in 2005. On the left is Andrezej Gussman, wearing a Plateau-style vest that he made from his original design. He is Polish and his wife Marie is Blackfeet, from the Blackfeet Res. in Montana where they reside.

CRAIG D. BATES is an author, prolific craftsman, and Curator of Ethnology at Yosemite National Park. He is an active member of CIHA. He is known for his efforts to help preserve northern Californian Indian culture, especially the ceremonies and material culture. He has expert knowledge on historic California baskets. He has been a frequent contributor to *American Indian Art* magazine and has also written numerous articles for *Moccasin Tracks* and other publications. (See *Four Winds Guide to Trade Goods,* pp. 173-175 for replica shields all made by Craig.)

LOUIS (Lars Roald) JULL served as art editor for *Powwow Trails* starting in 1967. Prior to this position, he also illustrated articles for *The American Indian Hobbyist* and *American Indian Tradition.* He joined *Singing Wire* as an artist in September 1970 and continued there until December 1973. He was born and raised in Seattle, Washington, where he lives with his wife Mary Lou, a Umatilla, Walla-Walla, Yakima Indian from Pendleton, Ore. Louis was a member of the local hobbyist group the Ikpoos (See p. 144). He loves to photograph Powwows and he has amassed a huge archive of photos and videos of Indian people from the Northwest and Plateau.

started work at Fairchild's Woodcraft Indian Store in North Hollywood, California. He assisted Win Fairchild, who was involved with Boy Scout dance teams at that time (see comments under Ty Stewart, who was also a member of this team, p. 146). As an active member of CIHA, Hans started a singing group, The 49ers, that same year.

He is a fine painter of realistic Indian portraits, and one of his Indian paintings is on the cover of *Singing Wire* (Vol. III, #5, 1969). He is well known as the ultimate craftsman because of his need for perfection! "…if his workmanship doesn't meet his exact standards, he'll rip it up and start again." ("Hobbyists You Should Meet," *American Indian Crafts & Culture,* Vol. III, #9, Nov. 1969, p. 5). His feather bonnets were superb (see photos), but he focused on beadwork after the law made it impossible to make or keep eagle feather bonnets. Hans has also made one of the most beautiful capotes we have ever seen, with every stitch hand sewn (see photo). He has consigned many superb beaded items for sale in our store that were pictured in *Four Winds Guide to Trade Goods*—quirts (p. 178), beaded knife sheaths (p. 162, upper right-hand corner), pipe bag (bottom half, p. 147), tack belt used in the movie *Maverick* (p. 138), his personal "old" mocs (upper right, p. 137) are just a few examples.

Louis Jull wearing a vest that he made, viewing a similar one at the Burke Museum in Seattle in 1985.

Hans Duddenhaus in Ojai, California in 1971, shown dancing and posing with a complete Powwow outfit that he made. Note the beautiful full trailer bonnet he is wearing. *Photos courtesy of Hans Duddenhaus.*

HANS DUDDENHAUS emigrated to the USA from Germany in 1931. His interest in Indians started while he was in Germany, where he saw an Indian show as part of a circus. He was a speed skater on the US Olympics team in 1939 (but due to World War II the Olympics were cancelled) and also tri-state archery champion. In 1944, he and his bride Betty bicycled from New York to California. (She took the train after two days!) Once there, Hans

Hans, holding a lance that he made, stands with the authors in front of their trading post in 2001.

Hans and the author pose in front of his Porsche, December 1988. Hans wears his capote with a fully-beaded belt that he made.

JACK HERIARD is publisher/editor of the longest running American Indian crafts magazine, *Whispering Wind.* The magazine has "evolved from a hobbyist publication to one devoted to American Indian studies." Today, the majority of readership is Indian, according to readership polls, and goes beyond the exclusive hobbyist interest. "I got my start through scouting, Order of the Arrow," notes Jack. "After attending a TIHA powwow in 1964, I was hooked. We began LIHA in 1967, at which time we hosted the first LIHA powwow." There have been two LIHA powwows annually since that first year. Jack started *Whispering Wind* as a newsletter for LIHA. He took over ownership in 1980, so there is no longer an affiliation with any hobbyist group. Next year will be the 40th anniversary for the magazine, which is a remarkable achievement given the changes that the hobbyist movement has undergone over the years. Jack has been able to successfully make the adjustment to a broader market. (Pers. comm., June 2006)

Detail of the beaded rosette on the capote.

Feather Dance Champions, Louisiana Heritage Assn. Powwow, 1976. (Left to right) Jack Heriard, Forest Luc, and Ron Bell. Jack did the featherwork and beadwork on his dance outfit. *Photo courtesy of Jack Heriard.*

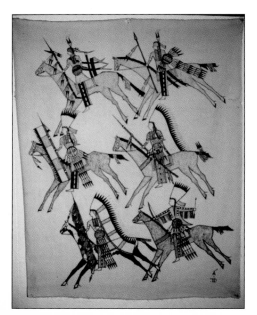

Pictographic muslin painted by Hans. *Author's collection.*

149

PETER DURKIN is currently the associate editor and a frequent contributing writer to *Whispering Wind* magazine. Growing up in western New York state, his earliest recollection of Native Americans was observing Seneca Indians in and around Allegheny State Park. This was an era of both movie and television westerns, and he always identified with the Indians and never the cowboys. "When my father was transferred to Pittsburgh, Pennsylvania, in 1957, I enjoyed ever more exposure to Indian culture through the Carnegie Museum and their impressive collection, which I visited often…While I did join Boy Scouts, our troop eventually disbanded due to a lack of adult leadership, so scouting was not a major factor in my Indian experience." In the 1980s, Peter read in a Houston newspaper about a group of Texans that attended a national powwow and the success they enjoyed at that event. This article got him in touch with the Texas Indian Hobbyist Association (TIHA), which he found very supportive to his growing interests in the hobby. He was especially interested in tipis and it was through TIHA that he first met Mr. and Mrs. Gordon Collins and Don Walske. Their tipis set such a high standard that he became determined to learn more, and to one day have an outstanding lodge. "I actually made my first tipi, following step-by-step, the classic Reginald and Gladys Laubin book, *The Indian Tipi*. While I am not a craftsman, I did meet Bill and Kathy Brewer, who, through their creative genius, helped me furnish my tipi with rawhide containers, backrests, and other items that made it look authentic." He travels often, which gives him an opportunity to visit museums, galleries, and native communities and learn more about his passionate interest: "I have met with notable authors, museum curators, hobbyists, and most importantly, native people, and everyone has been willing to share their wisdom and experience." (Pers. comm., June 2006)

ALLEN CHRONISTER is a craftsman, historian, and author of numerous articles in *Whispering Wind* and other books and publications on Plains material culture and photographs, as well as material culture of the fur trade. He is a frequent speaker at Plains Indian conferences, Montana Historical Society, and Lewis and Clark Interpretive Center. Allen says that his interest in the "hobby" began in fifth grade, when he found a copy of Ben Hunt's *Big Golden Book of Indian Crafts and Lore* in the classroom library. Other influences were books by Solomon, Mason, Laubin and *American Indian Tradition* magazine, which he subscribed to in the 1960s. "It was a major influence because it combined scholarship with a desire to make and do." His first article for that magazine appeared in September 1972. Allen was an Eagle Scout and earned the Indian Lore Merit badge. He was a counselor at a Boy Scout camp for two summers, where the counselors donned war bonnets and did Ben Hunt dances to a narrated story played over the loudspeaker. He used some things that he made but all the costumes were owned by the camp. (Pers. comm., March 2006) See his photo with the authors at Fort Union on page 187 of *Four Winds Guide to Trade Goods*; many of the high quality replicas in this book were made by Allen. He is known for his perfect appliqué beadwork and prolific production of replicas. See his Crow-style toy horse, page 134, as well as other items on pp. 17 (bottom), 18 (top), 19 (left), 20, 111, 114, 115, 117, and 121 (bottom).

MARK MILLER is best known for his authentic replication and restorations of Indian artifacts. As a result of his expertise, he does restorations for many of the top galleries in Santa Fe and other high-end dealers around the nation. His replicas are sold to artists as props, as well as to museums for "hands-on" exhibits and to private collectors. He got his start at age seven, when his schoolteacher mother gave him a copy of Ben Hunt's book *Indian Crafts & Lore*. There were no Boy Scout troops in the small Wisconsin town where Mark grew up, so he had no peer group to share his interests with. He was influenced by visits to the Parson Indian Museum's large Indian artifact display in nearby Wisconsin Dells, and later went to work for the owner, Duane Counsel, who encouraged him in his interest in Indian culture and crafts. He subscribed to *American Indian Tradition* in 1961. After college, he went back to art school and started making replicas as props for his own American Indian paintings. For reasons of aesthetics, he developed his own aging and patination processes for his reproductions. Parfleche work was an early focus, because of his need to outfit his own tipi. (Pers. comm., May 2006) Mark is known to be fastidious about his selection of the "right" materials, whether it is cloth, buckskin, beads, or rawhide. He is an occasional speaker at Plains Indian seminars and several magazine articles have been written about him, including one in *Art West*, 1983. (See his Crow-style knife case, p. 131.)

Mark Miller at his Kalispell Montana studio with his current parfleche projects in 2005

Pre 1840-style doll made by Mark for his daughter Margaret, c. 2001.

Intermontane-style war shirt, 1860-1870 period. The shirt and beadwork with quill-wrapped and yarn wrapped fringes was made by Mark Miller. *Photo courtesy of Mark Miller.*

Detail of war shirt, showing the double-lane quill-wrapped horsehair strips, sinew-sewn, made by Teri Llovet. *Photo courtesy of Mark Miller.*

Intermontane-style otter skin bow case and quiver, 1860-1870 period. Made by Mark Miller, an original design based on several old examples. Beadwork is all sinew-sewn. Old saved list cloth, silk ribbons, brain-tanned otters. *Photo courtesy of Mark Miller.*

JERRY FARENTHOLD. Indian material culture and powwow dancing led him to move to Montana, where he made brain tanned hides for eighteen years. "My first interest came with the Boy Scouts in the Alamo Area Council in San Antonio, Texas, when I got into the Indian Lore merit badge, purchased the simple kits, and learned from Ben Hunt's *Indian Crafts and Lore.* From there I ordered Grey Owl kits." His interest was increased by the Order of the Arrow activities. "I had much fun doing the ceremonies at summer camp—Rickenbacher Scout Ranch and Indian Creek Scout Camp—and eventually was honored as a Vigil member of the Aina Topa Hutsi Lodge. (See "Indian Dance Teams," p. 142 for his experiences in TIHA's Hunka Indian Dance Team.) "I lived in Munich, Germany in 1972 and joined a German group, 'The Arizona Boys,' in order to meet the white hobbyists there at 'Indian Council' near Frankfurt. I saw numerous private and club collections, such as that of the 'Cowboy Club Munchen' collection and of collectors such as Hermann Vonbank of the 'Tzaeltgemeinshaft' and the 'Hundepuntz,' or Dog Soldiers. In 1969, Steven Collins and I traveled the Pow-wow Highway to Crow Fair, Rosebud Fair, visited Dennis Lessard's first Trading Post in Mission, South Dakota, went to Pine Ridge Powwow and Sun Dance, Sheridan Indian Days, and ended up at Tecumseh Lodge Powwow in Indiana. Other hobbyists, such as Jill and Peggy Redmond, Ron and Eddie Head of Massachusetts, and others joined up with us at various events. After this much exposure, I had to move to Montana to be closer to the great Northern Drums, such as the Porcupine Singers for the dancing. I met Frank Andrews, Thom Meyers, and other non-Indians who came from the East and taught me more and told stories of the great Monroe Powwow in New York. I also met and visited members of the Porcupine Singers and learned much from them in South Dakota. The Walks Over Ice family invited me to camp with them at Crow Fair and I did so for many years." (Pers. comm., June 2006) See Jerry's photo in *Four Winds Guide to Trade Good & Replicas,* p. 191. He is wearing "Best Indian Outfit" at Ft. Bridger, WYO Rendez-vous, 1984.

BILLY MAXWELL is a craftsman, cultural anthropologist, USDA Forest Service interpreter, and historian. Billy was active within the Boy Scouts and became an Eagle Scout and an OA Vigil member. He belonged to the Neusiok dance team and the Croatan dancers for his lodge (next level up), and was a BSA Camp Program Director. "I started crafting in June of 1979 with a mostly beaded pair of mocs…and a full deer toe bandoleer. In August 1979, I took a road trip to St. Louis from eastern NC to the National OA Indian Seminar. It was the first of several I would attend. In one week I learned to do brained hides from Dave Christensen, seven forms of quillwork, eight form of beadwork, silverwork basics, antler work and powwow singing, basic pattern and style recognition of most North American cultural areas, the different etiquettes for Plateau, Northern and Southern Plains, Iroquois, finger weaving, and more. It was one of the most intensive things I have ever done…" (Pers. comm., June 2006) Billy and Pam Lemekin headed the first and second Material Culture of the Prairie, Plains and Plateau conferences in Great Falls, Montana in 2001 and 2002. He is currently employed as an interpreter at the Lewis and Clark Interpretive Center in Great Falls, Montana.

NANCY FONICELLO is a quillworker-restorationist-researcher. She is one of the founding advisors for the Material Culture of the Prairie, Plains and Plateau and was chairman for this conference in Bozeman, Montana (2004) and in Rapid City, South Dakota (2005). She initiated and maintains a web site by this group on Yahoo. (See photo of Nancy on p.156.)

PRESTON MILLER. "I wasn't born in an Indian Trading Post. I lived in a row house in York, Pennsylvania, and until I was about fourteen years old, I was still wearing cowboy suits, shooting Colt cap guns, watching Gene Autry on T.V. and going to Roy Rogers movies. It wasn't until 1953 that my interest in the American Indian was ignited. Across from the "Baseball for Boys" field lived an old gentleman, Frank Flory, whose house was full of Indian artifacts. Some of us boys would sit on his front porch and he would show and tell us his experiences of finding artifacts and when he worked for the Buffalo Bill Wild West Show. When he died, a public auction of his collections was held on March 28, 1953. The auctioneer stood on the front porch and sold all Mr. Flory's belongings to bidders standing on the sidewalk. I was fourteen years old and had $15.00 to spend, and I purchased several box lots of stone relics. My dad, sensing my interest, purchased a glass display case for me, which I placed beside my bed. That was the beginning of my lifelong interest in the American Indian.

"My parents were amateur antique collectors and on many weekends we would take long drives to visit antique shops. Needless to say, my collection grew quickly and I soon had pottery, moccasins, Navajo rugs, etc. usually purchased for just a few dollars. My dad often had people stop by the house to buy antiques and I joined in the fun. My ninth grade printing class project was our "MILLER AND SON" business card. In 1954, when I was fifteen years old, I joined The Tuckahoe Indian Dancers, who were part of the Boy Scouts Tuckahoe Order of the Arrow Lodge #386. Soon I was dancing and making Indian outfits. [See "Indian Dance Teams," p. 142 for more information.] In 1954, I subscribed to Norm Feder's *American Indian Hobbyist* magazine and still own a complete set of all issues. This would be the first time I thought of myself as an Indian hobbyist. In 1958 and 1959, I was the Indian crafts and dance counselor at Camp Wynakee, a private children's camp in Dorset, Vermont. By the 1960s, I had attended most of the Indian hobbyist powwows held in the eastern states. In 1964, I won the first place ribbon for the best "Old Style Dancing Senior" at the famous Monroe Powwow. I made many Indian outfits and built a furnished Indian tipi, which won the first place award at the 1966 Monroe Powwow held at Plume Trading Post in New Jersey. After a tour of active duty in the U.S. Navy, Bill Krieger, a fellow hobbyist, and I made a trip to the west. We carried my tipi poles on the roof of my station wagon and attended numerous powwows in South Dakota, Montana, and Canada.

It was this trip that convinced me to move west to real Indian country. In 1967, we packed up and moved to the Rocky Boy's Reservation in Montana. My ex-wife and I taught school there for two years, and all the while I was busy selling beads and buying moccasins and other crafts, which I sold through my Four Winds catalog. In 1970, I moved to the Flathead Reservation in St. Ignatius, Montana, and started Four Winds Indian Trading Post as a full-time business. So this is how I became an Indian hobbyist, Indian trader, school teacher, craftsman, author, historian and collector."

Preston Miller is shown wearing an Indian outfit he made about 1957 when he was eighteen years old. The outfit is a mixture of tribal styles and includes a Plains war bonnet, vest, and moccasins. Preston started this outfit several years earlier and when the photo was taken had not yet finished the fully beaded vest. The leggings, breechclout, and gloves are in Chippewa-style patterns. Later in life, all these pieces were sold or traded and Preston thinks they are now probably in someone's collection, a museum, or maybe worn out and discarded!

CAROLYN COREY. "I grew up in the suburbs of Chicago, and it wasn't until I moved to the Southwest in the 1960s that I had any real awareness of Indian culture. It began when I took my young children to the 'Rez' in Arizona to see Indian dances and rodeos. Later, when I moved to New Mexico, I worked for a turquoise/silver jewelry manufacturer along with a girlfriend whose parents were 'high-end' Indian dealers. I tagged along doing Indian shows and soon started my own business stringing necklaces and selling small items to retailers in California, where I would make frequent trips. I loved doing flea markets in New Mexico when Indians from Santo Domingo and other pueblos would sometimes sit and wait for me to make a sale so that I could buy their silverwork. This led to trips to Santo Domingo pueblo to trade manufactured jewelry, fox hides etc. for their diversity of hand-made jewelry, etc. My girlfriend and I were the only woman traders at that time! Simultaneously, I attended the University of New Mexico, where I studied Indian art history, but I thought I wanted to be an archaeologist, and no digs were open (except to grad students) in the Southwest at that time.

"When I later moved to California, I was thrilled to enroll in a UC Berkeley extension course in archaeology at a Coastal Miwok site near Novato. I lingered after the course and was a regular every weekend at this excavation for over three years until it was closed in the late 70s. As a volunteer, I was one of a handful of people from the dig who catalogued the same Coastal Miwok material when it was turned over to the Lowie Museum (now the Phoebe Hearst). When I enrolled in UC Berkeley as an anthropology student, my most fulfilling course was with JoAllyn Archambault (now with the Smithsonian in D.C.), who was a major influence in encouraging my interest in material culture. She arranged for me to photograph Plains items for her class that hadn't been out of the Lowie museum storage areas for years. We both attended the second annual Plains Indian Seminar in Cody Wyoming. I had met Keith Gilbert, a 'super' hobbyist, who knew both Norm Feder, who used to live in his house, and Bill Holm. As a result, when I met both men at Cody we had a mutual acquaintance. Keith took me to my first rendezvous after we read Laubin's book together cover to cover. I bought my own tipi, which I would set up myself—the poles fit great on my old Pinto station wagon. I also traveled to CIHA Powwows in southern California. Keith showed me how to make capotes, following Bill Holm's diagram in AIH magazine. Now I started selling items at local rendezvous made by Mark Miller, (who I also met at Cody) and capotes made by Hans Duddenhaus and started my own mail order business, 'Metis Mercantile,' selling reproductions. Keith got me interested in making white selvedge trade cloth and after hours of experimenting I finally discovered "the method." Twenty-five years later I divulged it in *Tradecloth Handbook.* I retired in 1997, after making hundreds of yards of "saved list" cloth for museums, movies, and hobbyists around the world." (See photo of Carolyn's strap dress on p. 112, and Cheyenne dress on p. 5.)

THE BREWERS: BILL, KATHY AND BOB. Today, the Brewers are widely known for their realistic re-creations of Plains artifacts made famous by their "Dances with Wolves" movie props. They have evolved from their childhood participation in Boy Scout dancing and crafts, as contributing artists to hobbyist magazines since 1969, and finally to the professional artisans that they are today. Bill and brother Bob painstakingly research and make exacting replicas that are one step beyond the "artifakes" such as those discussed previously by Bill Holm. (In *Four Wind Guide to Trade Goods and Replicas,* 1998, this new style of "artifakes" was described as "enhanced replicas.") Here is what Kathy Brewer has to say about their craft: "We never used the term artifaking, and didn't come across that term until the Cody Seminar on "Artifacts/ Artifakes" with that term in the title in 1984. [see p. 157 for more info on this seminar.] It was after that seminar that we started signing our pieces. We always called the pieces we made 'reproductions' or 'replicas.' 'Aging' items was always done merely for aesthetical reasons. Bill wanted to make things that looked like what he saw in museums." It wasn't until they were in college and learned about patinas and patination (a perfectly legitimate artistic process) that they really began to "age" items. It took them years of experimentation until they got the patina down so that the pieces had the museum look they were searching for. (Kathy Brewer, pers. comm., April, 2006). Their expertise has gained the Brewers a reputation: "Is it real…or is it a Brewer?" can be heard at auctions and Indian shows around the country. Kathy keeps photo albums documenting every piece they make in case one comes into question as possibly being old.

Bill and his brother Bob became interested in Indian costumes and culture as early as age four when they "played Indian" wearing the Indian suit that their father wore as a child. (Many years later, they concluded that it may have been made by the local firm of DeMoulin Bros. & Co, makers of the Red Men Society regalia! See article on Red Men costumes and kids wearing them in *New Four Winds Guide to American Indian Artifacts,* pp. 174-181.) Later, in fourth grade, a fellow student brought in some artifacts for "show and tell" which got the brothers started making things. They also had copies of books by W. Ben Hunt and Bernard S. Mason, which were strong influences. (Bates, Craig D. "Bill & Kathy Brewer: Artisans of Plains Indian Cultures," *Moccasin Tracks* Vol. II, #7 pp. 4-7.) Kathy says "I didn't get into Indian lore until I met Bill in college. Bill and Bob were full-blown hobbyists by then, having already started their own dance team in high school…making all the costumes and singing dance songs learned from records. Bill and Bob and two friends formed their own society within their Boy Scout troop, called 'American Indian Dog Soldier Association.' A pivotal book they recall reading from the grade school library was *Here's Your Hobby; Indian Dancing,* by William K. Powers. That book listed all of the hobbyist magazines in the back, which is how they first learned about them. (Kathy Brewer, pers. comm., Feb. 2006).

See photo of Bob Brewer in *Four Winds Guide to Indian Trade Goods and Replicas,* p. 191, in which he is holding the pistol case seen on p. 195 of the companion volume, *Four Winds Guide to Indian Artifacts.* On that same page is a Blackfoot knife case replica that Bob made.

Staff artists

Bob Brewer, art editor/artist for *Singing Wire* (later called *American Indian Crafts & Culture*) as of May 1969- Dec. 1973. Bill Brewer joined Bob as an artist from Jan 1972-Dec. 1973

Whispering Wind artists. Bill Brewer started in 1967, joined by Kathy in 1980 and they are still on the staff there. Bob Brewer did an article in 1980.

Brewer movie credits in chronological order (not including 16 more TV and movie titles)

Dances With Wolves, 1990 (Kevin Costner's knife case; Wes Studi's war club; principle Indian props – lances, shields, quiver and bow cases, clubs saddlebags; tipi set decoration – parfleches, dolls, horn cups, painted tipi liners; some costume – necklaces, buffalo horn headdresses)

Son of the Morning Star, 1991 TV (Crazy Horse props; principle Indian props, including weapons, shields, painted hide, costumes, dog soldier bonnet)

Thunderheart, 1992 (costumes – ghost dance outfits; props – ghost dance props, turtle rattle, old time pipe and pipe bag)

Northern Exposure, 1993 TV (Athabaskan babiche bag and sewing kit)

Last Of The Mohicans, 1993 (research for costume designer)

Maverick, 1994 (Mel Gibson's Indian outfit, feather bonnets, button vest, and other costume pieces)

Return to Lonesome Dove, 1994 TV (hand drum, shields, bladder bags)

Pontiac Moon, 1994 (Eric Sweig's quilled and beaded charms, imitation eagle feathers)

Legends Of The Fall, 1994 (Brad Pitt's hat band, buckskin leggings; Anthony Hopkins' beaded gauntlets, moccasins, other costume pieces)

Indian In The Cupboard, 1995 (principle Indian costumes with exception of Litefoot's leggings, which were made by Michael Terry)

Last Of The Dogmen, 1995 (principle Indian costumes, including full dog soldier outfit and quilled girl's dress; principle Indian character's props)

The Alamo, 2004 (costumes – Billy Bob Thornton's beaded vest, Dennis Quaid's beaded sash, bead and ribbonwork on his caped coat, knife case on stage performer)

The War That Made America, 2006 TV (props – ball headed clubs, lacrosse sticks and balls)

Seraphim Falls, not yet released as of this writing (costumes – Pierce Brosnan's buckskin coat, Liam Neeson's buckskin trousers)

Musquakie-style trunk. The construction style of this trunk is unique to the Mesquakie. Bill Brewer made this replica of the 1880 original, which is in poor and collapsed condition. (See photo of the original piece #186, collected by Milford Chandler, in *Art of the Red Earth People, The Mesquakie of Iowa,* Torrence & Hobbs Univ. of Iowa: 1989). When author Gaylord Torrence showed a slide of this rare object at a Plains Indian Seminar in Cody, Wyoming, Bill was able to demonstrate the puzzling construction to a fascinated audience! *Author's collection.*

Bill Brewer at home in the early 1980s working on beadwork.

Sioux-style shield made by Bill Brewer. Note aged buckskin and feathers attached with genuine old "saved list" cloth. The small twisted rawhide shields are to catch the enemy in the web. *Author's collection.*

Bill and Kathy Brewer set up at National hobbyist Powwow in the early 1980s.

Ball headed club, movie prop for *The War That Made America* (PBS-TV, 2006). Bill also made lacrosse sticks for this movie. *Photo courtesy of Bill & Kathy Brewer.*

Bill Brewer made the grizzly claw necklace on p. 118 (lower left). Bob Brewer made the Sioux-style parfleche on p. 138.

JANET CONNER is an expert quillworker-brain tanner. She got started in the business selling hides at Rendezvous in the early 1980s. She was influenced by Ben Hunt's books but also learned beadwork from Preston Miller's *Four Winds Beadwork Book.* (Pers. comm., March 2006) Later, she consigned or sold quilled items to Four Winds that were included in *Four Winds Guide to Indian Trade Good and Replicas,* pp. 152-3 and 161, parfleches pp. 158-60. She made the "enhanced replica" quilled bag by copying it from a disintegrating old one pictured in *Four Winds Guide to Indian Artifacts*, p. 196. She also made items in this book on p. 116 (vest), p. 126 (bags, top right), and page 133 (knife sheath, center left).

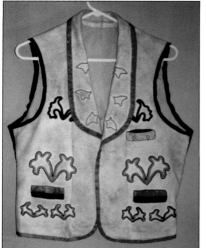

Davy Crockett's vest for the 2004 movie *The Alamo,* worn by Billie Bob Thornton throughout the film. The original is in the Alamo Shrine, San Antonio, Texas. *Photo courtesy of Bill & Kathy Brewer.*

Janet Conner shown at the MCPPP conference in 2005, wearing and holding items that she has made.

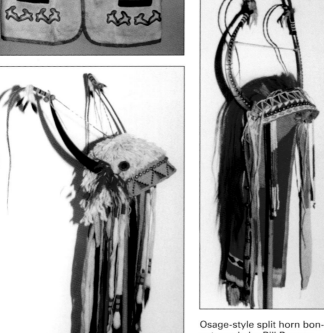

Osage-style split horn bonnet, made by Bill Brewer. *Photo courtesy of Bill & Kathy Brewer.*

A quilled frock coat made by Janet Conner. The original is in the Smithsonian Archives. *Photo courtesy of Janet Conner.*

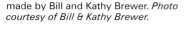

Sioux-style split horn ermine bonnet, made by Bill and Kathy Brewer. *Photo courtesy of Bill & Kathy Brewer.*

LINDA HOLLEY is an expert beadworker, researcher, consultant, teacher, and lecturer. She is currently writing a book that will be a complete guide to everything you want to know about tipis. She also sponsors two web sites for those who want to know more about tipis: www. tipis-tepees-teepees.com and www.tipis.org.

"My interest in Native American materials started in the early 1950s when my family took me to see the sites in downtown Seattle, Washington where there were Northwest Coast carvings in the shop windows and on the streets. Totally fascinated by these images, I just had to know more…Westerns at the movies and on early TV also piqued my interests in Indians. My first book was Ben Hunt's *Indian Crafts and Lore.* From those pages I began to make my first Indian items, such as loom beadwork and war bonnets. My study of Native American Culture and Art started in earnest about 1971 in Jacksonville, Florida, when Jack Butler introduced me to a new group called NFICS or North Florida Indian Culture Society, started by David Hart, Fred Glennon, and others who were Boy Scouts, Indian enthusiasts (hobbyists), and Indians living in the area. From 1972 through 1996, this group put on the largest dances in the Southeastern USA. Other groups I belonged to or worked with were the Florida Indian Hobbyist Association and West Coast Powwow Club. There were no totally run Native American dances in the Florida area until the later 1980s."

"Dancing at Powwows was a great learning experience," says Linda, "but I was interested in the tipi camping part." This led her in another direction, to rendezvous of the 1840s time period, "…where there was lots of tipi camping and you could dress up all the time in the period clothing. My first group was the NAPR or National Association of Primitive Riflemen (1974) and then the NMLRA or National Muzzle Loading Rifle Association (1975)…with my Powwow background, I could incorporate both [groups] in my life for studying the Indian culture. From 1978 to 1995, I began sewing the first tipis for my business, Alligator Trading Company, and I made over three hundred lodges. During all these years of making tipis, going to rendezvous, powwows and campouts, doing beadwork, and making tipi accoutrements, I was also studying—doing research and listening to those knowledgeable about tipi life. In 1987, I won the Les Bircher award at National Powwow and numerous crafts competitions across the country at dances and events. Today I am still an active member of the Powwow group AICA (American Indian Culture Association of North Carolina)." Linda is known for her exquisite traditional beadwork using very tiny beads.

In 1977, the annual Plains Indian Seminar was started by George Horse Capture, then curator at the Buffalo Bill Historical Center in Cody, Wyoming. The emphasis was on material culture artifacts, which was an excellent venue for a wide range of speakers and related subjects. I first attended in 1978, and found the one-on-one interaction between speakers and audience very rewarding. For one evening, the author organized a "show and tell" at the historic Irma hotel, which was a venue for participants to display their handicrafts. The following photos were taken in 1992:

Art and Sara Jensen show some of Sara's beadwork, including her tiny miniatures.

Mike and Gwen Fedor display a variety of traditional beaded replicas for sale.

Gary and Louella Johnson show Gary's Metis beadwork. See also his Metis vest on p. 12 of the companion volume, *New Four Winds Guide to American Indian Artifacts.* More about this interesting couple can be found on p. 192 of *Four Winds Guide to Indian Trade Good and Replicas.*

Nancy Fonicello stands next to her multi-quill plaited decorated dress.

Linda Holley at a TIHA dance in 1978, wearing a buckskin dress that she made and beaded. She won the TIHA buckskin contest that year for this dress. *Photo courtesy of Linda Holley.*

(Left to right) Bill Holm and Bob Laidig, with Gwen Fedor's beadwork in the foreground.

In 1984 the conference subject at Cody was "Artifacts/Artifakes". One of the speakers, Richard Edwards, addressed the legal issues of the new phenomenon of "artifakes" in the marketplace. (This new definition of the term "artifake" differs from the original term discussed by Bill Holm in which there is no "antiquing" or aging.) "While hobbyists <that is, non-professional craftsmen>have made Plains Indian-style items for many years, what is relatively new is the emergence of the *professional* non-native craftsman." He states that the time period for this change was 1971, when Parke-Bernet (Sotheby's) Auction House sold the Green Collection of American Indian Art.[2] "It is only since that time that the market prices of original pre-1900 beaded pouches and clothing have risen above the costs of materials.." which resulted in a market for high-quality reproductions made by skilled professionals. After the Green sale, the number of dealers and collectors in Plains Indian art rose drastically while the amount of genuine artifacts available remained the same. "As the demand increased for old items, inevitable contemporary craftsman-made material was marketed as antique.. after it had passed several hands." (Edwards, Richard W. 1993:9-10). In spite of this notorious use of antiqued replicas, MOST of these replicas are not misrepresented but are sold as contemporary pieces to fill a recognized need by collectors, museums, etc. for an otherwise too expensive or non-attainable item. (See p. 10 for an in-depth look at replication identification). It is important to note that if there is a deception, it is not initiated by the craftsperson, and often not recognized as newly made by the dealer or collector who passes it off as "real". This led the Brewers, Mark Miller and other honest craftspeople who age their work for aesthetics to sign their pieces. (Unfortunately, unscrupulous individuals can remove these markings). Kathy Brewer keeps meticulous photo records of their pieces and she is always on the alert for their work showing up in auctions. She has been known to call Sotheby's to inform them when a mis-representation of their work as genuine appears in one of their periodic sales catalogs; Sotheby's would then immediately withdraw that item.

Current Organizations, Publications, and Conferences

The Order of the Arrow (O/A) has evolved to include women in their membership who take an active role in powwow dance competitions at the National Order of Arrow Conferences. There are classes specifically oriented for the women, such as shawl making, ribbonwork, fingerweaving, etc. Jack Heriard says that "Of the 8,000 0/A members attending the 2006 National Order of the Arrow Conference in Lansing, Michigan, 2,000 were registered in American Indian activities (AIA). Within the AIA at the 2006 conference there were Native American attendees either as registered participants, invited 'elders,' honored guests and singers." (Heriard, pers. comm., August 2006)

The Koshare Indian Museum's original 1949 structure is now a registered state historic site of the Colorado Historical Society, housing a collection of Native American art and artifacts representing tribes from the Plains to the Southwest regions of the United States. A program of visiting artists features an exhibit of a different Indian artist each month throughout the year. The organization's web site (www.koshare.org) notes that "…the museum remains true to its origins, providing an active and varied educational youth program through Scouting…as a troop meeting location, a youth center, an overnight hostel for thousands of Scout and school youth throughout the year, a center for many local Scouting and civic activities, and a performing arts center, not only for the famous Koshare Indian Dancers but for other artists as well." Today, the Koshare Indian Dancers do all the things a regular Scout troop does and are active participants in the Order of the Arrow. Boys from other troops, crews, and posts may also join the them. The Koshares perform between fifty and sixty shows, trips, and special events, plus travel all over the country. According to the web site, "[a] particularly enjoyable event comes when we travel to powwows or to dance with our good friends the Kwahadi Dancers of Amarillo TX or the Kossa Dancers of Sulphur LA, who also come to the Koshare Indian Museum to dance with us…In addition to our Summer and Winter Ceremonials and other shows at home, the Koshare Indian Dancers are available for performances anywhere in the world…"

The word "hobbyist" is rarely heard anymore, as Colin Taylor stated when defining the movement in Europe: "although the term 'hobbyist' is useful, it is generally disliked by most of the individuals to whom it is applied, and just as in North America, it is rejected by many who feel that the interest cannot be equated to other leisure activities [hobbies], since it usually involves a very deep commitment." (Taylor: 1988, 562) Note that Bill Holm is pleased to be called a "hobbyist" today, even after all of his academic accomplishments (see bio above). But in 1961, the *American Indian Hobbyist* was changed to *American Indian Tradition*, purportedly due to protests from Native Americans who viewed the use of the term "hobby" as derogatory to their culture. (Deloria: 1998,145) "In 1972, the New England Hobbyist Association, under the direction of Ron Head, voted to change its name to the American Indianist Society." (Powers, 1988: 561).

After *Moccasin Tracks* ceased publication in 1987, *Whispering Wind* became the only available publication "devoted to the same interests addressed by Feder in the original *American Indian Hobbyist.*" Almost twenty years ago, Powers named it as "...the longest lived hobbyist publication in North America." (Ibid, 1988: 561). Jack Heriard started *Whispering Wind* as a newsletter of LIHA (Louisiana Indian Hobbyist Association). In 1990, LIHA's name was changed to Louisiana Indian Heritage Association to better reflect its changing membership of Indian people. (Heriard, pers. comm., May 2006)

In the early 1990s, Jack Heriard, editor of *Whispering Wind*, encouraged Peter Durkin to begin writing a feature called "Tipi Corner" for that magazine. Durkin believes that the quality of the tipis and the knowledge of the practitioners improves each year, although he regrets that the number of tipis seems to be steadily declining at powwows and other related events. (Durkin, pers. comm., July 2006) The 2005 National Powwow 13 had only 15 tipis set up in camp, whereas at the same site in 1975, at National Powwow 3, there were approximately 100 tipis. (Durkin, Peter, pp. 36-38, "Tipi Camp," *Whispering Wind* Vol. 35, #4, Folsom, LA, 2006)

A "grass roots" organization was started by like-minded people who wanted a new venue for discussions and presentations on the subject of historic ethnographic material of Native American peoples. As a result, *The Material Culture of the Prairie, Plains and Plateau* (known as MCPPP) *Conference* was first held in Great Falls Montana in 2001 and 2002, in Bozeman, Montana in 2004, and in Rapid City, So. Dakota in 2005. It is a non-affiliated open forum that promotes interaction between all participants: academics, students, "hobbyists," Native Americans, etc. A web site is maintained by this group on Yahoo.com, which enables daily ongoing active discussion about Indian material culture issues, with participants sharing ideas from around the globe.

Endnotes
[1] Other groups were Girl Scouts, Camp Fire Girls, YMCA, and Boys' Clubs.
[2] This large collection of baskets and Plains materials was started by Civil War surgeon George G. Green in 1870. *The Green Collection of American Indian Art–Part I* (New York: Parke Bernet Galleries, 1971, p. 9).

European Hobbyist Movement - England, Germany, Italy, and the Netherlands

Colin Taylor wrote that in Europe "...There has long been a fascination for American Indians...which began soon after the discovery of America." (Taylor 1988: 562.) The tiny seed beads first traded to native peoples of the New World four hundred years ago were made in Venice.

By the turn of the 20th century, the barbaric and wild image of the American Indian was transformed into the concept of the "noble savage," as influenced by Longfellow's poetry, i.e., *Hiawatha*, James Fenimore Cooper's *Last of the Mohicans*, and, in Europe, the enormously popular novels of German writer Karl May—all of which inspired local artists and poets to write about American Indians. (Kristek 2003)

England
George Catlin's writings were a major influence in England in the mid-19th century; his ethnographic exhibits in London were viewed by a wide audience. "Later editions of his books were published in large quantities, many being aimed at the young reader..." They formed a major influence for "...several generations of readers in the U.K. until the mid-20th century." (Taylor 1988: 562)

Several British authors also wrote about American Indians in the 19th century. By the early 20th century, Ernest T. Seton's books were readily available. (See books, p. 139 for more info.) Grey Owl, whose real name was Archibald Belaney (1889-1938), wrote many widely read books on nature conservation and American Indians. He personally pleaded the cause of the American Indian to King George VI in 1937.

As mentioned in the introduction, the British Boy Scouts never developed Indian lore to the extent of their American counterparts; for example, there is nothing comparable to the Order of the Arrow. The Indians of America were represented at the Boy Scouts' Jamboree in London in 1920 but it wasn't until the English Westerner's Society[1] was formed in 1954 along with the affiliated *Brand Book* and *Tally Sheet* that organized groups of hobbyists emerged in the United Kingdom. Coincidentally, 1954 was the same year that *The American Indian Hobbyist* magazine got its start, but Colin believes that the Westerner's publications had more influence in England until the late 1960s. Research papers in the *Brand Book* and exhibitions of Indian artifacts belonging to the founding members began in 1960, and the American Museum at Bath hosted the Westerners' Society annual exhibitions. (Taylor 1988: 562-565).

Ian West says that after the 60s, "...the whole thing blossomed with several groups of youngsters who were making their own costumes and doing Indian dancing; hence the beginnings of the English Powwows." (Pers. comm., 2004). Colin did a survey of hobbyist groups between 1971-1984. There were four initial groups that were all in Southern England. Dancing was the principal activity, but collecting, research, and craftwork were also important. In 1965, a Sioux Dancers club was formed, "combining ethnology with dancing." This young group was guided by the older members of the Westerners' Society and came to America to meet other hobbyists as well as ethnologist John Ewers (Taylor 1988: 562-565).

COLIN TAYLOR. Craftsman, collector, prolific author, and lecturer. An English scholar and world-wide recognized Plains Indian expert, he authored numerous books and articles on this subject for over forty years. John Ewers was his mentor and lifelong friend, who had a profound influence on Colin's research and dedication to Plains Indian studies. At seventeen, Colin became the youngest member of the Royal Anthropological Institute.

English Group of "Hobbyists" at Woldingham, Surrey, U.K., 1960. (Left to right) Susan Milliner, Colin Taylor, Ted Blackmore, Ian West, Ann Robinson, and Russell Robinson, who at this time, was Chief Armourer at the Tower of London. *Newspaper photo for the Croydon Times, courtesy of Ian West.*

Grey Owl's books were a major influence in Colin's early years. He later founded the Grey Owl Society in 1982 in his home town of Hastings, Sussex, which is also where Belaney (Grey Owl) grew up. (Ian West, Obituary, *European Review of Native American Studies* 18: 2, 2004, p. 57.)

Colin is best remembered by his many American friends for his frequent trips to the U.S.A. Colin's personal appearances were a highlight of annual No. American Indian and fur trade seminars throughout the years. I first met him in 1981 at the Buffalo Bill Historical Center in Cody, Wyoming, when he generously gave me his letters from the Hudson's Bay Co. that began my trade cloth research. His spirited enthusiasm and dedication to the subject of the material culture of the Plains Indians expanded our knowledge, while his engaging personality, buoyant cheerfulness, generosity, and friendship touched us all.

Colin Taylor shown here at his childhood home of Brighton at age nineteen, wearing a bonnet that he made. *Photo courtesy of Ian West.*

Colin and lifelong friend Ian West pose in their Indian costumes at Dover, Kent in 1963. Colin is proudly wearing a feather bonnet that belonged to Iron Tail, the famous Sioux Chief of Buffalo Bill Show fame. He purchased this bonnet in England and donated it along with most of his Indian artifacts to his local museum in Hastings, England where he was to become the curator. Colin holds the Sioux Catlinite pipe that he won in a contest for writing the best article for *American Indian Hobbyist* titled "The Plains Indian Shirt." (Vol. III, #7 & 8, March 1957) *Photo and information courtesy of Ian West.*

EDWARD H. BLACKMORE. Lecturer, craftsman, teacher, collector. He was influenced by Philip Godsell, an emigrant to Canada in 1903 who worked for the Hudson's Bay Co and sent him many Canadian Indian photos from 1940-1961, and his Mohawk friend, singer Oskenonton, who played the role of Hiawatha at the Royal Albert Hall in London, 1930-1945. Through Oskenonton, Blackmore obtained raw materials for craft work, i.e., eagle feathers, beads, and buckskin. In the following photo, he is shown wearing a double trailer bonnet that he made. Ernest T. Seton invited Blackmore over to America to teach the making of war bonnets at Seton's College of Indian Wisdom in Santa Fe. After his death in 1983, Blackmore's Indian collection was sent to the Hastings Museum in Sussex. Colin states that Blackmore was instrumental in fostering scholarly as well as hobbyist interest in Indians in Great Britain, especially after 1938. (Taylor 1988: 563-534).

Claverton Manor, Bath in 1966. (Left to right) Colin Taylor wearing all genuine Sioux garb; Ian West, all old items except tomahawk and pipe bag; E.H. Blackmore, shirt, pipe bag, and moccasins are genuine. Ian says "most of our 'dressing up' in the early days was done in conjunction with exhibitions of our various collections." *Photo and information courtesy of Ian West.*

Dover, Kent in 1963. E. H. Blackmore is "making fire by friction," while (left to right, standing) Ian West, John Dalton, and Colin Taylor look on. *Photo courtesy of Ian West.*

IAN WEST. Craftsman, writer, and collector. Member of the English Westerners Society and President of the Grey Owl Society in England. He has written articles for the American hobbyist magazine *Powwow Trails* as well as for *American Indian Art*. He is the author of *Portraits of Native Americans*.

Claverton Manor, Bath c.1967 (Left to right) E. H. Blackmore, Colin Taylor, and Ian West. Ian is wearing a Blackfoot-style shirt that he made and leggings with old Blackfoot-beaded strips. He is holding a Blackfoot rifle scabbard that he obtained from Norm Feder, collected in 1924, when Norm was curator at the Denver Art Museum. Note tipi set up behind them. *Photo courtesy of Ian West.*

Ian West is shown here in 1974 holding a Crow-style shirt that he made, now owned by Richard Green. *Photo courtesy of Ian West.*

Colin Taylor at Richard Pohrt's residence in Flint, Michigan in 1969. He is wearing an original quilled war shirt from the Pohrt collection. *Photo courtesy of Ian West.*

MICHAEL G. JOHNSON. Author, researcher, advisor, and collector. His interest in North American Indians, specifically the French & Indian Wars, began with school history projects in the 1950s. The first person to influence him was Albert "Dennis" Burdett, through his knowledge of the British Museum & Pitt Rivers Collection at Oxford. "Subsequently, I formed friendships with other enthusiasts, notably Colin Taylor, John Dalton, Ian West, William Reid, Jack Hayes, and more recently Richard Green."

Michael studied Indian material in museums throughout the U.K., esp. Cambridge University, where he researched the extensive collection of Canadian Plains material and discovered the Mesquakie collection of Alicia Owen, which had been lost in storage for over fifty years! His discovery and notes on the collection were later published by Torrance, Hobbs & Brown. His main influence became James Howard, through correspondence and a few meetings in America. These letters were so informative that Michael sent copies to the Milwaukee Public Museum to accompany Howard's collection there. Michael introduced the first Annual Indian Arts and Crafts exhibition in 1964 at the American Museum at Claverton, Bath, Somerset in England. This event followed an exhibit of his own collection there in 1962. Over the years, he and Ian West have been the main participants, who still display their collections at this annual event. (See photos of Colin and Ian at this museum in 1966). Michael has written articles for *The Grey Owl Society Magazine* in Britain and *European Review of Native American Studies*, Christian Feest's magazine in Austria and now Germany. He was a contributing writer to American hobbyist magazines, former associate editor for *Powwow Trails* 1966-1970, and for *American Indian Crafts and Culture* from 1972-1975. He is currently a contributing writer to *Whispering Wind*. Michael wrote *Encyclopedia of Native Tribes of North America,* for which he received the Denali Press Award in Chicago in 2000. He has also published several American Indian titles for Osprey Press in association with Richard Hook and Jonathan Smith. His special interests today include native demography, linguistic relationships and 20th century Pan-Indianism, with a continued interest in Iroquois history and material culture. (Pers. comm., June 2006)

Michael G. Johnson's collection displayed at the American Museum, Bath, England, June 2006. *Photo courtesy of M.G. Johnson.*

RICHARD HOOK. Illustrator, collector. His interest in Native Americans began in his childhood, when he purchased a pair of Iroquois baby moccasins that he still owns. Today he is an internationally known freelance illustrator specializing in military history; his favorite subject is American history, particularly Native Americans. He earns a living doing military illustrations, but his true passion and hobby is painting American Indian subjects. (Pers. comm., May 2006) In 1999, Richard did a dynamic painting of Joe Medicine Crow's World War II war exploits, which Colin Taylor and other English friends presented to Joe during a Plains Indian Conference at the Buffalo Bill Historical Center in Cody, Wyoming. (Taylor 2000: 69-74) Recently, Richard was commissioned to do a painting for the Oneida nation of regalia that had been recently given back to the tribe. He refused payment because "he did it for the love of it. My interest in American Indians has given me a lot of pleasure and I wanted to give something back." (Susan H. George, *The Oneida Indian Nation News,* March 2005) A lifelong interest in Native American culture has led to his selection as illustrator for a number of books on the subject including Michael Johnson's *Encyclopedia of Native Tribes of North America* (see below left) and *Warriors at the Little Bighorn 1876.*

Michael G. Johnson (right) at the British Museum in London with Guy Wood, who holds Michael's prize winning book, *Native Tribes of North America. Photo courtesy of M.G. Johnson.*

Oil painting by Richard Hook, titled "Mr. and Mrs. Spotted Tail," Brulé Sioux. *Photo courtesy of Richard Hook.*

RICHARD GREEN. Craftsman, collector, author, curator. Of his earliest childhood memories, he says that "like so many other kids growing up in the late 50s and 60s, I grew up watching Hollywood movies… Somewhere deep down, however, I sensed there was much more to this oft-repeated cinematic tale than met the eye!…I shared the interest with other like-minded English enthusiasts, such as Mike Johnson, (the late) Dennis Burdett, (the late) Colin Taylor, Ian West, Richard Hook, (the late) Ted Blackmore, Kim Oakeshott, and Ray Wilkes, amongst others. Each has had his own particular slant or area of specialism within the interest, though most of us came from a background of hobbyism. In many respects, it could be said that we were the hobbyists that could not dance! … As a young boy, I met up with most of the above at annual summer tipi camps at nearby Kinver Scout Camp, in the West Midlands, the highlight of which was a special weekend of dance performances and exhibitions of Native collections…which made a lasting impression on me! … In my student days, I was in the regular habit of frequenting the Portobello market at Notting Hill, London…in the hope of stumbling upon some small treasure of Native American origin…I was naturally engrossed in news coverage of the occupation at Wounded Knee on Pine Ridge Reservation in 1973, and corresponded throughout with a Sioux family closely involved in events there. I made my first visit to Sioux country in 1979, then spent four months over the summer of 1980, following my graduation from Reading University."(Richard Green, pers. comm., May 2006)

In 2004, Richard wrote a book entitled *A Warrior I Have Been*, a catalog for the exhibition that he curated at Birmingham Museum & Art Gallery on Plains Indian cultures, which featured his personal collection. He has also contributed to a number of other exhibitions. Richard has been a contributing writer for *Whispering Wind* magazine since 1983.

Crow moccasins made by Richard Green for American hobbyist friend, Sam Cahoon. *Photo courtesy of Richard Green.*

FRASER PAKES. Writer, speaker, advisor, and dancer. Although he emigrated to Canada in 1969, he was actively involved in hobbyists' groups in England during the 1960s, where he was associate editor of the English Westerners Society. From 1969 to 1998, he devoted his time exclusively as educator and ethnologist to Native Canadians, on the Blood, Piegan, Cree, Chippewa, and Stoney Reserves. His research interests are Plains Indian art, body art, imagery, and stereotyping. He has given talks on these subjects at Plains Indian conferences in the United States.

Germany

German "hobbyists" were inspired both by the writings of Karl May (1842-1912), who wrote about American Indians, and the European tour of the Buffalo Bill Wild West Shows. There are numerous German publications; the earliest was *Der Dakota Scout*, which led to *Kalumet* in 1969. The earliest documented event where Germans dressed as Indians was in the late 19th century near Leipzig, at the annual Taucha market. (Taylor: 1988, 567-8). The first Indian and Cowboy club was formed In Munich in 1913, followed by the Buffalo Cowboy Club in Freiburg in 1919 and many others in major cities throughout the country. (Belden, Chas. J., "German Fair" in *American Indian Hobbyist,* 1960: Vol. 6, #7-8, p. 95).

Larry Wettstein tells us that these early functions led to the first "Indian Council" held in 1951 in Karlsrue with forty people and only three tipis. Expanding every year, these were held in a new location and grew to a full tipi camp with hundreds of traditionally dressed participants. The expansion was due to the founding in 1969 of the Western Bund (Union) Germany, which is the central organization for all the "Western" clubs of Germany; there are approximately 150 different Indian, Cowboy, and Mountain Man clubs (as well as a few U.S. Cavalry and Confederate), principally from Germany but from other European countries, such as Switzerland, France, Belgium, Netherlands, England, and Czechoslovakia, as well. The "Indian Council" is actually a unified event of all the Western clubs joining to meet every May or June. By 1988, this annual event was held in a permanent location at Hundsdorf, Westerwald. (Exception, in 1993 it was held again in Freiburg.) Wettstein says that in addition to the Indian Council, there are various meetings throughout the year of each club visiting the other in different towns. German Indian hobbyists portray Indian life the way it was 150-180 years ago, living in tipis, tanning hides, doing bead and quillwork, and learning Indian songs and dances. "Many hobbyists have had good connections to different Indian reservations in the USA and Canada for many years." He says that even before the "wall" came down in Eastern Germany there were already many Indian clubs. They meet each year for "Indian Week" in August with a large tipi camp with only Indian hobbyists, no cowboys! (Larry Wettstein, pers. comm., March 2006)

Larry Wolfgang Wettstein at the 53rd Indian Council in Hundsdorf, Westerwald area, near Koblenz Germany, in 2003. He is standing in front of his Blackfoot-style tipi, which he painted with his own unique design. His wife, Pat (see next photo), tanned the hides for this shirt, which Larry constructed and painted. A member of his club did the quillwork. Larry started the Indian hobby when he was fifteen years old. He took the Blackfoot name for black bear, Sik-o-kayo. Later, in 1996, upon a visit to the Canadian Kaina Blood Reserve near Stand Off, he was given a new name by an 86-year-old elder of the tribe: "Nitanee," meaning say it once (you only have to say it one time to me). He took this new name with great pride. *Photo courtesy of Larry Wettstein.*

Patricia Wettstein is shown wearing a side fold dress that she made and husband Larry painted. She is pictured here at the 43rd Indian Council in the Black forest area of Freiburg, Germany in 1993. The store and saloon fronts in the background are part of the Western town Abilene, depicted in 1867. It was built by the eight different Western clubs of Freiburg. This particular Indian Council has 2,304 participants, 235 tipis, 232 lodges and 292 cowboy tents. Pat started her Indian hobby in the 1960s and was one of the first woman in Germany to tan hides the old Indian way (brain-tanned leather). For many years, she and husband Larry have been board members of their local club "Prariefreund Koeln," which translates as Prairie Friends of Cologne. Since 1996, she has been the secretary for the Western Bund (Union) Germany. *Photo courtesy of Larry Wettstein.*

Netherlands

HENRI VAN DE ESSCHERT. When he was a young boy of seven to eight years old, Henri read cartoons and stories about the Wild West. He was very sympathetic to the Indian people, which fostered his later interest in reading Indian history books. In the early 1990s, he met Andre Ebbers, also from the Netherlands, who taught him how to make Crow-style beadwork, Andre is most familiar with that tribe, having been adopted by the Little Light family. From that time on, Henri has made many Indian replicas, including his war shirt that was sold in Four Winds Auction (shown on p. 113). (Pers. comm., March 2006)

Henri Van De Esschert wearing a Crow-style outfit and holding a rifle scabbard that he made. *Photo courtesy of Henri van de Esschert.*

Ehrenfried Hoppe, a German hobbyist, is shown wearing a headdress that he made at Indian Council in 2005. *Photo courtesy of Ehrenfried Hoppe.*

Henri and his friends from the Netherlands at Indian Council near the town of Beerse in Belgium in 1996. Dutch hobbyists travel to Belgium or Germany, where there are large "Indian camps." *Photo courtesy of Henri van de Esschert.*

Italy

SERGIO SUSANI started in the "hobby" as a young boy, but Indian books were rare so he relied on objects he saw in the movies. At present, he says there are no real Italian hobbyist groups nor are there Indian camps as in Germany. There is an Indian magazine published in northern Italy, "AKO," which is mostly political with a little about craftwork. There are isolated people doing craftwork but no organized groups.

Sergio started his collection of what he calls "real stuff" in 1986, which soon became the basis for his own private museum display (see photo following). He now has about 150 Indian objects, including pipe bags, pipes, moccasins, war shirts, roaches, belt bags, a dispatch bag, and a tomahawk from the Speyer collection.

Indian Council Camp, at Hundsdorf near Ransbach-Baumbach, Germany in 2005. This council was organized under the leadership of Western Bunde. C. 1969. *Photo and description from Ehrenfried Hoppe.*

Many of his items were purchased from the late German collector, Herman Von Bank, with whom he had a long friendship. Sergio added replications that he has made to his museum collection using "the right materials and patina." He is proud of the time that Colin Taylor came to visit and could not tell his replicas from the authentic pieces! Sergio dressed all of the mannequins himself and made all but one of the eagle feather war bonnets as well as some of the beaded items. He feels that his most significant item is a horn spoon signed by Sitting Bull and obtained at a local county fair in Arezzo. He says that it most certainly came to Italy during Buffalo Bill's Circus exhibition in 1906. (Pers. comm., February 2006)

Sergio Susani, shown here with the authors, on one of his frequent visits to the USA, at a Missoula, Montana Powwow in 1991. *Photo courtesy of Sergio Susani.*

Sergio says it was his good fortune to meet the late German collector Hermann Von Bank, from whom he purchased most of his genuine Indian items for his Indian Museum. Most of the items are real but some items, i.e., feather bonnets, beadwork, etc., Sergio has replicated for his museum. He welcomes visitors to the museum, located in Della Chiana, Italy. *Photo courtesy of Sergio Susani.*

Author's note: The Czech Republic is covered in the next section, pp. 165-176. Many other countries, not covered here, also have active Indian hobbyist groups. (For information on hobbyists in other countries, see Taylor, 1988.) Also, there are many more people involved as hobbyists whom I would have liked to have included, but I was limited by space and readily available information. I have presented here what I believe to be a representative cross-section of activities and people exemplifying the movement around the world.

Acknowledgements: Thanks to all who shared photos and their personal stories for this history of hobbyism. I would especially like to thank those who sent me additional information on group activities: Jerry Farhenthold, Jack Heriard, Bill Holm, Benson Lanford, Ty Stewart, and Ian West; Ian West for the lengthy loan of his original photo collection from England.

Endnotes
[1]"A member of Westerners' International, the English Westerners' Society, was founded in November 1954, the ninth such group organized and the first outside the United States. It is an educational, non-profit organization whose object is to pursue and promote the study of American Frontier History. To this end, the Society issues publications and holds meetings." The National Cowboy Hall of Fame is currently the headquarters of Westerners International in Oklahoma City. Their website is http://www.westerners-intl.org

History of the Czech Hobbyists

It was the summer of 1995 when Daniel Hoffman and his hobbyist group from the Czech Republic arrived at our trading post for the first time. We were amazed at the array of high-quality Plains-style sewn quilled replicas available for our purchase, at wholesale prices! This was an unprecedented experience—we had never seen this quantity of fine quill and beadwork for sale. It was the beginning of a decade of annual visits by this group and other Czech quill and bead workers who were able to finance their trip to America by selling Indian-style craftwork.

By 1840, large quantities of Czech manufactured seed beads, known as "Czechoslovakian" or "Bohemian" beads, were being traded to America for the Indian trade. The first Czech anthropological museum, the Naprstek Museum in the capital city of Prague, was founded in 1862. In the late 19th century, several Czech noblemen traveled to North America and brought back collections of Native American objects for their curio cabinets; these included Prince Ferdinand d´Este at the Konopiste Castle (unfortunately, most of the collection was lost after the Communist overthrow in the 1950s) and Josef II Colloredo-Mansfeld at the Opocno Castle.

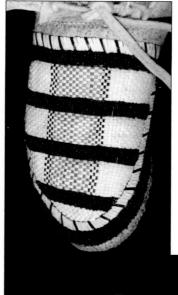

CROW MOCCASINS c. 1850
The original pair is from the Opocno Castle Museum, Czech Republic. They are one piece construction, according to Colin Taylor. Also, the originals have brown vegetable fiber instead of black/brown dyed quills. See Taylor, *Buckskins & Buffalo*, New York: Rizzoli International, 1998, p. 112-113.

CROW-STYLE QUILLED & BEADED MOCCASINS
These are Czech-made replicas of the above moccasins. Unusual checkerboard-style sewn quillwork in white, orange, and black/brown. Stripes are hard-to-find pony trader blue seed beads.
SOLD $650(99)

Daniel Hoffman and his original craftworkers group from the Czech Republic at Four Winds, summer 2000. (Back row, left to right) Daniel Hoffman; Carolyn Corey; Preston Miller; and Ludik Nykles, AKA Vikki (Badger), beadworker. (Front row) Xenie Rajnochova, quillworker; Hana Novotny (Petr's wife), beadwork; Petr Novotny (Perry), pipemaker and beadworker; Ales (Vikki's son), beadworker; and Radek Jirousek, beadworker. *Photo courtesy of Petr Novotny.*

The visitors for the most part spoke very little English, except for their interpreter, Petr Novotny, who discussed Czech history with us. We were wondering how this craft industry came about and why, of all places, in Czechoslovakia??

Thanks to Jan Kristek and Bohuslav Svara for their article titled "Indian Hobby in the Czech Republic," which relates the unique history of the Czech hobbyist movement. The following is an adaptation of their article from the website http://www.woodcraft.cz, hosted by the Woodcraft League of Czechoslovakia:

EARLY QUILLED WAR SHIRT c. 1840
On display at the Opocno Castle Museum, Czech Republic. Multi-quill plaited strips and simple band sewn quilled rosette. Note red "saved list" bib with double-wide white selvedge, which is at least 1.5" wide*. *Photo courtesy of Xenia Rajnochova.*

Here, as in North America, the Boy Scout movement led by the British Sir Baden-Powell and Canadian E. T. Seton was a strong influence in encouraging Indian lore amongst youth groups. Seton left the Scouts and established the Woodcraft movement at the turn of the 20th century (as noted previously on p. 139). Both organizations found multiple followers in the then Czech provinces of the Austrian-Hungarian Empire. It was the Woodcraft League led by M. Seifert there that primarily put forth the idea of the noble North American Indian as an example of a free, physically and mentally strong man living in accordance with nature. M. Seifert and his boys were the first ones to set up a tipi in the Czech lands in 1913, inspired by the idea published in Seton's *book Two Little Savages.* (However, Buffalo Bills Wild West Show had visited some Czech cities on their way to Vienna several years previously with a tipi camp.)

In 1918, following World War I, Czechoslovakia became an independent state. "Many independent groups of young men and women, so-called 'tramps' or 'Backwoodsmen,' traveled on weekends to the woods where they sometimes established log cabins, many of them felt the Indian influence and made Indian-style beaded objects. The sight of a single tipi or small tipi camps became gradually quite common in Czech valleys and forest meadows."

However, when Czechoslovakia was occupied by Hitler during World War II (1939-1945), activities were severely curtailed; besides others, all youth organizations including the Boy Scouts and Woodcraft League were forbidden. Many activists fled the country but in spite of life-threatening persecution, small groups and individuals continued their activities underground. The Communists won and the democratic state was overthrown in 1948, so that the same situation was repeated during the 1950s: "Remnants of involved people survived hidden by inactivity. During the early 60's a small number of people, primarily around the Naprstek Anthropology Museum in Prague…who studied the Native American (and other indigenous) cultures… wrote popular books on the true history of Indian wars and Native American culture. In the meantime, dispersed groups…and individuals, usually with historic ties to pre-WW II organizations, camped here and there in tipis and gradually during the 60's…a new generation of the backwoodsmen reappeared to become a massive movement during the late 60's and 70's." In the 1970s, the first groups of young people evolved that could be called "hobbyists" in the present sense of the word. From them came the first "Meeting in the North" in 1980, an event that brought together different individuals and clubs with an interest in American Indians to make personal contacts and to share hard-to-find information, because the Iron Curtain blocked access to sources published in the West.

"In those times it felt like a kind of resistance to do something outside the government-controlled organizations, a sort of adventure and gasping a little breeze of freedom…the half-secret Indian-style camps were one of the ways how to gain the feeling." (Kristek & Svara: 2003)

Many old techniques, customs, habits, and philosophic principles were adopted by the members of this, and other similar groups. "Meeting in the North" became a tradition with Plains Indian style camps ca. 1840-90 period apparel and tipi furnishing with dances, hunting expeditions, food, innumerable contests, and celebrations.

The impact of Native American religion, mostly Lakota, should be mentioned; treasured books by Black Elk or Lame Deer had been smuggled over the nearly impenetrable border and translated. Manually rewritten copies then passed through many a hand and found a resonating response in many hearts. Due to suppressed lack of communication enforced by the Communist government, all newly discovered information was a community treasure.

At that time, the traditional Native American moral standards, way of life, and fight for liberty provided strong motivation and inspiration for many such communities and individuals in their resistance against the Communist establishment and quest for their own freedom. (Kristek & Svara: 2003) The relatively small group of Indian hobbyists grouped together during their "Meetings in the North" to publish the magazine *Winaminge.* It contains articles by both professional and amateur scholars of the North American Indian. (Taylor 1988: 568).

In 1980, the "White Wampum" club was founded and member Daniel Hoffman soon became its leader. His group then set the pace and standards in a large part of the Czech and Slovak Indian hobby until its dissolution in 1999. In 1989, the Communist regime fell, frontiers opened, and the Indian hobbyists formed a group called "Czech Indian Corral" as part of the Westerners International organization, which is based in Oklahoma City. (See p. 164 for more info.)

Daniel (Wanblitanka) Hoffman wearing a Czech-made quilled shirt, summer 2002. He died suddenly in November of the same year. *Photo courtesy of Jan Kristek.*

"The high quality and relatively low prices of the Native American-style craftwork… led to the establishment of commerce among some craftworkers who produce beadwork, quillwork and other crafts predominantly for the German Indian hobby market." As a protest against this commercialism, saying that "Indian life was not made by just beading 12 hours a day," several groups left Indian Corral in 1993.

In the early 1990s, Daniel Hoffman and some others organized "factories," which mass produced a large quantity of beaded and quilled items. "Daniel had a fine taste and was able to make the people do the work in the way he wanted it." The group provided craftwork to merchants, primarily in Germany and the United States. Later, some of the craftworkers broke away to become independent and sold their own work.

Indian Corral has published the following magazines: *Indian Hobby Courier, Euroindian Magazine,* and *Posel-ství svta v kruhu* (Message of the Circle) that continues till now. All of them follow the thread that was started by the old Winaminge of the early 80s mentioned above. The Indian Corral organized the first modern style pow-wow with guests from Germany, Slovakia, and Native American friends in 1996. Major events organized by Indian Corral are the annual summer and winter camps, which take place every year at a different location.

Some Czech hobbyists have close ties to their colleagues in Germany and the U.S., and take part in their activities. There are quite a few Czech hobbyists who have accomplished their dream and gone to the United States, met the real Native Americans, and confronted their imagined ideas with reality, sometimes having to heavily adapt their rather naive image of what it truly means to be Native American.

In 1990, the Woodcraft League was reestablished, with many of the groups called "tribes" dealing with the Indian hobby to some extent. It is very active and publishes the magazine *Buffalo Wind,* as well as a handbook on *Camping in Tipi,* published as a second edition in 2002. The Woodcraft League survives to this day and is one of the strongest Woodcraft organizations in the world.

And, finally, let us thank the Indian people of America, whose courage, pride, aesthetics, philosophy and resolve to keep their freedom inspired many a white man on both sides of the Ocean. (Kristek & Svara: 2003)

Bibliography for Hobbyist Section

Brown, Steven C., and Lloyd J. Averill. *Sun Dogs & Eagle Down. The Indian Paintings of Bill Holm.* Seattle, WA: University of Washington Press, 2000.

Corey, Carolyn. *The Tradecloth Handbook.* St. Ignatius, Montana: Four Winds Indian Trading Post, 2001.

Deloria, Philip J. *Playing Indian.* New Haven & London: Yale University Press, 1998.

Edwards Jr., Richard W. *Artifacts/Artifakes Plains Indian Art Reproductions: The Law.* Cody, Wyoming: Buffalo Bill Historical Center, 1993.

Feder, Norman, editor. *American Indian Hobbyist Magazine.* Vol. I, #5. Los Angeles, Calif: Jan. 1955.

Feest, Christian, editor. *Studies in American Indian Art —A Memorial Tribute to Norman Feder.* Seattle, WA: University of Washington Press, 2001.

Holm, Bill. *Artifaking: Perception Enhancement by Doing.* Los Angeles: American Anthropological Association Conference, 1978.

Hunt, W. Ben. *The Golden Book of Indian Crafts and Lore.* New York: Simon & Schuster, 1954.

Kristak, Jan, and Bohuslav Svara. "Indian Hobby In the Czech Republic." (http://www.woodcraft.cz) 2003.

Miller, Preston, and Carolyn Corey. *The New Four Winds Guide to American Indian Artifacts.* Atglen, PA: Schiffer Publishing Ltd., 2006.

Powers, William K. "The Indian Hobbyist Movement in North America," pp. 557-561, *Handbook of North American Indians Vol. 4, History of Indian-White Relations.* William C. Sturtevant, gen. ed., Washington D.C.: Smithsonian Institution, 1988.

Taylor, Colin F. "The Indian Hobbyist Movement in Europe," pp. 562-569, *Handbook of North American Indians Vol. 4, History of Indian-White Relations.* William C. Sturtevant, gen. ed., Washington D.C.: Smithsonian Institution, 1988.

——. *Hoka Hey! Scalps of Coups: The Impact of the Horse on Plains Indian Warfare.* Wyk auf Foehr, Germany: Tatanka Press, 2000.

Czech hobbyist gathering at the small village of Hamiltony, near the city of Brno, Czech Republic, Spring 2000. (Top row, left to right) David Stasny; Radek Jirousek, beadworker; Petr Novotny, pipemaker; Tomas (Wabi) Denek, quillworker; Daniel Hoffman; Petr Geryk; unidentified member; Frantisek Popelka; and Cantekata. (Bottom row) Katerina Stasna; unidentified member; Xenie Rajnochova, quillworker, with her two children; Jarka Nikesova; and unidentified member. *Photo courtesy of Petr Novotny.*

Petr Mouka at a gathering in the Czech Republic. *Photo courtesy of Jan Kristek.*

Czech-made Reproductions

The items shown here were made by the following artisans from the Czech Republic, who visited Four Winds in the period between 1990-2006: Tomas Danek, Ivo Frydrych, Petr Geryk, Tom Giesl, Radek Jirousek, Krocak Ladislav, Petr Mouka, Petr Novotny, Ludik and Ales Nykles, and Xenie Rajnochova.

Clothing

CROW-STYLE QUILLED WARSHIRT c.1860-style
The original is on display in the Opocno Castle Museum Czech Republic. Multiple sewn quill "checker weave"* plaited shoulder strips (2.5"W) bordered with white and old-stock pony trader blue seed beads; quill-wrapped horsehair sleeve strips (1.75"W) have same border. Sewn onto brain-tan buckskin strips with white pony beads.

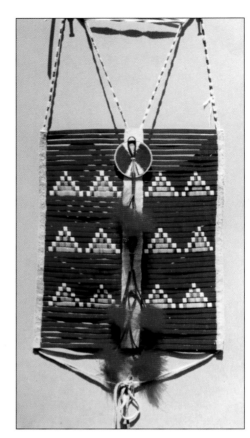

SIOUX-STYLE QUILLED BREAST PLATE
1/4" quill-wrapped rawhide slats, pred. red with natural white, purple, gold, and lt. blue step-triangles; center ornamented with 2.5" sewn quilled rosette and three quill-wrapped drops with red feather fluffs. Buckskin bound sides; buckskin ties with partially quill-wrapped red top thongs. Pristine condition.14"L x 11.5"W panel. Est. 1450-1800

Quill colors: yellow, varying pale-med. red-orange, varying pale to med. blue looks like natural dyed. Very few craftspeople are skilled in these techniques. Heavy golden (looks yellow-ochred) comm. buckskin shirt. Painted dk. red ochre with war exploits, which probably relate to the specific individual who wore this shirt. Back has similar motifs including rifles (not shown). Neck opening has heavy red wool laced with thong. Shoulder W. 24". Chest 52". 39"L. Est. 1200-1800 **SOLD $1200(99)**
*See Orchard, p. 33, for quill technique; also see Taylor, 1994, p. 195 for photos and descriptions of this specific shirt.

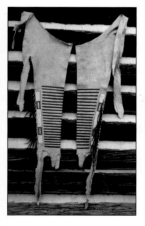

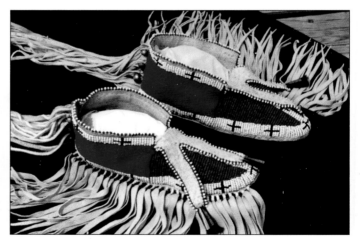

NO. PLAINS-STYLE QUILLED LEGGINGS
c. 1840-style
Note that the buckskin makes use of appendages which are common on the earliest garments. Lt. smoked brain-tan has warble fly bites indicative of a far Northern habitat. Painted stripes are deep red; human hair fringes are quill-wrapped (pale to med. yellow). Simple band quill technique strips (1.5"W) are pred. yellow with early-style box forms in red and lt. blue. 35" in seam L. Exc. cond. Est. 600-950 **SOLD $500(99)**

See the original pictured in Taylor, 1994, p.33. "...Regalia of this type distinguished the wearer, proclaiming his achievements and tribal standing."

UPPER MISSOURI RIVER-STYLE 1840-STYLE MOCCASINS
Similar to ones formerly on display in the Heye Fdn. NY. Pony-beaded flashy pair in dramatic colors: pony trader blue, white, and black with red wool overlay. White edge-beaded front tabs have red horsehair/tin cones. 8"L side fringes with partial white quill wrapping. Hawk bell heel embellishment at 20"L buckskin fringes. Est. 600-950 **SOLD $475(00)**

Pipes

CATLINITE FIGURAL PIPE & QUILLED STEM
Catlinite elaborate lead inlaid pipe with fantastic carved double figures trading whisky; dog head at front! Expert workmanship. Carved stem is 1/2 spiral and 1/2 "puzzle" style with quilled wrapped checkerboard pattern in red, white, purple, and yellow. Pipe 6"L x 3.5". 31" total L. Est. 1250-1850 **SOLD $1400(99)**

(Top to bottom) **SIOUX-STYLE QUILLED PIPESTEM & LEAD-INLAID PIPE**
Wrapped 1/16"W plaited quillwork in early box motif: dk. red, varying indigo, and pale yellow. Wide soft green rayon ribbon holds red horsehair. 25.5"L x 1.75"W. Pipe is Catlinite horse with fancy inlay. 6.5"L x 3.5"H. Total length 32"L. Exc. cond. Est. 1500-1900

SIOUX-STYLE QUILLED & CARVED PIPESTEM & CATLINITE PIPE
Carved stylized bear claw motifs on wooden stem plus finely (1/16") plaited wrapped quillwork double thunderbird motifs in orange, black, and white. Red rayon ribbon and buckskin drops. 25.5"L x 1.5"W. The speckled Catlinite t-shaped pipe is an old one that shows use and age. Pipe is 7"L x 3.5"H. 32" total L. Est. 800-1500 **Pipestem alone SOLD $550(06)**

SIOUX-STYLE PLAITED QUILLED STEM & CATLINITE PIPE
Bold motifs of abstract butterfly-like designs are white on richly varied hues of red-orange and dk. brown finely (1/16"W) plaited wrapped quillwork. Wide dk. green ribbon attaches 12"L. red horsehair. Flat wood stem is 1.75"W x 26.5"L. Catlinite pipe has concentric grooved circles 6"L x 3"H. Looks like an old original. Est. 700-925

CLASSIC SIOUX-STYLE CARVED & QUILLED PIPE STEM
There are many variations of these carved animal symbols of turtle, elk, and buffalo heads found on old pipe stems but unusual to see whole figure of a bighorn sheep as well. Masterfully carved 3D figures. Triple "puzzle" portion is wrapped quillwork: orange with black and white difficult checkerboard pattern. 26" total L. 2"W. x apx. 3/4" thick. Exc. cond. Est. 500-800

169

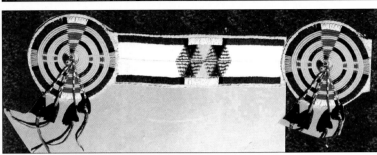

UPPER MISSOURI-STYLE FULLY-QUILLED BLANKET STRIP
Mandan-Hidatsa Style. Quill-wrapped horsehair rosettes and multi-quill diamond pattern. ALL SINEW-SEWN. Rosettes are yellow, red, black, and lt. blue; connecting strips same colors + white. Lane-stitched seed-bead borders are stripes of pony trader blue, Crow pink, white, and black. Thong drops partially-quilled with dew claws hanging from rosette centers. Rosettes 5.5" diam. Strip 3.25" W. 55"total L. Est. 2500-4000
SOLD $2500(03)

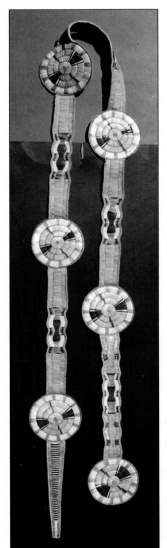

NO. PLAINS-STYLE FULLY-QUILLED BLANKET STRIP
Replicated from the original in a museum in Copenhagen, Denmark, where it is mounted on a painted buffalo robe. Rosettes are simple band with unusual undulating zig-zag quillwork on connecting strips. Subdued colors are varying corn yellow/pale yellow, white, lt. periwinkle, and varying rich cinnamon brown and dk. brown. 67"L. Rosettes are 3.25" diam. Strips are 1.25" W. Est. 1750-2500

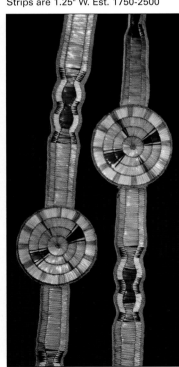

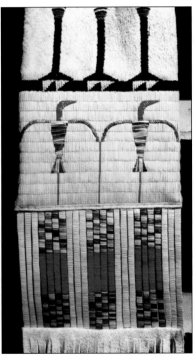

(Left) **LARGE CHEYENNE/SIOUX STYLE QUILLED PIPE BAG**
Simple-band panels each side have double thunderbird motif: pale yellow bkgrd. with varied lt. and med. blue and red (same both sides). Quilled bottom slat panel is wrapped in same colors. Soft buckskin top is beaded in black, brick white hearts, and white; roll beaded top same colors. ALL SINEW-SEWN. Buckskin bottom fringes. Hangs 36"L. 6.25"W. Est. 1000-1500 **SOLD $1000(99)**
(Right) **EARLY UPPER MISSOURI-STYLE QUILLED PIPE BAG**
Multi-quill plaited panel in yellow with black and white (both sides). Incredible perfect, flat quillwork. ALL SINEW-SEWN. Bottom buckskin fringes and side thong drops are individually white quill-wrapped with hand-made tin cones with red horsehair. Buckskin top has pony trader blue seed beads bands and triangular motifs with white. 5.5"W. Hangs 32"L. Exquisite piece. Est. 900-1200 *Author's collection*
    See *Four Winds Guide To Trade Goods & Replicas*, p. 126, for more info. on this quillwork style.

SIOUX-STYLE FULLY-BEADED PICTOGRAPHIC PIPE BAG

Original is in Denver Art Museum. * Crow pale blue bkgrd. with overlapping horses and male figure on one side, female and tipi on the other. Bead colors are white, pale gr. yellow, gr. blue, pony trader blue, and t. rose. "Rainbow" forms are also Cheyenne pink, t. bottle green, and t. lt. green. Large 7"L quilled wrapped slat panel in red with faded indigo and corn yellow blocks. Long side quill-wrapped drops with dk. red horsehair in tin cones. Four corners of beaded panel have white quill-wrapped drops, hawk bells, and red horsehair in tin cones; bottom row has tin cones with dk. red horsehair. Long bottom buckskin fringes are 18"L. Vertical side has single lane stripes: white, t. green, gr. yellow, and pony trader blue; same on top roll beaded edge. 6"W x 44" total L. Nicely aged. Est. 1200-2500 *Author's collection*

*See Conn, p. 112, plate #83. Also pictured in *American Indian Art Magazine*, Vol. 16, #1 Winter 1990. Dennis Lessard wrote a convincing article for this unique style of beadwork originating from Cheyenne River Sioux ONLY to later retract his findings in AIA magazine, Vol. 16, #4 Autumn 1991 as being made by a single craftworker, Edith Claymore, from Standing Rock Res. A photo of her other pictographic work is seen in the book *Yuto'keca: Transitions The Burdick Collection.*

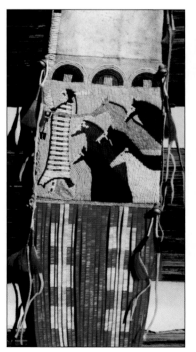

SIOUX-STYLE FULLY-BEADED PICTO-GRAPHIC PIPE BAG

Very long pipe bag with one fully-beaded and two partially-beaded pictorial panels on front; back fully-beaded pictorial panel. Vertical stripe patterns on top are white, red w. heart, t. cobalt, and gr. yellow. Double lane-stitched horizontal borders pred. Chey. pink with Sioux green and gr. yellow triangles outline in cobalt. Bottom quill-wrapped panel in varying shades of yellow with faded indigo and red cross motifs. Roll beaded top. Entire bottom row has tin cones with dk. red horsehair. Long bottom buckskin fringes are 18"L. 6" W. apx. 50"L. Spectacular piece. Est. 1500-2750 **SOLD $1300(03)**

SIOUX STYLE LARGE QUILL "ANTELOPE" BAG

Simple band quill technique is all sinew-sewn on white heavy buckskin. Quill stripes and border are red. "Antelope" motif has yellow horns with med. blue beaded top and bottom borders; gr. blue with cranberry w. hearts, dk. cobalt, and white. Quill-wrapped handle is red; yellow quill-wrapped side drops have tin cones with yellow horsehair. Quill-wrapped bottom slats are red with yellow and blue box motifs; tin cones and yellow horsehair bottom fringe. Brass hawk bells trim; bead edged in gr. blue ponies. Added bonus is interior painted with parfleche design. 15.5"L. (incl. bottom tab and fringe) x 7.75"W. Est. 750-1200 **SOLD $750(99)** See *Spirits in the Art,* pp. 124

NO. PLAINS-STYLE FULLY-QUILLED ROSETTE BAG

Beautiful simple band sewn quilled large rosette in white, dk. orange, lt. blue, and varying dk. red. Outer beaded lane is t. dk. navy, white, and gr. blue. Red wool bound top binding. All-around 1.5"L fringes are pumpkin colored quill-wrapped. Central navy wool appliqué circle. Side drops (10"L) are silk thread wrapped with lt. red dyed horsehair with tin cones. Strap is alt. white/pumpkin quill-wrapped. 9" diam. + fringes. Hangs apx. 16"L. Est. 750-950

EASTERN-SIOUX-STYLE QUILLED PIPE BAGS 1835-style

Quilled panels with double deer? motifs each side in sewn zig-zag bands. Quilled strips along side. ALL SINEW-SEWN. White quill-wrapped bottom buckskin fringes. Est. 800-1150 each (Left) Panel and sides are white with black figures and orange bands with red and black. Six prs. of white quill-wrapped suspensions have hand-made tin cones with orange horsehair. Top is bound with red trade wool sewn with pony trader blue beads. Bottom fringes have pony trader blue spacers. Hangs 32"L. 5"W. Fringes are apx. 18"L. Nice smoked buckskin, very light patina.
Est. 800-1200 **SOLD $850(04)**
(Right) White with black deer? and lt. orange bands. Six prs. of pale orange quill-wrapped drops with hand-made tin cones and lt. orange dyed horsehair. Top has white seed-bead edging on tabs; eight prs. of tin cones with red-orange horse hair. Pony trader blue bead spacers betw. bottom buckskin fringes. Buckskin is painted dk. grey and quillwork has heavy patina. 5.5"W. Apx. 35"L. Looks like a museum piece. Est. 800-1200 **SOLD $625(01)**
*See Taylor: 1994, p. 133 for photo of a quilled cradle collected by George Catlin in 1835, with these same animal motifs.

GROS VENTRE-STYLE QUILLED PICTORIAL BAG

Unusual rooster motif in faded indigo, pale yellow, and dk. red with stylized floral and star motifs in red with pale green. Pale yellow quilled border. All simple band sewn. Bottom slats are quill-wrapped in pale yellow with four concentric box motifs in white and lt. periwinkle. Bottom has aged tin cones with dk. red horsehair and buckskin fringes. Handle and four side drops are quill-wrapped in dk. red, pale yellow with faded indigo and dk. red horsehair. 8"W. 12" bag hangs 19"L. Est. 850-1100

NO. PLAINS-STYLE FULLY-QUILLED RO-SETTE BAG

Unusual fully-quilled bag in simple band sewn rosette; striking contrasting colors in classic early design: black, white, pale yellow, and dk. red. Quill-wrapped handle and surrounding drops with dew claws and quill-wrapped loops. 8.5" diam. Hangs apx. 16"L. Est. 750-950 **SOLD $750(04)**

SIOUX-STYLE QUILLED BAG

Fully-quilled simple band sewn early concentric box designs, pale yellow and varying faded indigo on bright red with lane-stitched beaded borders of lt. periwinkle, mustard, and t. "Montana" blue stripes and edge beaded. Tin cone bottom fringes have red and natural buckskin fringes (5"L). Side drops are tin cones with red buckskin fringes. Carrying handle is red quill-wrapped. Every detail is perfect and expertly done. Hangs 14.5"L. 4.75"W. Est. 400-650

SIOUX-STYLE QUILLED BAG

Sewn simple band fully-quilled front is pale yellow with red and varying indigo step triangle motifs. Beaded lane-stitched borders are t. red with t. dk. cobalt and mustard box motifs. Black edge beaded. Tin cone buckskin fringed bottom. Quill-wrapped handle in red and pale yellow with tin cone yellow fluff drops. Same on bottom. 4.5"W hangs 17"L. Pristine cond. Est. 400-650

Weapon Cases

NO. PLAINS-STYLE BUFFALO HAIR-ON QUILLED QUIVER 1830-style

Splendid in its simplicity and elegance. 20"L quiver tab is red wool embellished with three lanes zig-zag sewn quillwork in striking pale varying orange, white and dk. brown; drops are five partially-quill-wrapped buckskin thongs with tin cones (7"L). Long buffalo hair hide back. Red wool drop and strip along quiver have white selvedge (saved list). Buffalo hide quiver and bow case are red wool bound sewn with pumpkin ponies. 22"L buffalo hide carrying strap has fully-quilled simple band drops in alt. stripes of pale orange and dk. brown with long buckskin fringes. Backed with red ochre painted muslin. Quiver is 24"L.; 35"L quiver; both with long buffalo hide fringe drops. Rawhide lines cases. Est. 1100-1500 **SOLD $1100(03)**

NO. PLAINS-STYLE QUILLED COYOTE? QUIVER

Spectacular piece has five sections of sewn quillwork over red saved list on flap. Quillwork is all yellow, red and black: two simple-band rosettes with partially quilled dangles; two rectangular panels of woven checkerboard-style quillwork; lower panel of zig-zag style quillwork. All panels on buckskin and outlined with pony trader blue "real" beads (old size 9). Same beads are used as edging for entire flap. White selvedge at top. Another strip of red saved list laced with buckskin over wood stick support. Two quill-wrapped slat panels hang from side. Fur carrying strap. 25"L quiver with 12" diam. top opening. Est. 1200-1600 **SOLD $900(04)**

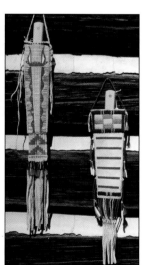

(Left) NO. PLAINS-STYLE QUILLED KNIFE SHEATH
Author's collection. This incredible sheath has four styles of quillwork incl. difficult multiple plaited central panel with single line, single band and lower panel of quill-wrapped slats. Colors are faded indigo, golden yellow, red and white with a few purple. The motif could be considered a female buffalo or antelope head. Trimmed with pony trader blue beads. Lower buckskin fringes have red horsehair with tin cones and top buckskin drops are partially red quill-wrapped with red horsehair tin cone drops. Rawhide insert. Sinew-sewn. 6" blade Green River knife included. Sheath 13"L. 2.75" top opening. Lower panel is 2.5" L + 8"L. fringes. Est. 750-950

(Right) UPPER MO. RIVER STYLE QUILLED KNIFE SHEATH
Red quill line simple band front with upper panel red, yellow, and black woven quill panel bordered with lane stitched Pony trader blue and mustard. Red quill-wrapped handle and side drops with tin cones and red horsehair. Bottom fringes wrapped with alt. red and yellow quills connected with pony trader blue. Buckskin covered heavy rawhide, sinew-sewn. Sheath 9.75"L x 3.75" top opening. 7" bottom fringes. Includes 6" blade Green River butcher knife. Est. 400-550

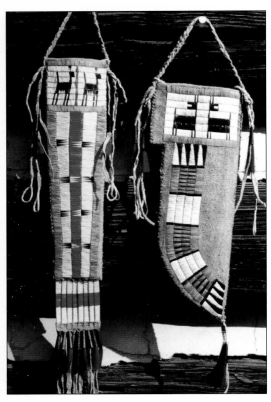

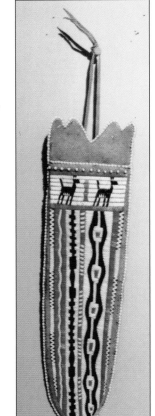

(Left) **EASTERN SIOUX-STYLE FULLY-QUILLED KNIFE SHEATH** 1835-style*
Zig-zag bands are white, red, and pumpkin with black 4-legged animals, deer or dogs. ALL SINEW-SEWN. Partially-quilled loop dangles at top have tin cone with red horsehair drops. 2" wrapped quilled slat bottom panel same colors. 14"L buckskin fringes with row of tin cones and red horsehair. Green River 6" butcher knife. Braided buckskin handle. Dark aged buckskin. Case 10"L +slats and fringes. Hangs 29"L. Est. 400-600 **SOLD $350(01)**
(Right) **EASTERN SIOUX-STYLE PARTIALLY-QUILLED KNIFE SHEATH**
Similar motifs to previous sheath. Est. 400-500
*See Taylor: 1994, p.133 for photo of a quilled cradle collected by George Catlin in 1835, with these same animal motifs. Also, see similar designs on quilled panel c. 1800, *Art of the Great Lakes Indians,* Exhibition Catalog, Flint, Mich. 1973: 4.

EASTERN SIOUX-STYLE FULLY QUILLED KNIFE SHEATH Early 1800-1820 style. *Spectacular copy of an original piece*. Two stylized deer on top border and beautiful zig-zag sewn quilled designs. Colors are orange, dk. brown, and natural white. White pony bead edging on all sides and front opening. Buckskin covered rawhide. Buckskin thong hanger. 12.5"L x 3.5"top W tapering to 2" bottom. Est. 500-800. *Author's collection.*
    *This is a mirror image exact copy of one in the book *Akicita*, p. 29, figure 26.

NO. PLAINS-STYLE BEADED KNIFE SHEATHS
Each is beaded in old-time bead colors: clear rose, gr. blue, gr. yellow, white, and t. dk. cobalt. Sinew-sewn buckskin over rawhide with twisted buckskin straps. Tin cone ornamentation. Exceptional craftsmanship. 10.5"-11"L. Est. 250-400 each.
Photo courtesy of Radek Jirousek.

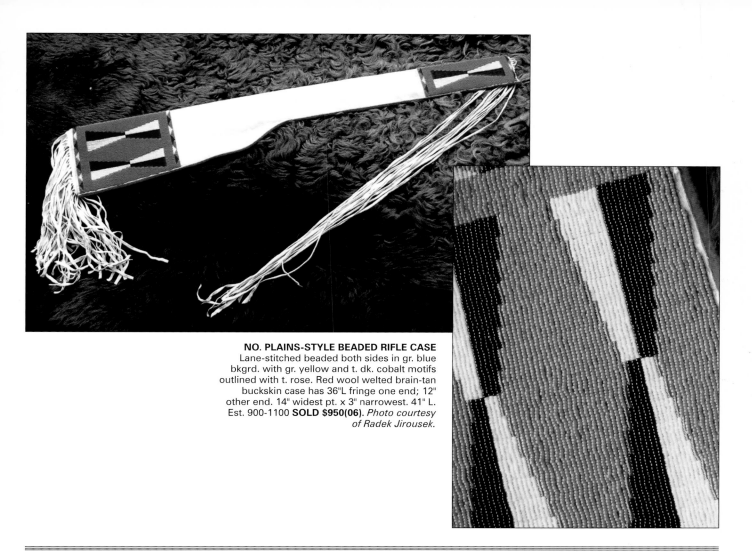

NO. PLAINS-STYLE BEADED RIFLE CASE
Lane-stitched beaded both sides in gr. blue bkgrd. with gr. yellow and t. dk. cobalt motifs outlined with t. rose. Red wool welted brain-tan buckskin case has 36"L fringe one end; 12" other end. 14" widest pt. x 3" narrowest. 41" L. Est. 900-1100 **SOLD $950(06).** *Photo courtesy of Radek Jirousek.*

Horse Gear

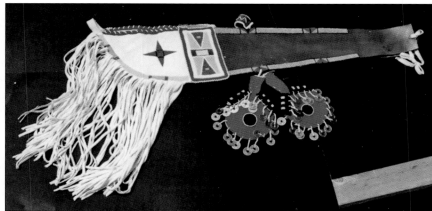

CROW-STYLE BEADED CRUPPER
Heavy latigo bordered with Crow pale blue with red w. heart, gr. yellow designs. Beaded panels are same colors plus Crow pink and white border. Buckskin has red 4-pt. star with pred. Crow pink with gr. yellow, red w. heart stripes. Red wool bound; 14"L buckskin fringes. Red wool covered rawhide ornaments have Chinese coin dangles; navy wool inlaid with Crow pale blue beadwork. 34"L. Est. 900-1250

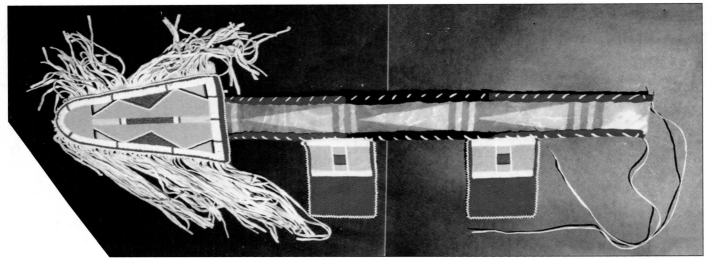

CROW-STYLE BEADED LANCE (or SWORD) CASE
Lt. blue appliqué bkgrd. Crow pink, gr. blue, corn yellow with white borders over red wool inlay. Painted rawhide case bound with alt. red and blue trade cloth buckskin laced. Tabs are red wool with Crow pale blue, white, corn yellow, and red w. heart panels; white seed bead edged. Apx. 40"L Est. 900-1200

CROW-STYLE WOMAN'S HIGH POMMEL SADDLE WITH BEADED STIRRUPS
Buckskin covered wooden saddle. Beautiful red and navy trade wool fully-beaded drops different each end; roll beaded pommel tops. Heavy harness leather cinch with iron rings. Est. 2000-2500